CUMBLER, John T. Working-class community in industrial America:
work, leisure, and struggle in two industrial cities, 1880–1930. Greenwood, 1979. 283p ill (Contributions in labor history, 8) bibl index
78-57768. 22.95 ISBN 0-313-20615-5. C.I.P.

The major strength of Cumbler's labor history is its social-intellectual
approach. Going beyond the bread-and-butter labor histories of the John R.
Commons school, Cumbler focuses on the total working environment in
Lynn and Fall River, Massachusetts. He discusses the impact of immigration on close-knit communities, the structure and demands of the workplace, and the nature of community. The close proximity of the Lynn
shoemakers while on the job, for example, created a work environment far
different from that of the Fall River textile workers who found themselves
isolated by the nature of their workplace. Lynn was a close city, built up
physically and culturally united; Fall River had a different class structure
and was more degraded. Throughout this well-reasoned study Cumbler
concentrates on the changes brought about by technological improvements
and the trauma caused by the influx of immigration. Recommended for
upper-division undergraduate libraries with labor, social, and/or urban
history collections.

Working-Class Community in Industrial America

CONTRIBUTIONS IN LABOR HISTORY
Series Editors: **Milton Cantor and Bruce Laurie**

Working-Class Community in Industrial America

Work, Leisure, and Struggle in Two Industrial Cities, 1880-1930

John T. Cumbler

Contributions in Labor History, Number 8

GREENWOOD PRESS
WESTPORT, CONNECTICUT • LONDON, ENGLAND

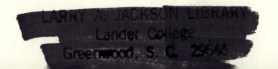

Library of Congress Cataloging in Publication Data

Cumbler, John T
   Working-class community in industrial America.

   (Contributions in labor history ; no. 8 ISSN 0146-3608)
   Bibliography: p.
   Includes index.
   1. Labor and laboring classes--Massachusetts--Lynn--History. 2. Labor and laboring classes--Massachusetts--Fall River--History. 3. Lynn, Mass.--Social conditions. 4. Fall River, Mass.--Social conditions.
I. Title. II. Series.
HD8085.L963C85   301.44'42'0973   78-57768
ISBN 0-313-20615-5

Library of Congress Catalog Card Number: 78-57768
ISBN: 0-313-20615-5
ISSN: 0146-3608

First published in 1979

Greenwood Press, Inc.
51 Riverside Avenue, Westport, Connecticut 06880

Printed in the United States of America

10 9 8 7 6 5 4 3 2 1

TO THE PILLARS I STOOD ON THROUGH
THE COMPLETION OF THIS STUDY:
JUDITH, ETHAN AND SAM

Contents

Tables

Maps and Illustrations

Acknowledgments

This work owes much to the characters and actors of the past who made the story of Lynn and Fall River. Without their daily struggles, there would have been no factories, no wealth, no poverty in these cities. This account is their history as best as I could re-create it. This work also has many debts in the present as well as in the past. Sam Bass Warner, Milton Cantor, and Bruce Laurie all deserve a great deal of credit for the completion of this work. Sam Warner as a friend and teacher taught me history, gave me a feel for the city, and developed my comprehension of how to complete a historical study. Moreover, he offered a model of a teacher, scholar, and friend which I take daily into the classroom, library, and home. The debt I owe Milton Cantor is one I share with a score of young social historians. As editor of *Labor History,* he encouraged our work, improved our scholarship, and pointed out weaknesses while finding our strengths. Both he and Bruce Laurie helped our writing and our careers, and the tireless and immense effort that they put into a generation of labor historians will be reaped by the profession at large if we continue where they led us.

Charles Tilly and Ray Shortridge contributed time and effort in making me more aware of both the weaknesses and strengths of this work. Professor Tilly made a major contribution in clarifying my thoughts on the conclusion; Ray Shortridge read and reread the manuscript, and got me beyond many a stalled intersection on the road toward completion.

The maps and photos were prepared with the help of Janet Dakan and Stewart Galley, respectively. Thomas Dublin and Charles Stephenson gave me important help in reworking the manuscript. Paul Faler and

Alan Dawley assisted through conversations and their own work. The Lynn Public Library, as well as Harold Walker and the Lynn Historical Society, provided tremendous aid in the research stage of this work. The workers of Lynn and Fall River who took time out to talk to me about their lives and struggles made my understanding of the histories of both cities richer and hopefully closer to the reality of their experiences. Others have helped, such as Lew Erenberg, John Sharpless, Sally Benbasset, Sue Benson, and Flossie Smith. As in everything I do, my family gave me a proper balance about the importance of other things besides history.

Working-Class Community in Industrial America

1

Introduction

In 1871, Joseph Cook, a Congregational minister, came to Lynn, Massachusetts, the national center of shoe production which was America's largest industry at that time. Reverend Cook delivered a series of lectures on factory reform. In trying to understand the presence of labor militancy in Lynn and its absence in Lowell and Lawrence, Cook noted that "a study of the subject at a distance might lead to the opinion that a shoe town and a cotton town are much alike; but the reverse is true. Each has a set of exigencies of its own."[1] He went on to argue that these differences in turn affected the behavior and attitudes of the workers themselves: "The periodical lulls in the activity of the shoe factories and the large percentage of changeable operatives [make] it difficult to introduce into the shoe factory system the admirable method of sifting operatives according to characters that has long been practiced in the cotton factory system."[2]

Reverend Cook may have been inaccurate in his analysis of the differences between the cotton factory town and the shoe town. Furthermore, his concern for reform devolved into a call for moral purity at the work place, segregation of the sexes in the factory, more church services for the wage-earners, and greater effort in the cause of temperance reform among workers. But, almost inadvertently, he did put his finger (for all its moral waving) on a fruitful area for research by urban and labor historians—the impact of ecological factors on class behavior and on collective action and consciousness.

Historians of the American working class, following the tradition established by John R. Commons, have written a history of labor organizations, the trade unions, and labor parties. They have emphasized, until recently, the materialistic goals of organized labor. Thus, they accepted

Commons' notion that, with the development of capitalism, self-interested unions, united only by the pragmatic needs of their members, were formed to advance the interests of these constituents.[3]

Such concern with bread and butter unionism led historians to a detailed analysis of the history and structure of the formal institutions of the American worker. Their work has contributed much to our understanding of the history of trade unionism and its uniqueness. Unfortunately, however, by focusing primarily on formal union institutions, their work has overlooked important cultural and social dynamics of working-class experiences.[4] Rather, these traditionalists have assumed that the worker had no unique culture of cummunity. The history of trade unionism was pictured as one of consensus and accommodation. Conflict was seen as confined to issues of "how much" or union recognition, and not as clashing ideologies, aspirations, even cultures.

Labor historians in the 1960s, following the lead of the English labor historian E. P. Thompson, have begun to break down many of the original assumptions about the American working class.[5] Unfortunately for those who are interested in modern urban or labor history, their efforts have tended to concentrate on the worker as a pre-industrial type, either immigrant or artisan. They have looked at him as a carrier of pre-factory values but not as an actor in the industrial community. Nor have they examined the formal or informal institutions which make up the industrial worker's environment. Not all wage-earners were newly arrived immigrant peasants, and those who were not only entered the industrial factory, but the urban world and the community of urban workers as well. They often joined established working-class institutions and became part of a complex of urban factors which affected their behavior.[6]

Researchers in labor relations, although not disputing the Commons school, also began to raise questions about community and social factors, and their impact on worker behavior and consciousness, in an attempt to understand labor conflict. In 1954, for example, Clark Kerr and Abraham Siegel argued that, although several factors help explain labor conflict, "strikes occur where they can occur, that is, where the working class community is closely knit and the workers forceful, and not where the workers are dispersed and subdued."[7] Although this argument appears fairly obvious and has several weaknesses, it points to the importance of understanding the worker's world, beyond his membership in a trade union.[8]

This study seeks to analyze that environment in order to understand how it functioned to preserve militancy; and how working-class community institutions, both formal and informal, have acted to maintain strong class solidarity as well as contribute to collective action. It examines the impact of urban factors such as geographic dispersion (or centrality) of the work place; the residential area of the labor force; and the demands, scale, conditions, technology, and discipline of the work place. Nor will it neglect immigration patterns and the modes of integrating newcomers into existing working-class community institutions which sustained class cohesion and provided the base for collective action.[9]

Lynn and Fall River, Massachusetts, from 1880 to 1930 serve as case studies for this analysis. Although both are eastern cities, the analysis developed here should be testable in other cities elsewhere in the country.

Lynn and Fall River were among the nation's leading industrial cities at the end of the nineteenth and early twentieth centuries. Lynn led the nation in shoe production and then became the center of a large electrical industry centered in General Electric. Fall River was first nationally in textile production in the late nineteenth century. In the 1920s, the city lost most of its textiles and came to rely instead on the garment industry. Both cities had ethnically mixed work forces but experienced different patterns of immigration. Furthermore, the structure of the urban environment, as well as the conditions and nature of the work, put different demands on the work force of each community.

Lynn and Fall River had the topography of industrial towns. For over a century, the work force of each was crowded together in deplorable tenements located in the most wretched districts. Yet, the cities differed significantly in their urban structure; and these differences related to the nature of their industrial development.

Lynn's shoe industry developed from early pre-industrial shoemaking, which was dominated by the merchant, jobber, and skilled craftsman. Before the Civil War, its master craftsmen worked in small shops called "ten-footers," with two or three journeymen or apprentices turning out shoes which were sold to markets or jobbers in Boston. In the 1830s and 1840s, Lynn's merchants began to centralize production. This process accelerated with the introduction of the sewing machine in 1852.

Following the Civil War, the factory system dominated shoe production, and the shops were bunched together in the downtown area. Such centralization was encouraged by the need of an industry that was highly seasonal and required low capital. It had to be close to both the financial and warehouse districts in order to have easy access to capital and to the urban labor pool. The independent real estate developers' practice of building factory structures several stories high and leasing out floor space to the individual shoe factories encouraged centralization. Thus, the historic and dominant role of the merchant and jobber in organizing the industry, coupled with the real estate interests' control over factory construction, drew the growing shoe industry to Lynn's central warehouse district. The walking city allowed manufacturers to make quick response, in labor variations and warehouse utilization, to the elastic and unpredictable market of the shoe industry.[10]

These same factors also contributed to the centralization of Lynn's working-class residential district in the fourth, fifth, and sixth wards. These wards comprised the so-called Brickyard located between the downtown warehouse district and the marshland southeast of town; Highlands, situated northeast of the Brickyard and the downtown; and east Lynn, which was east of the Brickyard and the downtown. Their location, like the manufacturers' shops, was determined by the highly volatile and seasonal labor market. These factors, which meant frequent job changes, required the workers to live within easy access of several shops, as well as of the downtown lunchrooms, cafes, and union hall. Thus the residential area of the work force, whether native or foreign-born, was centralized next to the downtown manufacturing district.

Fall River developed differently than Lynn because its industrial structure and requirements were different. The city's residential and commercial sectors grew up around the original mills which were located along the Quequechan River. The central recreational areas for the working class, before the late 1880s and 1890s, were located along Main Street which intersected the river and the mills. Here the workers built their union halls and their cooperative stores, and carried out their political and social functions. As Fall River expanded and switched from water power to steam, the mills moved away from the river and sought spacious waterside sites on the urban periphery. The textile mills, unlike the shoe shops, required large amounts of water and space, and did not have the fluctuating labor demands of the shoe industry. They were constructed by the corporations which operated the mills. Although subsequent urban growth absorbed these originally peripheral or isolated locations, the scattering of the mills decentralized the city and contributed to residential and industrial dispersion.[11] Residential areas began to spring up around the various mills, some of which were several miles from the central district, with many homes being built by the textile companies themselves to accommodate the growing work force in these peripheral areas. Such residential neighborhoods took on characteristics of their own, so that by the end of the century Fall River was known as a collection of villages. These villages, such as Mechanicsville, Bowenville, Border City, and Flint Village, evolved their own institutions. Their workers were less likely to go downtown to socialize or to interact with workers from other villages.

The wage-earners in these cities lived in working-class ghettos. In the late nineteenth century, Fall River's ghettos took on ethnic characteristics. Immigrants first settled in areas around the mills which had attracted them to the city. The French Canadians, for example, who were brought in as strikebreakers by the American Linen Company, settled near its mills. As an area became identified with a particular ethnic group, workers in other mills moved, if they were able, into the ghetto of their fellow immigrants. This trend concentrated certain ethnic groups within certain areas and mills. Conversely, in Lynn the centrifugal forces of the working-class residential area discouraged ethnic segregation.

Working-class communities in both Lynn and Fall River attempted to deal with the problems confronting labor, ranging from job procurement and unemployment (two to four months of every year for Lynn shoe workers) to child care. They developed their own institutions to meet these problems, in the shape of formal institutions such as unions and benefit or fraternal societies, or informal ones such as child care arrangements for working mothers, lunchrooms or pubs for social activity, and job information for the men. Through these institutions, the working class in the two cities built their communities and passed on their culture and history from generation to generation.

These working-class community institutions were the focal point in collective action and class cohesion. They became multifaceted and served as integrating agencies for wage-earners, whether these were youngsters or immigrants from abroad. But such institutions could prove to be vulnerable to massive or rapid changes in urban, demographic, and industrial processes. When strong and healthy, they could support and direct collective action by the working class; when weak and disrupted, they could act as segregating agents and disrupt or weaken collective action. Under pressure the community could segment, and class-based community institutions would then break down and be replaced by ethnic and craft subcommunity institutions. The viability of the working-class institutions affected the ability of the community to hold itself together over time, to maintain class solidarity, and to sustain collective action among its members.

This study focuses on three specific urban factors: centrality or dispersion of the urban setting; demands of the work place; and the nature of immigration, and how, depending upon a whole configuration of elements, it can strengthen or weaken community institutions. Community members had needs, created by the structure of the work, which reinforced community institutions. These institutions in turn affected the job through worker-group action which the community supported.

The historical experiences of Lynn and Fall River were in sharp contrast. In the nineteenth and early twentieth centuries, Lynn was characterized by relatively small shops, regular breaks during the work day, seasonal slacks in the trade, intershop discussions among the workers, some control over the work place and job conditions, and an integrated relationship between leisure, work, and home due to the centrality of the work place and residence. As a result, Lynn developed and maintained strong class-based community institutions which reinforced community solidarity and cohesion, and minimized the stress associated with integrating new members into the work force. Beginning in the late 1920s, the electrical industry dominated Lynn with its large work force, prison-like working conditions, and the use of Taylorism and efficiency management procedures. In addition, the federal housing policy encouraged suburbanization of the skilled work force. Consequently, the community was disrupted, class-based institutions were weakened, and collective action was more difficult to sustain.

Fall River in the late nineteenth and early twentieth centuries had a large work force, decentralized work and residential areas, excessive on-the-job pressure, a machine-tending technology that limited the worker's control and participation in the production process, and excessive noise and concentration that prevented intershop communication and encouraged after-work socializing. These factors, together with the pressure of immigration and severe job competition, led to the disruption and segmentation of the work force. Ultimately, the work force was fragmented into isolated ethnic and craft subgroups.

It is important that the reader understand the use of two key concepts, community and class, throughout this work. Intellectual historians have sometimes used the term *community* to indicate a feeling of commonality and distinctness, but on the whole it has been employed to refer to an aggregate of people who occupy a common and bounded territory within which they participate in institutions related to the geographic area, such as schools, churches, and municipal elections. In this study, the term is used in a sociological sense to describe a set of bonds among those people of the community; the people may or may not occupy a common territory. The "community" also entails a feeling of commonality and cohesiveness created by that interaction. Thus, as used here, community refers not to the city of Lynn or Fall River but to the *workers* within who felt a common identity with each other.

"Class" has been defined in many ways by historians and sociologists since Marx first developed the term as a means of analyzing social structure and economic development. To avoid confusion and sidestep the arguments which can undermine an otherwise sound study, this study defines "class" as "the real aggregates of people who share some characteristics and group interests, who favor each other in social relationships, and who exhibit varying degrees of group-consciousness."[12] Simply put, in this study the term can be understood largely to refer to occupational characteristics.

No history of a community can be complete and comprehensive. In the course of developing some aspect of a community, other aspects are neglected. In this study, the political behavior of the working-class community has been slighted. The role of the Socialist Labor party, the People's party, the Socialist party, and the Communist party, not to mention that of the Democratic and Republican parties, is not covered in this study of the working-class communities. Clearly, the socialist parties played a social role for the radical and politically active members of the community. The various parties sponsored rallies, parades, and dances which were attended by many Lynn workers. Fall River in the nineteenth century sprouted several independent working-class political organizations, although none matured into long-term viable alternative parties. The radical Italian anarchists had an active, if small, group in Lynn.

The Democratic and Republican parties also managed to activate working-class voters, especially around specific working-class issues such as the use of police during strikes, shorter hours, and legislation for women and children. This study does not discuss the role of the party machine, ethnic or ward politics, or the political boss, for the impact of political parties on the community is not the province of this work. Nineteenth-century statistics indicate that political parties, despite the big city ward boss and his machine, had little effect on low-income groups, especially the foreign-born. In Fall River in 1885, for example, out of a possible 14,341 voters in the city, only 9,426 were registered and only 4,421 voted in the gubernatorial race of that year.[13] The percentage of voters falls off rapidly among the foreign-born. In 1888, only a little over 10 percent of the legally eligible French Canadians, one of Fall River's largest foreign-born populations, voted. Forty-two percent of the English did not vote, and 31 percent of the Irish stayed home. The newly arriving Portuguese participated even less than the French Canadians.[14] In Lynn, with a smaller percentage of foreign-born, the working-class community was more active in elections, but not significantly so. In 1880, Lynn workers did turn out to the polls to elect a shoe worker for mayor, following a bitter strike in which police were used against the workers. In 1890, workers in the city again mobilized to dump the mayor and elect a union man to the highest city office in the midst of a bitter strike. This political activity notwithstanding, electoral parties did not turn out large percentages of workers to the polls. In 1885, under 50 percent of Lynn's legally eligible voters actually cast votes.[15]

Voting behavior does not, of course, measure the full impact of electoral politics on a community. Politics clearly had an influence on the working-class community. Working-class leaders were oftentimes drawn into politics either as leaders of workers or as a means of upward mobility, and sometimes as both. For example, George Sanderson, a leader of the shoe workers' strike of 1860, failed to lead his fellow workers to victory on the streets, but they carried him to victory as mayor in the election of 1876. Robert Howard, leader of Fall River's spinners, took the cause of textile workers to the state house in Boston as a successful politician. Yet, the political success of those leaders often failed to contribute to the workers' daily struggle for dignity and bread. Their electoral success often meant their loss to the community. And their failure to deliver benefits observable to the workers frequently led to cynicism at the local level.

Thus, it becomes apparent that many studies in labor politics may have overemphasized the influence of party politics on the working class. This study has avoided party politics in order to investigate community interaction from a perspective outside political activity. Where political behavior does intersect with community activity, such as in the Lynn leather workers' strike of 1890, the dynamics of the electoral politics is outlined.[16] For those interested directly in the relationship between class, class consciousness, and politics, this study will be a disappointment.

As indicated already, this study is basically urban and behavioral in orientation, focusing on the influence of ecological factors on working-class collective action. More than a purely behavioral study, it is also an assessment of working-class community and the change that community experienced at the end of the nineteenth century and the beginning of the twentieth. As a community study, it is also interested in the workers' culture and ideology. Workers' behavior is determined not simply by changes in space, working conditions, and makeup of the work force, but also by perceptions of those changes. Although as historians we can never be sure of how workers perceived themselves and their community, we cannot ignore the question.

2

Lynn: Queen City
to Zero Defects

Reverend Joseph Cook's lectures of 1871 evoked praise from the middle class and hostility from the workers. Cook pointed to the phenomenal success of Lynn in the twenty years after 1850. It was, he believed, the product of "the large factory system," with its "subdivision of labor." Yet, Cook feared that success because it eliminated the old system of independent shoe workers and replaced it with opposing classes: "an operative class and an employing class."[1] And the factory system pictured the operative class as morally deprived.

This factory system which Reverend Cook saw maturing in the 1870s grew to dominate the whole of downtown Lynn by the late nineteenth century. Huge five- to ten-story buildings were so bunched together that when the secretary of the Lasters Union was denied entrance to a fifth-floor factory in 1896, he called instructions out to the lasters from the fifth-floor window of the adjacent factory.[2]

By the mid-1920s, the massive factory buildings were nearly empty. In 1924, a real estate agent claimed, "there are now thousands of feet of vacant floor space in Lynn formerly occupied by shoe manufacturers."[3] By the 1930s, the General Electric complex dominated the western part of the city, and Lynn was again forced to adjust to a new factory system, this time one which was a huge single-company industrial complex.

The developments Reverend Cook noted in 1871 were only part of the story of a rapidly changing city, which transformed Lynn from the "Queen Shoe City" to the home of General Electric "where zero defects are a way of life."[4] Yet, this change transformed not only the urban topography, but also the environment and working conditions for urban wage-earners. Lynn changed from a city of shoe workers to a place where tasks were reduced to their simplest form without "defect." That change affected what workers did, how they perceived themselves and their labor, as well as their ability to influence their conditions and define themselves as part of a community. Thus, the history of the changing city was also that of the changing lives of Lynn's workers and had a direct effect on how they organized themselves. This chapter tells the story of Lynn's evolution and its impact on the work force.

Industrial Lynn emerged out of a small satellite manufacturing town located along the Massachusetts Bay just north of Boston. It lacked the natural advantages of a good harbor and fertile land, and turned early to the making and selling of shoes. By 1651, the town was giving cordwainers added acreage in recognition of their skill.[5] Yet, another century passed before shoemaking became established as a local industry. In 1750, a young Welshman, John Adam Dagyr, set up shop in the community and began training cordwainers. Lynn's proximity to Boston gave it easy access to both labor and raw materials, as well as to markets and trading centers. What the local farmers could not supply in leather, ships coming into Boston could. Boston also contributed capital for Lynn's growing industry.[6] Its capital so dominated Lynn that, when the new city hall was dedicated in 1867, all of Lynn was said to have been mortgaged to Boston at one time.[7]

Before the Revolution, Lynn shoemakers exchanged their shoes for other products of local origin in the surrounding New England towns. Even as late as the 1830s, a group of Lynn shoe workers were known as the "bag bosses" because when they produced a few shoes they piled them into bags and disposed of them in Boston as best they could, taking mostly leather stock and truck for payment.[8]

With the coming of the Revolution, Lynn cordwainers expanded their markets outside of New England, competing with Newark and Philadelphia in the production and sale of shoes to national markets. Lynn merchants began traveling through the South peddling shoes. In the late 1830s, Lynn's shoe shops, making "an inferior" but cheaper product, cut seriously into Newark's control over southern markets. By 1810, the city was producing a million pairs of shoes a year, and by 1830, production exceeded over 1.5 million. With the aid of the sewing machine, introduced in 1852, Lynn shoemakers were producing almost ten million shoes yearly by the mid-1850s.[9]

Lynn's population increased with the increase in shoe production. By

1830, the population had grown to over 6,000, and in 1850, to 14,257. After the introduction of the sewing machine, the city grew to almost 20,000, not including the towns of Swampscott and Nahant, which broke off from Lynn in the 1850s.

In the early nineteenth century, Lynn shoemakers worked in shacks known locally as "ten-footers." In these shacks a few journeymen, "jours," and apprentices would work under the master cordwainer. The master would cut the leather from which his apprentices and jours would fashion the shoes. The master took over the cutting job because the high cost of leather required that the largest possible number of pieces be obtained from the hide. A poor cutter could waste away the profits in scraps. Within the early shed there was much exchange of information and comradeship. One worker would read newspapers to the others, and if there was a good show in Boston, a collection would be started up to send one of the crew, who would report back in his most imitative manner.[10] These ten-footers were not the utopian social forums of later reminiscence: as early as 1810, local citizens were complaining of the overcrowding of journeymen in the shoe shops.[11]

As the markets for Lynn's shoes expanded, the technique for producing them became more specialized. The master workmen withdrew from the shops and set up special central shops to do the cutting. At this point, merchants also began organizing shoe production, supplying leather, hiring cutters in the central shops, and "putting out" the uppers. The stitching together of the upper parts of the shoes also became separate from the making and lasting of the upper part of the soles of the shoe. The stitching became women's work, first done by the wives or daughters of the early shoemakers and later by the wives of the farmers and fishermen of the surrounding countryside.[12] By 1829, women shoe workers had become so much a part of the shoemaking process that together they were receiving $60,000 in wages annually.[13]

Verses from the following nineteenth-century poem by Lucy Larcom, "Hannah's Binding Shoes," reflect Lynn's putting-out system and the use of these women workers in shoemaking. Under this system, the cut leather was shipped to the countryside for the women to stitch. In this case, the worker is a woman from the small fishing village of Marblehead, just a few miles up the coast from Lynn:

Poor lone Hannah
Faded and wrinkled

Sitting stitching, in a mournful muse,
Bright-eyed beauty she once was,
When the bloom was on the tree;
Spring and Winter
Hannah's at the window binding.

With the development of the putting-out system, control over the total work process passed from the master workman and the artisan shop to the merchant. The merchant now began to play the role of manufacturer, controlling the production process through his manipulation of the sources of raw material and markets, and his subdivision of labor. The shoe industry moved into the stage of manufacturing capitalism. Although the workers were divided according to separate tasks, through their hand power and skill they continued to create the shoe and give it its value. While they may have been performing only one part of the creative process, collectively they remained unique.[14]

In 1848, with the introduction of the kimball last, the skill required for lasting shoes was but one of a series of processes which further transformed shoemaking in Lynn. Now shoemakers were not only divided up and removed from the source of raw materials and markets, but they were also beginning to be separated from the source of power itself. They were embarking on a new stage of organization of production—industrial capitalism.[15] Under this stage, the power of production and the skill involved in it became increasingly part of the machine, while the worker more and more became an extension of the machine. What shoe workers were experiencing at midcentury, textile workers had experienced in the early part of the century. Textile workers in Fall River were already extensions of machines, and the memory of when they produced finished cloth through their own power was distant for some and totally unknown for most. For the shoe workers of Lynn, however, the transformation from artisan to manufacturing capitalism to industrial capitalism occurred within one generation.

Although journeymen shoemakers combined as early as 1844 to secure better wages and conditions, they were not strong enough to prevent women workers from coming into the factory or the assembly line operation for heels. The introduction of the sewing machine in the 1850s created several small stitching shops around the city. Sometimes these shops were small buildings standing by themselves in imitation of the ten-footers of the shoemakers, but more often they became rooms in the shoe factory, whereby industry was beginning to centralize in one building.

Further specialization occurred when the heelers (jours trained specially to make and attach the heels to women's shoes) were separated from the rest of the shoemakers. Between 1830 and 1855, fashion eliminated the heel from women's shoes, but after 1855 heeled shoes were again in style and manufacturers began employing journeymen to heel the shoes. Soon heelers, like cutters and lasters, became specialists in their own branch of the industry and knew nothing else but heeling. After the Civil War, heeling itself became divided within the factory into "nailing," "blacking," and "polishing."[16]

Although these moves toward the factory system took place before 1860, it was not until the great shoe strike of 1860 that Lynn lost the ten-footers, the putting-out system, and the old pre-machine method of shoemaking.[17] The strike marked the beginning of the modern factory system in Lynn. While the strike was called in response to wage reductions, a more basic issue was the journeyman's fear of losing his status under the developing factory system.

In 1862, soon after the strike, which was centered in Lynn and was the biggest strike in America up to that time, the McKay stitcher was invented as a modification of the sewing machine. The McKay stitcher reduced the effort of stitching the uppers to the soles and cut the number of seams in half as well, by sewing directly through the inner, upper, and outer soles. The old hand method required an hour for a skilled worker to finish one pair of shoes. Powered by steam, the McKay stitcher could finish up to eighty pairs an hour.

In 1858, John Wooldridge introduced steam power for making heels in the Lynn factories. After the war, steam was introduced to power the McKay stitcher. The factory system, and in turn the further division of labor, dominated shoe production in Lynn. By 1880, the labor had become so divided that it took thirty-three different jobs to complete the shoe. Beginning with the sole cutter, it took a stripper, a sole cutter, a sorter, and a tier-up to complete the bottoms. The upper stock required an outside cutter, lining cutter, trimming cutter, and dier out. In the stitching shop, the shoe went from lining maker to closer, to seams rubber, to back stayer, to closer on, turner, top stitcher, buttonhole cutter, corder, vamper, and bottom sewer on. The uppers and bottoms then moved to the fasting room where they passed by the stock fitter, laster, sole layer, stitcher, beater out, trimmer, setter, liner, nailer, shaver, buffer, burnisher, and channeller. It is no wonder that a Lynn shoemaker, Horace Eaton, testified in 1908 to the United States Industrial Commission that shoemaking in Lynn had become so specialized that a shoemaker had little sense of other parts of the shoemaking process besides his own. If a shoe worker was thrown out of work, he had to seek another factory which had "identical work" for him to do.[18]

The factory system grouped large numbers of workers in multistory buildings which housed the machines operated by workers brought in from the ten-footers and surrounding countryside. Lynn was transformed from a small satellite community of gardened cottages into an industrial city of triple-deckers and boarding houses crowding close to the rising multistory factories in downtown Lynn (see Photograph 1). David Johnson noted that a few years after 1855, "vacant shops were seen all over the city, until most of them were transformed into hen-houses or coal-pens, or were moved and joined to some house to make a snug little kitchen."[19] Some of the larger ones were transformed into mean tenements for the overcrowded operative class which came to the city to work in the new factories.[20]

By the late nineteenth century, Lynn was the leading shoe manufacturing center in the country. Already in 1880, the city had over 174 shoe factories employing over 10,700 shoe workers. At the turn of the twentieth century, Lynn was described by a shoe worker as "distinctly a city of laborers from the greatest to the least of us."[21] William Betts, in an article about Lynn at the turn of the century, described the regimentation of the work force: "As the whistles blow the hour of closing and the streets resound to the trampling of feet hurrying from the doorways of the great factories . . . home life is resumed till the morning whistle hurries the Army of homemakers to wage-earners."[22]

Lynn attained early success as an industrial city because of its efficient use of technology and the factory system. But that same technology traumatized the city. The city looked back with regret at the loss of the ten-footers and the purported social equality of the old system. By 1880, the local historians had begun publishing nostalgic works on how the city had changed. These works glorified Lynn's success as an industrial city but bemoaned the means to that success, the factory system. The theme of nostalgia for the old system with its social equality and comradeship between master and journeymen runs throughout all these

1. Highlands Housing

1. In the background are the shoe factories where hundreds of the Highlands residents found employment in the late nineteenth and early twentieth centuries. They walked to work and back or to Central Square just this side of the shoe factories in the background. As shown here, both the city of Lynn and the shoe workers' community were highly compact.

works. The loss of the supposedly high mental, political, and social quality of the craftsman's milieu was believed to be a high price to pay for the new industrial success. This sense of loss was shared by shoe workers, shoe manufacturers, and especially the middle class. The dedication of David Johnson's work on Lynn in 1880 reflects this yearning for the past: "To . . . the members of the gentle craft of St. Crispin, Who like the author spent their early days in the old-time shoemaker's shop."[23]

For the middle class, the new system seemed to bring with it what they feared most: an antagonistic working class which felt no ties to the old community. The phrase "floating population" recurred continuously in the literature the local residents wrote about Lynn and the new system. In 1884, an old shoe worker complained to the *Lynn Item* that the city was filling up with an "unorganized floating population," who came when business was good, taking jobs from local shoe workers, but left for their farms in the offseason.[24]

Lynn's anxiety about its new success was demonstrated most dramatically by Reverend Cook's lecture series which was held under the auspices of the First Congregational Church, Lynn's most middle-class church. (The Protestant working class went to the Methodist or Baptist churches.) Listeners packed the Music Hall, Lynn's largest auditorium, where several hundred were forced to stand and many others were turned away. The lectures reflected the ambivalence of the middle class. For example, the first lecture began by praising the city's great success and growth:

This city has been greatly prospered in the last twenty years! . . . There is a new Lynn. It is visible enough in the midst of old Lynn. The City Hall costing $350,000.00, new school buildings, new churches, new business blocks, new factories, fifty-five railway trains a day, have made a new Lynn.[25]

There was also fear of the new Lynn: "Old Lynn was just the same as ever in its moral standing. But the transition state of the shoe business from the old to the present factory system has called in a floating population which has changed the general character of the place."[26]

The people were awed by the change in the industry and by its great production capacity:

Invention has followed invention. The supply of the wants of the new system of factories has taxed the skill of the best experts in machinery in New England. The McKay sewing machine, the shaving machine, the pegging machine, the sole-molding machine, the cable-wire machine, the self-feeding eyelet machine, are but a fraction of the recent inventions not only patented but in use.[27]

However, with the machines "the small shop system has been abandoned and the large factory system has been adopted. . . . A great subdivision of labor has taken place." This change eliminated "the old shoemakers," who "were largely independent in the management of their businesses, each family attending to its own for itself. The large factories have introduced an operative class and an employing class."[28] The middle class, and even many skilled workmen and manufacturers, feared that this change would give rise "to grave moral and industrial perils and abuses."[29]

This point of view was not particularly that "of the capitalist," "of the manufacturer," or "of the Crispin Lodges," as Cook phrased it. Rather, it reflected that of the very anxious middle class which prospered with the city, but at the same time feared the consequences of that prosperity. Rather than confronting the contradictions of capitalism which brought about the "floating population" and the great extremes between the wealth of the owners and the poor conditions of the "operative class," Reverend Cook looked to moral reform as the answer to Lynn's dilemma. He called for missions for the poor and attacks on the "club rooms . . . gambling rooms, and dwelling house sabbath drinking parties." He also advocated the separation of male and female operatives in order to establish "good order in the working class . . . and regularity in industry."[30]

With the factory system came the centralization of the city. This centralization was encouraged by the need of the highly seasonal and low-capital shoe industry to be close to both the financial and warehouse districts of the city in order to have easy access to capital and to the urban labor pool. The centralization of shops was also enhanced by the very process of factory building. Real estate interests such as the Lynn Realty Trust built the multistory factories and then leased out the floor space to each concern (see Map 1). The shoe shops would occupy one, two, or three floors in a six- to ten-story building. As many as three or four shoe shops would be housed in one structure. Manufacturers in these late nineteenth-century factories commonly employed one to two

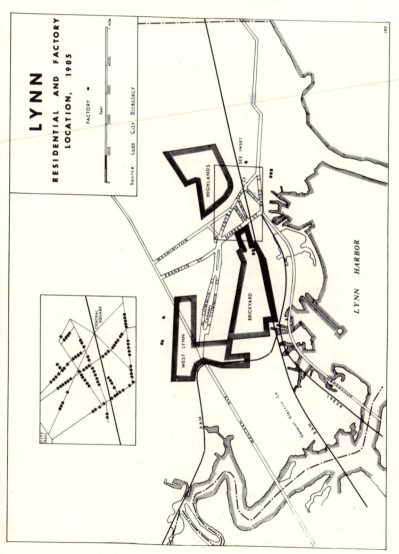

Map 1. Lynn: Residential and Factory Location, 1905

hundred workers.[31] By 1890, Union Street, a main downtown street, was dotted with boarding houses inhabited by the recent arrivals who came to the city for work.[32] A few blocks away adjoining the factory district, Lynn's tenement district, known as the Tenderloin or Brickyard (see Map 1), soon developed into an overcrowded interethnic, working-class slum, "as in the most thickly settled section of New York. . . . The houses are smaller, but many of them are crowded and in a neglected condition. Spaces between and around the houses are filled with debris and the streets, unsightly, ugly, squalid and mean . . ."[33]

The population steadily increased from 15,713 in 1855 to 38,274 in 1880. Before 1870, three-quarters of the male shoe workers commuted into the city from the surrounding areas because of the housing shortages in Lynn or family ties in the neighboring towns.[34] In the 1880s, Lynn's railway connections to Boston further tied the labor market into Boston. Indeed, local residents complained that the rail ties would bring "all the riffraff of Boston to our back doors."[35] Despite these concerns, most workers lived in the city of Lynn by 1890.

The workers who came to live in the tenements and work in the shops were mostly native Americans. Unlike the growing Massachusetts textile industry, which after the Civil War came to depend upon Irish, English, French Canadians, and, later, Eastern European and Portuguese immigrants, the shoe industry relied primarily upon native workers who traced their beginnings to the early putting-out system and whose fathers had been part-time farmers or part-time fishermen. This transitional stage was eased by the seasonal nature of shoe work, so that in the early stages of the factory system, rural New England farmers moved to Lynn for the rush seasons and then returned to their farms during the slack periods. *The Boston Evening Transcript* of November 13, 1886, reported that "probably not more than one half of the [Lynn] operatives would have more than eight months full work if they had that amount."[36] As farming became less viable in New England and families became more dependent upon factory wages, these workers took up permanent residence in the city. In 1880, almost three-fourths of all boot and shoe workers in Massachusetts were of native stock, followed by the Irish and the British Canadian. Even as late as 1895, native-born workers were predominant in the shoe industry.[37]

With the growth in population and in shoe manufacture, the demand for labor increased (see Tables 1 and 2). Connecting railway lines helped

1

POPULATION OF LYNN, 1860-1960

Year	Population	Year	Population
1860	19,083	1915	95,803
1865	20,747	1920	99,148
1870	28,233	1925	103,081
1875	32,600	1930	102,320
1880	38,274	1935	100,909
1885	45,867	1940	93,123
1890	55,727	1945	105,153
1895	62,354	1950	99,738
1900	68,513	1955	99,020
1910	89,336	1960	94,478

SOURCE: United States Decennial Census, 1860-, for each decade; Massachusetts State Census, 1865-, for odd years.

2

NUMBER OF SHOE WORKERS IN LYNN, 1880-1923

Year	Number of Workers	Year	Number of Workers
1880	10,679	1905	11,402
1890	12,478	1905	12,500
1900	10,082	1923	8,221

SOURCE: United States Decennial Census 1880-1920; Massachusetts State Census 1905; and Robert Billups and Phillip Jones, *Labor and Conditions in the Shoe Industry in Massachusetts 1920-1924*, for the 1923 data.

bring in shoe workers from Boston to the factories and gave the workers the option of commuting to Boston jobs during slack times. But Lynn became progressively more dependent upon foreign immigrants as a source of labor. Although shoemaking was dominated by the native-born worker until the early twentieth century, by 1920, 62 percent of the population was either foreign-born or had one or more foreign-born parents.[38] The Irish immigrant came first and dominated the foreign-born population from 1865 to 1895, but this migration fell off slowly after 1905. English and French Canadians came after 1875, followed by a steady but slow German and Scandinavian immigration beginning in 1885. By 1905, Polish, Russian, Italian, and Austrian immigrant groups grew rapidly in Lynn.[39]

These immigrants were not all peasants; they often came over with shoemaking experience. On the national level, over 40 percent of the immigrants entering the shoe industry had been shoe workers before arriving in the United States. In Lynn, the percentages were even higher. Forty-six percent of the French Canadians, just under 49 percent of the Russian Jews, and 88 percent of the Italians had prior shoemaking experience.

Not only immigrants but also larger proportions of women began to fill up the ranks of the working class, especially during the rush seasons. The number of women laborers in the shoe industry in the state rose over 136 percent from 1875 to 1885, with Lynn the leader in that growth.[40]

The influx of immigrants continued what the introduction of the factory system had begun—the transformation of Lynn into a city of tenements. The influx gave rise to large numbers of lodging houses, boarding houses, and overcrowding within the tenements as a result of the practice of taking in lodgers. Between 1908 and 1914, the number of boarding houses increased from 192 to 226.[41] In 1909, the United States Immigration Commission noted that

> although a considerable proportion of the wives with families the heads of which are connected with the shoe industry, as well as other female members of the families, seek regular employment outside the home as a means of contributing to the family support, a much larger proportion of wives add to the earnings of their husbands by taking boarders or lodgers in the home.[42]

The increased cost of tenements exacerbated the crowded conditions. For example, in order to stay in a tenement at the same cost, a worker had to switch from a six-room tenement in 1878 to a four-room tenement in 1897.[43]

Families with large numbers of children had the greatest trouble securing housing. Many residents of the Brickyard complained to the local settlement house worker that they could not find decent housing and were forced to pay exorbitant rents, including an extra fifty cents a child per week to the landlords. Thus, even greater crowding resulted from the high rents and the discrimination against families with children, since these families were often forced to take on boarders or live in poor and over-crowded conditions.[44]

Housing quickly began to eliminate open space in Lynn. A 46,000 square foot plot of land in west Lynn, which had been an orchard with a small grocery store in 1905, had over eight tenement houses "packed like sardines" and supporting over 377 people by 1910.[45] The shortage of housing and the continual overcrowding put tremendous strains on the working-class families; at the same time, it helped break down isolation and increase the workers' sense of interdependence. Although the shoe trade was divided into several isolated tasks, within the same house and especially the same neighborhood these workers were thrown back together again. Although a skilled cutter or channeller would not necessarily be forced to take in boarders, next door his co-worker might be forced, because of illness, unemployment, or misfortune, to take in a semiskilled or unskilled shoe worker as a boarder.[46]

Despite the rapid and dramatic growth of the American economy and the immense fortunes made by Lynn manufacturers, clearly visible in the diamond district, Lynn shoe workers had to struggle for subsistence even in the best of times. The study of working people's budgets by the Massachusetts Bureau of Statistics of Labor in 1875 clearly shows the fine line between a comfortable living without luxury, which some of the skilled workers were able to maintain, and bare survival. In the study sample, a skilled worker such as the well-off American shoe channeller could live with some security, although prolonged sickness in the family or too many children could often mean the difference between debt and comfort. He earned $714, $681 of which went for expenses for his family of four. He was able to support his family and maintain his membership in various fraternal organizations, and to pay out $6 a year for newspaper and journal subscriptions. His family ate well on his income in a tenement of six well furnished rooms, with a garden attached. He worked eight and a half months a year and was able to save in case of sickness.

The channeller was one of the lucky few. More typical was an American laster who earned $495 and had to pay out $520. Work cutbacks and accumulated debts forced his family to live in an overcrowded tenement in a rundown working-class neighborhood. Other shoe workers with incomes below $500 a year lived comfortably if they could either limit the size of their family or send their children into the shops to supplement the family income. An Irish family of five managed by adding the $196 income from a fourteen-year-old daughter to the $508 of the father. For large families, the difference between debt and comfort was usually the income of children. An English shoe worker with two children, aged sixteen and fourteen, both of whom worked in the shops, managed to live in relative comfort and save for the future but only through the income of the children. Even though the father's job involved skill, he and his family were directly involved in the interests of unskilled labor in which his children were employed. A wage cut and deteriorating conditions for the unskilled workers affected the skilled workers who depended upon the income of the total family for survival.

Some workers were even more oppressed. Workers in the sample with children too young to work, or because of sickness or a slack in trade, were forced to live in excessively overcrowded, polluted working-class areas with overflowing outhouses and "unbearable stench." Such families simply could not afford the resulting sickness.[47] They could expect little improvement until the children were old enough to enter the shops. The budgets of these families did not allow for complete meals, much less for membership in societies.

Conditions for shoe workers did not significantly improve by the end of the nineteenth century. Between 1872 and 1881, they experienced a general decline in wages. While wages began to increase between 1881 and 1897, they still remained below the 1872 rates. Prices for food and dry goods also declined during this period, leaving workers in only a slightly improved situation over that of twenty years before. By 1911, a shoe worker able to work fifty weeks a year (which was unusual) could earn $750, but most of this added income, which was $230 more than that of the average shoe worker in 1890, was eroded by the increased cost of living during the first two decades of the twentieth century. Living costs jumped 13 percent between 1900 and 1910 and 172 percent between 1910 and 1920. Thus, it is not surprising to find that a shoe worker was brought to court in 1908 for not having beds for his children. Both parents were shoe workers but could not support their six nonworking children in their overcrowded tenement in the Brickyard.[48]

For the shoe workers who could remember the days before the great fortunes or the stories of older workers, the contrast between the wealth of the shoe manufacturers and their own bare subsistence struck a bitter chord. They worked hard and yet reaped little material benefit. For the more radical, the obvious reason was "the wealth of the manufacturers."

Although it was not impossible to rise from worker to manufacturer in Lynn, it became progressively more difficult to do so as the nineteenth century wore on. The early cutter could, with the aid of friends and a local bank, rent a floor in one of the old buildings or set up his own ten-footer, either buy or rent a stitching machine, hire a few dozen workmen, cut his own leather, and move up from worker to manufacturer. This mobility gave rise to Reverend Cook's statement in 1871 that "our prosperous manufacturers are men from the common walks of life."[49] As the century progressed, division of labor became more acute, machinery more integral to the production process, and upward mobility more difficult—particularly because the laborer was able to save so little.[50]

Despite the increasing difficulty of moving from worker to manufacturer, the manufacturing class was not a completely closed group. The shoe industry, unlike textiles or iron, required a low level of liquid capital investment. The shoe manufacturer did not have to build his own factory; he could actually rent a few floors from a realty company. Machinery did not have to be bought; it could be rented from the United Shoe Machinery Company. With little investment in either space or machinery, technological innovation could easily be incorporated into the new and old factory. The large number of new, although small, shops started each year indicates the relative ease of entering shoe manufacturing.[51]

Although moving up to the manufacturing class was less difficult in Lynn than in a textile center, there was a certain continuity within the manufacturing class. The diamond district around Ocean Street, as the residential area of the manufacturing class was called, was not an open area. The city directories from the late nineteenth through the early twentieth centuries reflect fairly continuous domination by a few groups of shoe manufacturing families.

The fact that shoe manufacturing required a low level of capital investment ultimately threatened Lynn's position as the nation's leading shoe manufacturing city. However, tradition, the skill of the shoe workers, and the convenience of closely located related industries kept the shoe industry strong enough through the early twentieth century. In fact, it continued to grow and expand until 1918. In 1914, the city was still the nation's leading shoe center, producing over eight and a quarter million pairs of shoes. By 1919, however, it had fallen behind Haverhill and New York City, and by 1921, although still in third place, its production had fallen off by over five million pairs a year, a loss of 29 percent from 1919. The new shops that were set up in Lynn were tenuous and small in comparison to the nineteenth-century shops. Although five hundred shoe manufacturing companies were established in Lynn in the first fifteen years of the twentieth century, only eighty-eight of these were there by the outbreak of World War I, and most of these shops employed only fifty to sixty workers. In the first four years of the 1920s alone, the city lost sixty-seven shops. Forty-six were old shops, some over twenty years in operation and many employing over a hundred workers. The closed shops accounted for over four thousand jobs. At the beginning of 1920, Lynn had one hundred shoe manufacturing concerns; four years later, only eighty-eight, including those set up during the intervening period, remained.[52]

In 1905, Lynn employed 11, 402 shoe workers, with 2,884 workers in related industries. By 1923, Lynn dropped to 8,221 workers, a loss of 28 percent (see Table 2).[53] The huge old shoe factory buildings began to display "floor space for rent" signs where help wanted signs once hung (as seen in Photograph 2). A real estate man stated in 1924 that "there were now thousands of feet of vacant floor space in Lynn formerly occupied by shoe manufacturers. . . . In 1920 all space in Lynn was in use."[54] The massive buildings, acting as warehouses and factory-outlet stores, became ghostly reminders of former activity. Downtown was no longer clogged at lunchtime with hungry shoe workers. Lunchrooms closed down, and central Lynn became a depressed shopping area. The city, which had been so overcrowded in the nineteenth and early twentieth centuries, thinned out with vacant flats opening up.[55]

While manufacturers claimed labor conditions as the reason for leaving the city, this was only part of the answer. Lynn's tradition as one of the strongest, most militant, and independent union centers in the country existed long before the 1920s. Its workers may have been tough union men, but they were also tough workers. To quote manufacturers who were thinking of leaving the city "to get away from labor conditions," the Lynn worker was "as skillful and efficient as workers in any other locality." Another manufacturer stated that "our [Lynn] employees are very efficient and do as much or more work per man per hour, and do it as well if not better than shoe workers elsewhere." Still another stated that "Lynn shoe workers are faster and more efficient and do a better grade work than workers in factories in nearby states."[56] Workers

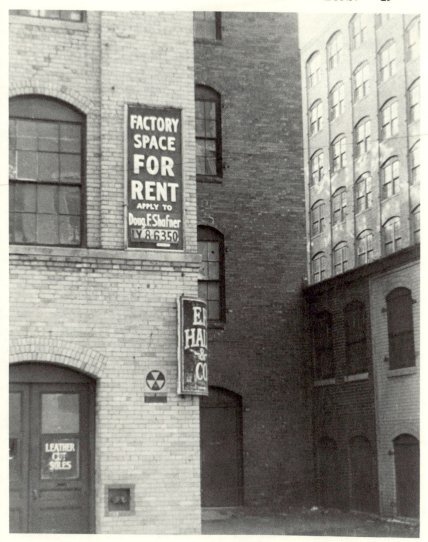

2. Factory Space for Rent

By the 1920s, many of Lynn's large factory buildings reflected both the past and the future of the city. Here the older shoe factory signs indicate more prosperous times, and the for rent signs point to the future of the shoe industry. Notice also the compactness of the factories.

in Lynn (although paid more than the national average) were paid less than shoe workers in Haverhill, which surpassed Lynn in shoe production by 1919.

Lynn lost its shoe industry because of many factors, the most important of which was the industrial depression which hit the New England industries before the rest of the country. Of the sixty-seven factories Lynn lost, only twenty-seven moved elsewhere, and forty went out of business; clearly, then, much of the loss stemmed from depression in the trade. Shoe shops were also closing down or running short-time in Brockton, Rochester, Cincinnati, Brooklyn, Chicago, and St. Louis. A second factor was the national trend among shoe manufacturers of moving out of the highly industrialized East Coast regions, and moving west and southward into the less industrialized fringe areas. This movement occurred in response to land costs, rental space available, and taxes, as well as to labor costs and unrest. The shoe industry was one of the first industries to move out because it was a low capital investment industry. Very little shoe capital was invested in buildings and machinery in Lynn. Its capital could quickly be liquidated, be put elsewhere, or be invested in a new shoe shop in Maine. Beyond the skill of the shoe workers, little else was needed which could not be quickly obtained in the new location.

As the shoe industry declined in Lynn, the remaining manufacturers became more hostile towards the workmen. This period saw the introduction of the yellow dog contract and union busting.[57] Manufacturers used the threat of closing to bring down wages and curb other demands. By the end of the 1920s, a shoe worker could no longer expect to pass the job on to his son.[58]

In an effort to protect their jobs, some shoe workers in the late 1920s began forming cooperatives or worker-owned shoe companies. In 1928, the workers of the newly liquidated Cushing Shoe Company asked James Daly, a shoe worker who had moved up through the ranks and had become a manager, to form a worker-owned shoe factory. The employees subscribed the stock among themselves and started the Golden Rule Shoe Company. Soon, other workers whose factories had gone bankrupt asked to join the cooperative venture. These new companies were model factories for the workers. All workers were required to have union cards, and when a worker called in sick, his comrades filled in for him to prevent loss of pay. Although the Golden Rule Shoe Company continued to expand during the difficult years of the late 1920s and early 1930s, such cooperative ventures were not permanent solutions to the nationwide depression in the trade and could do little to stop the continuing loss of jobs in the Lynn area.[59]

Well before the decline of the shoe industry, Lynn industrialists began looking elsewhere to invest their capital. In 1883, Charlie Coffin, a shoe manufacturer, purchased the American Electric Company of Bridgeport, Connecticut, and brought it to Lynn. Later, in 1892, the Thompson-Houston Company of Lynn, as Coffin's new company was now called, joined with the Edison Electric Company to form the General Electric, with large plants in Lynn and Schenectady, New York. The General Electric plant in Lynn quickly grew into a large complex of massive buildings giving employment to several thousand workers. By 1930, General Electric employed more workmen than the shoe industry.

As the shops shut down, many shoe workers moved into the General Electric plant, which had expanded greatly in the late 1920s. Many more shoe workers either retired early, picked up marginal jobs, or tried to secure another position in the remaining shoe shops.[60] Unemployment ran high in Lynn during the Depression and, except for a brief interlude during World War II, it continued high, especially for shoe workers.

As Tables 3 and 4 indicate, in the early 1920s shoe workers typically attempted to stay within their trade, despite the industry decline. Instead, their children left the industry. Most of the retired shoe workers interviewed for this study in 1972 stated that they learned the trades of their parents but that their own children went into other work. Thomas Coleman, an eighty-year-old retired shoe cutter in Lynn, the son of a shoe laster, reported that almost all the children he knew as a child went into the shoe trade: "that's all there was . . . there was plenty of shops to get a job (at)."[61] A commentator in 1901 noted that Lynn children

were born in the business of shoemaking. . . . That they should one day or another join the ranks of the shoemakers of the city was with them a matter of course from childhood. The children on the street practically knew nothing but shoes, and let a boy at the age twelve or fourteen start to work and ninety-nine out of a hundred you will find that it is within the walls of a shoe factory. He meets his companions and they ask him what he is doing, the chances are that he will tell them that he is inking edges, cementing channels or something of a like nature with the result that the other

3

OCCUPATIONAL MOBILITY OF LYNN SHOE WORKERS
DURING THE SHOE INDUSTRY DEPRESSION

Shoe Workers	1925	1935	1940
Shoe Workers	200	72	37
General Electric	—	—	3
Laborer	—	5	10
Mechanic	—	3	1
Clerical	—	1	2
Telephone Company	—	—	1
Other	—	9	8
Retired	—	1	3
Unemployed	—	14	27
Lost to the Directory[1]	—	95	108

1. "Lost to the Directory" does not indicate that the workers left the city. Any number of factors may account for the failure of these workers to be lost to the Directory, such as loss of a job, change of address, failure to be home, lack of a telephone, or poverty. When cross-checking Odd Fellows with the City Directory, underenumeration was found to be between 30 and 50 percent.

SOURCE: *Lynn City Directories,* 1925, 1935, 1940, random sample.

4

OCCUPATIONAL MOBILITY OF WOMEN SHOE WORKERS
IN LYNN DURING THE SHOE INDUSTRY DEPRESSION

Shoe Workers	1925	1935	1940
Shoe Worker	40	10	4
General Electric	—	—	1
Retired	—	—	2
Other	—	2	1
Unemployed	—	8	13
Lost to the Directory[1]	—	20	19

1. See Table 3, n. 1.

SOURCE: *Lynn City Directories,* 1925, 1935, 1940, random sample.

youth goes home to his family and asks for a chance to go to work the same as his neighbor.[62]

The shoe workers' children who entered the work force during the Great Depression did not enter the shoe trade, but either went into the General Electric plant or left Lynn altogether.[63] The case records of the Associated Charities reflect the attempt of the older generation of shoe workers to hold on to their jobs and of their children to look elsewhere during the Depression years. Steven Miller, an Armenian shoe worker who worked for the Brofy Shoe Company for fifteen years as a vamper, got a job at the Walsh Shoe Company when Brofy closed its doors. His children stayed out of the shoe business.[64] Rose Morcelle's husband, a laster, left his family to find a job elsewhere when the shops shut down, and she was forced to seek work at General Electric.[65]

Other shoe workers remained in Lynn but commuted to the remaining shops in the nearby cities of Boston, Beverly, Chelsea, Danvers, and Salem. The move not only cost the worker his fare, but also often meant poorer working conditions, longer hours, no union protection, and lower wages.[66]

By remaining in the shops as long as possible, and either sending children and wives to other jobs or removing them from the job market, the Lynn working class made a slow transition from the shoe industry to the electrical industry. During the Depression, shoe and leather workers in Lynn who could not find enough work supplemented family income by taking home piece work which the whole family, especially the mother and children, would work on at night. The practice was first noticed by grammar school teachers who complained that their pupils were falling asleep in class.[67] Ironically, the workmen were returning to the work patterns followed by the artisans who worked in the ten-footers.

Other shoe workers who lost their jobs and could not make the transition fell back on methods which the working-class community had long since developed for dealing with depressions within the trade. The worker who could afford the dues looked to his lodge or club for support. Boarders and relatives often helped when jobs were scarce. If the husband lost his job as a shoe worker, but the wife worked as a waitress or kept boarders and lodgers, the family could manage to remain in the city in hopes that a shoe job would open up. Often, if the wife lost her job as a shoe worker, she stayed out of the job market or looked elsewhere for work. When the head of a settlement house asked questions of occupation during the Depression period, many residents of the working-class district responded that a "brother (or other relative) works."[68]

With the loss of the shoe shops, life in Lynn was unavoidably altered. Despite the attempt of many workers to hold on to the older patterns of work and leisure, it became increasingly impossible to do so, especially for younger workers who were soon forced to find work in other sectors of the economy. The empty factories ultimately created empty lunchrooms and cafes. Living in the working-class communities bordering on central Lynn became less viable for workers forced to commute outside the city, and the central city institutions became less patronized by workers in west Lynn's General Electric plant (see Photograph 3). By 1910, with over ten thousand workers, General Electric had almost as many employees as all the city's shoe factories, and by 1920, the number of electrical workers surpassed the number of shoe workers.[69] By the end of the Great Depression, General Electric dominated the city, as the shoe factories had seventy-five years earlier, though symbolically not at the center but at the western edge of the city.

3. General Electric Riverworks, Lynn

The Riverworks at the extreme western edge of Lynn reflect the large scale and
the distance between the workers' community and the place of work which the
General Electric workers found by the 1920s.

3

Worker and Community

The workmen who came to Lynn's shoe shops and factories, beginning with the artisans in the first half of the nineteenth century, developed a sense of community solidarity which was passed on from generation to generation. The system of formal and informal institutions which these workmen built provided a basis for their community, giving it flexibility and continuity. The workers taught the new members of the work force, both those from Europe and from rural New England, the strength and power of unionism, class solidarity, and community cohesion. They integrated the new workers into the community, instilling in them the idea that Lynn was a union town and that the strength of the workers lay in the union and the community. Immigrant workers and children of immigrant workers were taught pride in their work and their community. They learned of past struggles and felt themselves a part of that past.[1]

The new worker was easily assimilated into the community partly because the old workers did not feel that the community was threatened by wave upon wave of "alien workers." Even when times were hard and job competition the greatest, older workers perceived that their interest lay in a united community, encompassing immigrant and native alike. The nineteenth- and twentieth-century immigrants came in small numbers and moved into Lynn's existing working-class neighborhoods. Their style of life and condition of work enabled them to be integrated into an existing class and community.[2]

The workers were able to keep their community alive and strong from generation to generation because they controlled a network of institutions upon which the individual workers depended, not only for higher wages

and job security, but also for the job itself, for social life, and even for
family security. As the new immigrants arrived, they moved into the common working-class ghetto, the Brickyard, where their neighbors were
native American, English, Irish, Italian, Greek, Scandinavian, and Jewish.[3]
Unlike other industrial workers who found themselves increasingly isolated
from their fellow workers, especially at the beginning of the twentieth
century—the very time in which most industries experienced new waves
of immigrant workers—shoe workers continued to work together. They
worked in small shops where they learned to know and depend upon their
co-workers (Photographs 4 and 5). "The man who joins a union does so
knowing full what is expected of him as a union man. He also expects
others to back him up in his line of work."[4] They filed into central Lynn's
lunchrooms for breaks, where they met more workers. For entertainment,
they went to the union hall to play cards, pool, and billiards, to sing union
songs, and to listen to the oldtimers' tales of past struggles.[5] They worked
and ate and lived side by side with the older workers and thus were accepted into the unions and social affairs of the working class.

   The shoe workers lived near the shops where they worked. In the
nineteenth century, families resided in the nearby working-class ghettos
of the Brickyard or Highlands, while the single men and women lived
in the boarding and lodging houses which lined Union Street and adjoining avenues and streets.[6] The lodging and boarding houses were within
easy walking distance of shoe shops in downtown Lynn. They were also
close to the social and activity centers—the cafes, lunchrooms, poolrooms,
and union halls.

   A typical nineteenth-century boarding house provided housing for nine
or ten people, both male and female, with the landlady keeping the home
"as one big family."[7] During their lunch hour, the workers could either
return to their boarding houses or go to the numerous cafes and lunchrooms in central Lynn. Many of the lunchrooms and cafes were open all
night long, providing a continual source of companionship, news, and job
information, as well as food.[8] These establishments were not the only
centers of social life for the working class. The unions played an important
part in welding together a community, serving both as wage and job condition negotiators, and as social centers. The union hall, the largest in the
late nineteenth century being the Lasters Hall, was not only a meeting
place for union business but also the shoe workers' center for social activity. After work, card tables would be set up in the main meeting rooms

4. Inside a Cutting Room, Circa 1900

This photo illustrates the close contact between the workers. Women and men worked together, sharing in the discussions which went on above the noise of the machines. As is obvious from the ties and suit vests of the cutters at the window, the cutters took great pride in their dress.

—*Courtesy of Lynn Historical Society*

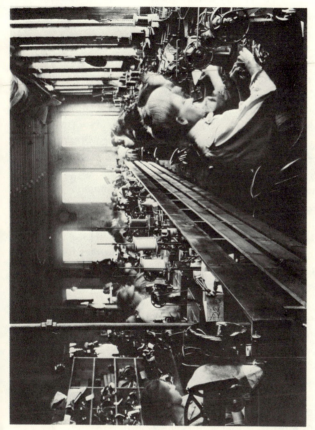

5. Inside a Stitching Room, Circa 1900

Like the cutters, the female stitchers worked in close proximity of one another. Conversations about social events and work went on above the hum of the sewing machines. The conversations, ranging from child rearing, marriage expectations, and dating patterns to job conditions and wages, were shared in by immigrants from Europe and native-born workers from Massachusetts, and based on their common experiences, they built up class loyalty.

—*Courtesy of Lynn Historical Society*

and the workers would play cards throughout the night with as many as fifty games going at once. There was plenty of talk and comradeship at the union hall. The Lasters Union Hall had a billiards room and poolroom which took in from ten to twenty dollars a week from members and friends who played there rather than in the other public poolrooms around Central Square.[9]

Unions also sponsored mutual benefit associations. The benefit association of the Lasters Union provided a library with local and national labor papers, a social center, and benefit affairs, banquets, balls, and concerts.[10]

The union hall reinforced the working class's sense of class interdependence, for it not only defended them on the job but it also provided for them off the job. The newspapers carried in the union library transmitted the message of class solidarity, and the experience of the workers in the union's social center strengthened that message. Their work place experiences were interpreted in the school of unionism, and the lessons were clear: Labor creates the wealth of the nation and the community, and only through collective support and solidarity can labor attain the fruits of its toil. To those who doubted this lesson, the more radical would point to the diamond district where the owners lived and would ask: "Where did their wealth come from and what have they given the worker for his labor? If the worker is in need, who supplied him with a loan or benefits? Who helps tide him over when the owners have callously thrown him out of the shops during the slack seasons?"

The union social center and the informal working-class social centers molded the working-class ideology which was passed on to other members of the class, especially recent arrivals. Typical of social center support was that given the women members of local 38 of the United Shoe Workers. This local was founded when the Reese buttonhole machine replaced the old Singer sewing machine, resulting in greater productivity and reduction in the piece rates. The local not only managed to raise the rates, but also provided a strong sense of comradeship among the members.

There was never a problem of a quorum at Lynn union meetings as there was for Brockton unions. While the Lynn union did not have sickness benefits, it provided food for sick workers, and if a member was in financial need a whist party or other social event was held to raise funds. The union sponsored a good deal of social activity, including monthly dances in which unionists from other locals were invited. Through these benefits and social events, the workers learned to look to their union's sisters and brothers for support. The interunion affairs also universalized the sense of class and union solidarity.

Unlike the textile towns of New England, Lynn was not ethnically segregated. A turn-of-the-century observer noted of the city that there was "no distinct race quarter. The social and housing problems were not those of race, but those that represent the ebb and flow of immigration everywhere."[11] Workers with families tended to live in the crowded working-class areas in the center wards. Over 55 percent of a random sample of shoe workers drawn from the Lynn City Directory of 1905 lived within a half mile of Central Square and the major shoe factories; 35 percent lived within a mile, again within walking distance of Central Square, and only 9 percent lived over a mile of the Square. Most of the shoe workers sampled were clustered in the Highlands, the Brickyard, or along Washington Street near the factories.[12] Although some of the workers were moving out into the newly settled areas of the Highlands or west Lynn, most working-class families lived within walking distance of their place of employment. The Brickyard or Tenderloin district of Lynn, just south of the downtown shops, was the center of the working-class community. Throughout the late nineteenth century, the Brickyard was known as a tough working-class area.[13]

When the weather was pleasant, shoe operatives would go down to Central Square where Simon's Poolroom, various bowling alleys, and numerous cafes were gathering points and sources of information for friends and fellow workmen. A retired shoe worker reminisced that "if you were to come down to Central Square in Lynn, the place was full of people, always a friend, if you go to a restaurant and have a cup of coffee, there was a half dozen friends at least, who were sitting down, having a cup of coffee or what not, something like that."[14]

If a shoe worker was laid off, he would spend his days at Hunt's Cafe which was known as "Crispin's Congress" because so many shoe workers spent their time there discussing the affairs of the trade and the world. They would commonly meet friends and ask for job information there, and in this way Hunt's functioned much like a French bistro.[15] Another popular spot was the Waldorf Cafeteria, which, as late as 1941, was said to be a place where shoe workers would gather to drink coffee and "analyze the city's ills and question the cutting of salaries of union job holders."[16] Local union reports carried advertisements for lunchrooms emphasizing the social and political aspect of the lunchrooms. Mac-

Kenzie's Lunch on Blake Street claimed to be "strictly a union house," and Wyman's Union Lunch on Monroe Street in the heart of the shoe manufacturing district was open all night for socializing and gathering. Wyman's also advertised "tables for women."[17]

In remembering how Lynn had changed over the last seventy years, retired shoe and electrical workers testified to the importance of this walking community in holding the working class together and in giving it a sense of its own community. They complained that the automobile had destroyed their community by pushing people outside of walking distance and thereby separating them from local "hand-outs," clubs, and social activity.[18]

> Shoe workers are not together the way they used to be,
> even in the shop. There is no more familiarity. One guy
> comes from Boston, another guy comes from New
> Hampshire, another guy comes from west Lynn, east
> Lynn and all them places. Years ago it seemed that every-
> body came from the Brickyard or something. You knew
> everybody who worked next to you, you knew him from
> somewhere, you either met him for coffee, or you met
> him for lunch.[19]

Some institutions were vital to the working class because they offered means of dealing with the constant fluctuations in employment in the shoe industry. In 1886, the *Boston Evening Transcript* estimated that not more than half of the Lynn operatives had more than eight months of full work.[20] In 1871, Reverend Cook in his *Music Hall Lectures* stated that during the lulls each year, thousands of operatives were dismissed from work.[21] During these lulls, which lasted throughout the nineteenth and the first part of the twentieth centuries, shoe workers had to look elsewhere for work or live off savings. Many became ditch diggers for the city or construction workers during the summer lags. It was important that they have access to job information, either in Lynn, Boston, or Salem, and for this information they depended upon friends and relatives and the social gathering places.[22] At the turn of the century, a woman who took a job in Lynn as a shoe worker noted that most of the jobs were passed on to friends or relatives. When there was a job opening at the shop, the news was spread at the local cafes, and friends' names were put in.[23] The workers' dependence upon each other for job information strengthened their sense of community, and the functioning of the community institutions reinforced already existing feelings of loyalty to the class. The boss, even though still the boss, did not provide the job or community that was provided by fellow members of the working class. The boss's exploitative role was not muted by a sense of dependence for the job.

These sources of information were important to both the permanent residents of Lynn and to the "floating population." In the early factory period of the second half of the nineteenth century, it was estimated that over 30 percent of the work force changed jobs annually.[24] This "floating population," most of which was made up of young workers, usually drifted between the local shoe towns of Boston, Brockton, Haverhill, and Salem. They would leave their native city in search of employment and adventure, especially during the seasonal lags, and would return to Lynn when work was available there. They would eventually settle down in the city and become permanent residents. Even before settling down, however, they would form close ties with the city, through relatives and friends, and they still maintained connections with Lynn's working-class institutions.[25] When these migrant workers returned to Lynn, they would go to the local lunchrooms and union halls for job information. "If you were looking for a job you had to go to the union hall."[26]

In the community itself, working parents developed a strong sense of community interdependence in order to meet the demands upon the family. With a large number of mothers employed in the shops, the working class became dependent upon each other for care of the children. An early twentieth-century observer noted that children of working mothers "are found in groups everywhere."[27] The working women relied on the neighbors to watch over the children. Relatives, grandparents, and neighbors were expected "to have an eye on the children too young to go to school. . . . A woman worker stated that 'any old woman who will keep the house is welcome, to look after the children while the mother works'."[28] In one documented case, neighbors cared for a working woman's children while she worked in a shoe factory. Later, she moved in with another widow and shared child care with the woman's "old lady."[29]

One mother who worked in a shoe factory, a widow with two children, prepared breakfast for the children before she left for work. On her way out at 6:30 A.M. she woke the children, an eleven-year-old girl and a younger boy. The children did the housework before school, and, when the mother came home from work, they had dinner ready. They saw nothing unusual about this pattern since "it was the life of the majority of [their] friends."[30] A social worker in 1908 became concerned when she learned that a two-year-old child, Bessie, was locked out of the house every morning when her parents went off to work. They left food for her on the lower step. Although the social worker was alarmed by this situation, people living in the Brickyard accepted it as necessary.[31]

Generally, however, children too young to go to school hung out in groups, with the peer group providing most of the protection and child care. At the foot of Astor Street in the Brickyard, "Bennet's pond" was a recreation area for the children. It was considered safe, for it was close to neighbors. In December 1907, some small children fell through the ice but were pulled out by the older children. The local paper reported that "the boys have pulled more than one boy or girl out of the water."[32] The groups, adopting names such as the "dirty dozen," the "wharf rats," and the "forty thieves," mostly provided the working-class children with group comradeship. The local authorities, however, viewed many of these peer groups as "gangs" and were particularly disturbed by their breaking windows in abandoned houses and factories.[33] During strikes, these gangs would often gather at the factories, break windows, and join in harassing the scabs.[34]

Thus, the children grew up depending upon each other, while their parents depended upon neighbors, lodge brothers, and union brothers and sisters to watch over the younger children, find jobs, and help out in tight times. When the children were older, they joined the lodges and benefit societies as their parents had before them.

Besides their unions, the working class had numerous clubs, societies, and lodges which tied them together. A turn-of-the-century observer stated that "the social side of the [Lynn] wage-earner's life seem[ed] to be developed through lodges and benefit organizations, some exclusively for men, more open to both sexes."[35]

The Independent Order of Odd Fellows was one of Lynn's strongest working-class lodges. In 1872, the Odd Fellows erected their first building. The early lodge provided its members with sickness, funeral, and death benefits, as well as with relief in times of need or during seasonal lags.[36] The by-laws of an Odd Fellows lodge stated that the lodge would provide "for death and funeral benefits for a brother," "health care and visiting nurse for brothers who [were] sick," and "benefits in other areas if a brother travel[ed] outside an area."[37]

The Odd Fellows lodges were a source of comradeship and activity, especially political discussion. The local lodge met the needs arising from the shoe workers' unique situation. The shoe workers were subject to two layoffs each year, and the lodges offered the unemployed worker assurance that his family would not starve during the off season. If he had to travel outside Lynn in search of a job during the seasonal recession, he knew that his lodge membership would give him contacts in the new area.

A new need for benefits occurred when the sole-cutting machines were adopted during the second half of the nineteenth century. The new machines, started by a friction buffey, were liable to switch on at any time. The operator of the machine had to feel all around the edge of the sole to determine that the machine had completed the cut. If the machine happened to start while the cutter was inspecting, that portion of his hand which was over the die would be cut off. Every stockroom in Lynn during the late nineteenth and early twentieth centuries had some men who had lost some portion of their hands.[38] These men needed the assurance that, after losing a finger or a hand, they would be taken care of until they were well enough to work or could find another job. The sole-cutting machine was one of a series of machines that, especially during the nineteenth century, endangered the operator's health or job. The workers in the leather industry, which grew up in Lynn during the nineteenth century to supply the workers with leather, were particularly prone to toxic fumes given off in the process. These men needed the benefits which the Odd Fellows offered them, as is shown in Table 5.[39]

As General Electric, with its heavy equipment and dangerous machines, became an important industry in Lynn, its workers also joined the Odd Fellows, as their shoe worker fathers had before them. By 1914, Lynn had fifteen Odd Fellows lodges, which provided members with job information, especially about the General Electric plant, before and just after World War I.[40]

The Odd Fellows was not the only lodge which had predominantly working-class members and served as an important social force in the working-class community. Lynn workingmen, confronted by the spectre of the factory system, formed several local benefit organizations to provide sickness and death benefits, as well as financial aid, during periods of

5

OCCUPATIONAL MAKEUP OF ODD FELLOWS
MEMBERS: LYNN, 1908, 1914

Occupations	West Lynn Lodge, 1908	Kearsarge Lodge, 1914
Shoe Worker	57	22
General Electric	30	92
Blue Collar (Other)	42	40
Skilled Worker	42	51
Craftsman (Watchmaker)	—	4
White Collar	52	40
Upper Class (Doctor)	6	12
Blue Collar[1]	171	205
White Collar[2]	58	52
Craftsman[3]	—	4

1. Blue Collar combines the occupations of Shoe Worker, General
Electric, Blue Collar (Other), and Skilled Worker.
2. White Collar combines the occupations of White Collar and
Upper Class (Doctor).
3. Craftsman is the occupation of Craftsman (Watchmaker).

SOURCE: Membership List of Odd Fellows, Lynn Lodges.

recession and seasonal lulls. These clubs and associations gave the workers
some control over their situation and security in the face of economic
instability. Workers who could remember when their parents worked on
shoes by hand or within the support system of the family realized the
importance of interdependence. When entering the factories of the new
era, they also looked for support within their community. Support and
aid was a major function of their unions and organizations. This aid
substantiated their belief in class dependence and solidarity. Without
that solidarity, they would be left to the mercy of the manufacturer and
to harsh and unsympathetic public charity. The institutional defenses
against injury and want also provided a basis for defense against the
manufacturer and gave experiential support to an ideology based upon
class loyalty.

The Lynn Mutual Benefit Association, formed in 1880, was one such
organization of skilled shoe workers and lower white collar members. The

Washington Mutual Benefit Association also had upper-working-class officers, with all its trustees being shoe workers. The Independent Order of Industry and the United American Mechanics were both working-class organizations without any middle-class officers or trustees. Most of the members were shoe workers as well as boarders. The Ancient Order of the United Workmen founded in 1881 was also a working-class benefit organization, consisting mostly of boarding shoe workers. These organizations offered the shoe workers who boarded a surrogate family and comradeship, giving them a place to go after supper to talk to friends and other shoe workers.[41]

The need for benefit organizations among the working class can be seen from the case of the "Jones" family which came before the Associated Charities in 1915. The husband worked full time at General Electric until January 1915, when he died of pleural pneumonia. The children were too young to work, and the family was forced to seek aid from the city's Overseer of the Poor when the mother's plan to take in boarders and do light work failed. The family received aid for a short time from an uncle in Nova Scotia, but his limited resources could not support the family of three. The family suffered continual want from 1915 until the death of the mother in 1940, despite the fact that the older daughter went to work in the shoe shops and the son periodically found employment.[42] Every working-class family was similarly threatened by poverty; consequently, the advantages of a benevolent association or lodge were not overlooked. These societies provided not only security but also a constant reminder of the reality of the poverty which the working class faced. The threat of poverty helped forge a sense of class identification within the different working-class organizations, helped explain the separation between middle-class and working-class lodges, and reinforced the workers' sense of class division. Their precarious existence on the abyss of poverty dramatically conflicted with the wealth in the city, a contrast which the Reverend Cook so aptly pointed out. The estates of the manufacturer overlooking the ocean were relatively new, and many shoe workers could remember the days before such wealth. Older shoe workers could recount to younger operatives the days when the Newhalls, Breeds, and Chases were just beginning to organize the shoe industry. For many, the causal relationship was plain: the wealth of the manufacturers came from the exploitation of labor. The workers believed that value came from labor, and if the manufacturers were gaining in wealth while labor was not, the reason was obvious: workers were being robbed. Given such a situation, labor had to look to itself for support and aid. Support institutions helped carry the ideology of working-class solidarity and the values of the worth of labor into the daily experiences of the workers of Lynn, not only during their direct struggles against the manufacturers, but also in their daily lives.

Some institutions within the city opposed these support institutions. For example, the Catholic church urged its members to avoid the lodges and benefit organizations. The Lynn church, which was very conservative on most labor and social issues, condemned all members in societies except for those sponsored by the church.

> Any Catholic who joins such organizations (Masons, Odd Fellows, Knights of Pythias, Sons of Temperance, and kindred organizations) and remains a member of the same ceases to be a Catholic in communion with the Church. It means that at the hour of death unless the member of such condemned society shall renounce such society . . . he dies in his sins, an enemy to God and his Church.[43]

The Catholic church in Lynn recognized that its working-class members joined to "enjoy a better fellowship in such societies" as well as for benefits. The church reminded its working-class parishioners that it sponsored its own societies, but few joined.[44]

The Lynn church did not enthusiastically support unionism or any other working-class political or social activity. It was "opposed to all principles of subversive human society whether they be known as liberalism, socialism, anarchism, or by any other term."[45] Although the church encouraged Catholics to "take a firm stand against Social Democracy which preaches the gospel of materialism and atheism," it accepted, with reservation,

> the endeavor of the workingmen to better their material condition by the formation of trade unions, but at the same time . . . exhort[ed] [the] Catholic workman to form special associations, the object of which [was] to provide also for their religious and moral wants and to instruct them properly on the social questions.[46]

Even as late as 1924, Reverend Father Maley, pastor of Lynn's largest
Catholic church, was calling upon the city's Catholic workers to eradicate
the "radical element" from the labor unions. Father Maley claimed that
the workers were voicing "the spirit that has brought the ruin of Russia
and other European countries." He called for "Americanism" in the
shoe shops, with "American" shoe workers carrying American flags and
purging "the foreigners . . . brought by these red leaders to regard the
employers as wicked enemies."[47] Despite these strong warnings and con-
demnations, the workmen, Catholic as well as Protestant, joined benevolent societies and lodges and unions. Although the Catholic church was
seen as a religious institution for the Irish Catholic population, the church's
conservative views undermined its importance as a class institution for the
Catholic working class. Since the church was unwilling to moderate its
antilabor and antiradical views and at the same time failed to provide
counter-institutions for the working class, Lynn's Catholic workers looked
to the stronger working-class institutions for support. This orientation was
facilitated by the lack of a strong nativist movement in Lynn and by the
fact that both Irish and Catholic workers were accepted into Lynn's
working-class institutions.[48]

Irish Catholic shoe workers did not overtly reject the Catholicism of
their ancestors, but neither did they embrace the cooperative antiradical
position of their clergy. Conditions in the shops and in the community
presented these workers with a different reality. From working with other
shoe workers, they learned the need and importance of labor cooperation.
Constant layoffs during slack times taught them that the employer was a
ruthless calculator of figures, and not a partner with labor. When times
were hard, labor, not capital, received the cutbacks; misery was not
jointly shared in the "partnership between labor and capital." In such a
situation, workers turned to those who offered aid and who knew the
reality they experienced. The union activists supplied aid during hard
times, shared in the workers' misery, and offered a partnership of equals.
While these activists were not always ethnic brothers and sisters, they
were brother and sister shoe workers. For the worker who saw the great
wealth of the manufacturers and the corresponding want of the shoe
workers, and who at the same time produced more and more shoes with
little increase in wages, the ideology which stressed the labor theory of
value made more sense than one which emphasized cooperation between
labor and capital.

Lynn's middle class, like its Catholic church, felt uneasy about working-class organizations. They believed these organizations were aggravating the "opposing classes" which, in their minds, had developed with the introduction of the factory system. Hence, they attempted to form their own benefit societies for the working class. In 1880, the town's upper middle class formed the Lynn Workingmen's Aid Association to encourage shoe workers to purchase land and build homes and thus make the working class respectable middle-class homeowners. The association had mostly middle-class support, with some skilled shoe workers as members. The organization floundered for a few years, with shoe workers losing interest when the members who were not shoe workers began to push it as a panacea for the working class.[49]

The middle class also directed much of its attention to the working-class children, in hopes of reaching them with the message of hard work, Christian self-discipline, and social order before the influence of the peer group "corrupted them." Through the "healthy activity" of the YMCA and the Boys' Clubs, the middle class strove to give these children a middle-class world view. Unfortunately, mostly middle-class children utilized the facilities, for both the YMCA and the Boys' Clubs were considered too expensive and Protestant for working-class children and young adults.[50] Nor did the Glenmere Mutual Benefit Association and the Young Men's Mutual Benefit Association, with their upper-middle-class direction and orientation, have any appeal among the workers.[51]

Lynn's largest lodge, the Lynn Ancient Free Accepted Masons, competed with the Odd Fellows but did not have substantial working-class support or membership. The Masons, although offering fellowship, attracted mostly middle- and lower-middle-class white collar members and a few skilled working-class members. The Masons, although offering fellowship, attracted mostly middle- and lower-middle-class white-collar members and a few skilled working-class members. The Masons did not provide the benefits of the working-class lodges; moreover, they explicitly prevented any discussion of issues pertinent to the working class. For example, the charter and by-laws of the Lynn Damascus Lodge of the Masons in Section Nine of the miscellaneous regulations states, "no political or other exciting topics shall be introduced for discussion in any lodge."[52] Because of these restrictions, the middle-class membership, and the lack of benefits, the shoe workers tended to avoid Masonic lodges.[53] Just as the clergy's argument about the partnership between labor and capital undermined the church's influence among the workers, so the argument used by middle- and lower-middle-class organizations destroyed any of their potential impact. In a world in which class conflicts were reenacted again and again on the shop floor in battles over batch size and wages and where class solidarity was reinforced daily, such as when one worker filled in for a sick worker, an organization which stressed classless ideas and discouraged the discussion of vital conflicts could have little appeal.

In addition to the benefit lodges, the workers formed neighborhood clubs which were combination pubs, lodges, and friendship clubs. These clubs, such as the Highlands Club, the Tremont Club, or the Elnore Club, were made up of shoe workers and other non-Crispin blue collar workers, and were adult extensions of the neighborhood gangs.[54] The working-class membership of these clubs reflects both the class segregation of the city and the class style. The middle-class clubs, such as the East Lynn Club, were not locally oriented, nor did they function as extensions of earlier gang activity.[55]

As in most industrial cities, the immigrant workers in Lynn founded ethnic clubs and lodges which helped them deal with the alien culture. The ethnic clubs offered friendship with people who spoke the same language, shared the same past, knew the same customs, and understood the same frustrations. They could also provide a contact where the immigrant could learn of housing and jobs. In many cities, they kept native customs and practices alive in the new country, especially for the younger generation.[56] In Lynn, unlike many other industrial cities, the ethnic clubs tended to be transitory, serving as agents for integrating the newest arrivals into the general community. The members were of the working class, unskilled, and mostly recent arrivals.[57] The clubs provided the immigrant with vital information, but he soon learned to depend upon other working-class organizations such as the union, lunchroom, or neighborhood club.[58]

The Independent Order of British Abrahams was a club for British immigrants, most of whom were shoe workers. The Robert Bruce Club and the Order of Scottish Clans were dominated by shoe workers. The Orangemen and the Ancient Order of Hibernians provided, respectively, for Protestant and Catholic Irishmen, with mostly unskilled workmen as officers in both clubs. The Scandinavian Benefit Association was a social and benefit club for Scandinavian shoe workers.[59] The Workingman's Circle, a national Jewish society dedicated to teaching Jewish culture and socialist thought, acted as a benefit society and organization "to improve the condition of the workingman" in Lynn. The circle sponsored many speakers on socialism and provided the Yiddish-speaking shoe workers with a socialist forum.[60]

These ethnic organizations were local chapters of national organizations which the new immigrant had heard of back home. In the case of the worker who did not know English, they served as centers of information about the city. Many immigrants coming from other United States cities already belonged to these organizations. The new immigrant used these clubs to break into the city. After he became familiar with Lynn and its institutions, he drifted into nonethnic-oriented lodges or neighborhood clubs and let his membership in the ethnic organization lapse. This trend can be inferred from the large number of officers of these organizations who were unskilled workers, a sign of recent immigration.[61]

This pattern can be seen in the development of the Young Men's Italian Club. The club was formed by a group of young first-generation shoe workers before World War I, and all its members were shoe workers. The club sponsored dances and foot races, but it became defunct after a few years as the members became more active in the union and the other social activities of the working-class community at large. Saturday evening whist and other card games at the union hall replaced ethnic dances.[62] This pattern was also true of other ethnic groups. As a young man, Nick Pappas was very active in the Greek ethnic community, but after he became a shoe worker (following brief careers as a boxer, a fruit vendor in Boston, and a typesetter for a Greek newspaper), he gave up much of his activity in the ethnic organizations and became involved in the organizations and activities of the general shoe-worker community.[63]

Apart from the ethnic and benefit organizations, the workers formed a special club just for shoe workers, the Prospect Club, at the turn of the century. The club sponsored dances, card games, and general get-togethers, and provided the workers with a center where they could discuss their problems and concerns in a sympathetic atmosphere. Unfortunately, the club's success proved to be its undoing. As more and more shoe workers joined, the club lost its intimacy, and the facilities could not hold the growing membership. Rather than turn the club into an impersonal formal organization, its members decided to disband it in the 1930s.[64] Many of the members drifted into the other lodges and clubs around the city, but many deplored the loss of a center purely for shoe workers.

The "comraderie" of the shoe workers was that they wanted
to be with shoe workers, they knew what they were talking
about, if you talked about shoes at least I could answer you,
but if you sat down with somebody who doesn't know to talk
about shoes you don't want to listen to him.[65]

Following World War II, a retired shoe worker began another club that
was exclusively for shoe workers. It was called the Pioneer A. A. Club,
simply because the originator had an old banner already inscribed with
that name. At first, the Pioneer A. A. rented a room on the third floor
of an old building, but since the stairs were too much of a hardship for
the older members, a first floor was rented across from the union hall on
Washington Street. The club included a bar and tables for cards, and
held dances on Tuesdays, Thursdays, and Fridays. It provided the type
of entertainment and activity that the union had offered during the late
nineteenth and early twentieth centuries.[66]

In addition, the workers formed a socialist club which met every week
to discuss politics and social affairs at Unity Hall. In the late nineteenth
century, the Lynn working class also supported a strong labor church. In
1894, the Reverend Herbert N. Casson started the labor church, which
functioned as a community center for the workers and was "composed
entirely of working men and women."[67] Casson's church not only provided
a platform for labor speakers, but also distributed thousands of labor
papers and pamphlets to the community. Although designated as a church,
it had no particular religious affiliation. It held meetings every Sunday
afternoon and, whenever an issue of importance to the community came
up, it opened its doors to the working class.[68]

Through these formal and informal clubs, lodges, and gathering places,
the workingmen and women learned of job conditions and wages, the
health and condition of their brothers and sisters, the strength and power
of the unions, and of past battles. The workers worked in relatively small
shops, but often rotated through different shops. They slowly learned
most of their comrades' faces. During lunch breaks, they filed out of the
shops into the lunchrooms to meet and talk with their friends.

The workers' periods of enforced idleness contributed to their sense
of community and comradeship. During these slack periods, the workers
would spend their time at either the union hall or "Crispin's Congress"
(Hunt's) socializing with other workers. When the work increased, many

workers would move into different shops, expanding their contacts and their sense of common identity with their fellow workers.[69] They also met and socialized with new shoe workers as they entered the work force. The new workers learned that Lynn was a union town and had been a union town since the great strike of 1860 (Photograph 6). Shoe workers of Greek or Italian parents, living in the Brickyard, learned the history of the city from the old union men who hung out at "Crispin's Congress," the Prospect Club, or the union hall. They therefore got a unionist's point of view and soon came to identify with the union movement.[70] As late as the 1970s, children of immigrants working in the General Electric plant talked with great pride of the strong unionism among Lynn's shoe workers. They identified with that unionism and felt that they were a part of it.[71]

The shoe workers were so totally integrated into the institutions which they developed that, with the exception of the "bosses" who lived in the diamond district, they assumed that the shoe worker and the Lynn citizen were synonymous in the early twentieth century. In response to a question about the middle class, a retired shoe worker stated that there was no such class in the old days, just shoe workers. Except for the bosses, this man recognized no one but shoe workers as legitimate Lynn residents.[72]

The shoe workers believed that the interests of the city and of the shoe workers were the same. They felt a common bond with all the workers in the city and on the basis of this bond built a powerful union movement. Life within and outside the shops contributed to the working-class community's sense of class dependence. That dependence gave support to the ideology which stressed class solidarity and the importance of the worker in the community. It centered the community around the worker and away from the manufacturer or the middle class. While they acknowledged that the middle class had a central role in the community, they regarded the middle class or manufacturers as enemies of the workers. In the eyes of the more radical workers, the manufacturers were parasites who were becoming wealthy off the labor of the working people.

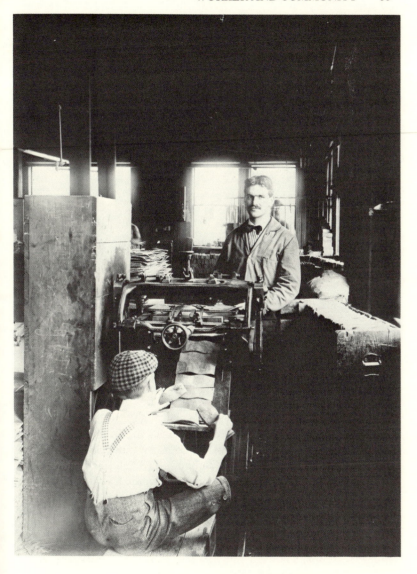

6. Inside a Sole-Cutting Room, Circa 1900

Notice the boy working under the more experienced worker through whom he learned his skill as well as his role in the production system.

—Courtesy of Lynn Historical Society

4

"Lynn Is a Union City"

*"One hundred per cent of your welfare
lies entirely in your own hands."*[1]

Labor organizations in New England's industrial centers had their roots
in local conditions and local support. In those organizations which were
part of larger units, local concerns often transcended national policies
and determined what direction the labor organizations took at the local
level.[2] When local rank-and-file interests conflicted with national directives,
secession and the formation of independent unions often resulted.[3]

The workers of Lynn were no exception to this pattern. Over the years,
they had built up a strong working-class community and a solid tradition
of militant unionism, both of which determined the direction of its unions.
To understand the actions of Lynn's workers, we must examine the nature
of that community and traditions. Although the Lynn workers belonged
to national unions—the Knights of Saint Crispin, the Knights of Labor, the
Socialist Trade and Labor Alliance, the Boot and Shoe Workers Union, the
United Shoe Workers Union, and, later, the United Electrical Workers and
International Union of Electrical Workers—local community and class
solidarity often took precedence over national policies.[4] The workers'
strong local community and unionism gave them a continuity with their
past, and that continuity kept their unions and class solidarity strong.
Although this strength helped the workers in their struggle with capital,
it also contributed to their parochialism, which severely hampered the

movement in the late nineteenth and early twentieth centuries. Tension between local militancy and national organization hindered the shoe workers for most of this period. The Lynn workers were not able to merge their local militant tradition with a national strategy against capital until the United Electrical Workers Union was formed in the 1930s.

The workers' strong tradition of unionism and solidarity predated the Civil War. In the 1840s, the Lynn operatives published the *Awl*, a working-men's paper which advocated the dignity of labor, freedom for the working-man, and the social equality of all producers. These workers formed co-operatives, debating societies, and clubs for journeymen cordwainers.[5] When the wages of these early nineteenth-century workers were cut, they fought back. In 1860, this militant independence, born in the early days when journeymen and masters were considered social equals, collided with the developing factory system. During the nation's largest strike to date, involving thousands of workers, Lynn became a focal point.

The shoe trade experienced recessions in 1852, 1855, 1857, and 1859. Wage reductions and layoffs accompanied these slack periods. After the slack period in 1857, the Lynn shoe workers began to organize. In 1858, they formed the Journeymen Cordwainers Mutual Benefit Society, an organization which immediately began building a strike fund from membership dues and daily assessments. The workers set up functioning committees and met with virtually every shoe worker in the city. Members poured in by the hundreds. In early February 1860, the shoemakers issued a "bill of wages" (a statement of wages demanded by the workers) which they pledged to fight for, planning even to withdraw their labor if the employers refused to sign the new bill. On February 22, thousands of striking shoe workers marched to downtown Lynn. They established administrative structures based upon neighborhoods, with committees elected from the various sectors of the city.[6]

By early March, thousands were taking part in the mass meetings and parades. Female binders voted to go out with the male workers, and they actively participated in the parades and rallies. The strike set a tone of class solidarity for the next half century in Lynn. Whenever workmen went out on strike after the great strike of 1860, they always made comparisons to 1860. Ultimately, the strike of 1860 ended in a mixed victory: some of the manufacturers agreed to the bill of wages, and the ranks of strikers began to break. But the outcome of the strike for the working class was not as important as the glory of the struggle itself: the parades, the rallies with the bands and volunteer fire companies, and the friends and neighbors who poured into the streets in support of the workers.[7]

In 1870, the Lynn workmen published the *Little Giant,* a newspaper dedicated to working-class solidarity and unity. In the same decade, they established one of the nation's strongest and most militant branches of the Knights of Saint Crispin, although the cutters did not join. The Knights of Saint Crispin not only negotiated for higher wages and acted as a militant spokesman for the interests of the Lynn working class, but it was a social center as well. According to a study by Alan Dawley, the Knights of Saint Crispin represented a cross-section of Lynn's work force and advocated militant unionism.[8] The Crispins provided community and fellowship for their members. Their extensive activities included picnics, dances, theatrical events, and lodge meetings. All elements of Lynn's working-class community, skilled and unskilled, were attracted to the unions. The Crispins continued to maintain their social functions, even after the loss of the strikes of 1872 and 1879 crippled the formal union. The social activities remained a base for later working-class organizations which continued the tradition of dances, banquets, concerts, and benefits throughout the later nineteenth century. The Lasters Union of this period maintained a billiard and poolroom, a reading library, and a social room well stocked with labor papers, and it sponsored a mutual aid society for its members.[9]

In the 1880s, the Knights of Labor replaced the Knights of Saint Crispin as the organizing force behind Lynn's shoe workers. The cutters, who had been looked down upon for not joining the Crispins, took an active role in building the Knights of Labor. In 1885, they formed an independent union that joined the Knights of Labor later that year. By 1886, the *Boston Evening Transcript* accused the Knights of having "almost absolute control in the workrooms of every important factory."[10]

The Knights, like the Crispins, were not concerned solely with issues of "pure and simple unionism," but also built community-based institutions which touched on the workers' social lives. After hours, shoe workers would file into the union hall to play cards or engage in other social activities. The union held picnics and parades and endorsed political candidates. Labor Day in Lynn was indeed a day of solidarity. The Knights would dominate the city with mammoth parades, rallies, union picnics, and dances until late in the evening.[11] The union hall was a common place to play cards, talk about the state of the industry, or "discuss on economic and political questions."[12]

The unions in Lynn were an important part of the worker's life, protecting him both on and off the job. The Knights of Labor acted as an "agency for the collection of money to assist the sick and disabled members." The unions saved "many a family from the humiliations of being forced to appeal to public charity for assistance."[13] The Lasters sponsored a mutual aid association for members, providing benefits in case of sickness, unemployment, or death.[14]

The unions were able to hold their members together not only because they offered social services but also because of the nature of the jobs. The shoe workers labored in small shops containing between fifty and one hundred employees who constantly discussed the conditions of the industry, their jobs, and the unions. The seasonal nature of the work induced the rotation of workers through different shops, and this rotation allowed the men to spread news of the union and wage scales. The on-the-job socializing and interaction continued off the job in the cafes, lunchrooms, and union halls. The social aspects of the union welded it to the community in a system of reciprocal support.

The Lynn unions were vigorously independent and militant, and were built upon local conditions and community interactions. They were suspicious of any custom which they felt would undermine their equality, democracy, and independence, whether it came from the boss or from the union itself. They would not tolerate interference with the rank-and-file wishes by the national union or by local officials. Horace Eaton, general secretary of the Boot and Shoe Lasters Union and ex-secretary of the Lynn Lasters Union, testified before the Senate Industrial Commission in 1901 that the national union leaders were more conservative than the rank and file: "Most of all the aggressive strikes . . . were due very largely to impulse of the rank and file which was in control."[15]

The Lynn workers were initially the major supporters of the formation of a national union of shoe workers. They felt that increased use of machinery in the shoe shops pointed to the need for an industrial union. Lynn shoe workers were instrumental in the founding of the national Boot and Shoe Workers Union, but Lynn's traditional militancy and independence soon led to conflicts between the workers and the Boot and Shoe Workers Union. For example, the cutters remained loyal to the Knights of Labor because they were suspicious of the Boot and Shoe

Workers Union leadership. When the Boot and Shoe Workers Union attempted to raid the Knights locals at the turn of the century, the anti-democratic and high-handed manner of the Boot and Shoe Workers Union turned the workers away, despite the fact that its national orientation appealed to the workers. In 1903, the Lynn working class, including the American Federation of Labor (AF of L) carpenters and plumbers, supported the Knights of Labor cutters against the Boot and Shoe Workers Union. Throughout the first decade of the twentieth century, various groups of Lynn workers broke from the Boot and Shoe Workers Union to form independent unions. In 1907, delegates from the independent unions formed the Lynn Joint Shoe Council.[16] In 1909, several members of the Joint Shoe Council formed the United Shoe Workers of America; by 1913, the organization had over eleven thousand members, and by 1919, twenty-five thousand, with Lynn as the leading center. In 1912, the Lynn cutters and stock fitters of the Knights of Labor joined the United Shoe Workers of America. They were followed by the buttonhole operators and stitchers who left the Knights the same year.[17] The new union was open to all: women, children, and men. It organized both mixed and craft unions, and was more democratic and decentralized than any union of its time. The organization was totally member-dominated, with officers having no vote. The new union continued Lynn's tradition of militant independence and class consciousness. The first general secretary of the union stated categorically that the shoe manufacturers were the "opponents" of the union and the workingman.[18] The Lynn shoe workers, even after they formed the United Shoe Workers of America, were continually calling wildcat strikes without consulting the union.[19]

Because of their dissatisfaction with the conservative leadership of the Boot and Shoe Workers Union, Lynn shoe workers also maintained other smaller independent unions, such as the Independent Union of Allied Shoe Workers which began as an alliance of three smaller local unions. By 1912, the Independent Union of Allied Shoe Workers had contracted all edgemakers and heelworkers in Lynn. These unions, like their predecessors, were involved in extensive social activity which interlaced the union and the community.[20]

In the 1920s, the United Shoe Workers Amalgamated joined with the other smaller independent unions and formed the Amalgamated Shoe Workers of America, with over five thousand members. The Amalgamated pledged itself to industrial unionism and to raise the workers to the position in society to which "they were justly entitled." This was Lynn's largest union, followed by the Boot and Shoe Workers Union, the Independent Lasters, the Shoe Workers Protective Union, Independent Stock Fitters, Independent Packers, and mixed unions. The Independent Stock Fitters and Independent Packers seceded from the Amalgamated when too much control was exerted from above.

The unions controlled not only wages and job conditions, but also the job itself. They furnished the workers for the shops through the permit system. If a worker found that there was a job available in a union shop, he went to the union for a permit in order to work there. If a worker found that there was a job available in a union shop, he went to the union for a permit in order to work there. If a worker went to work in a nonunion shop, he would lose his union membership and his permit to work in any other union shop in town.[21]

Lynn workers were the first in New England to join or form unions, but they never docilely followed union orders they considered undemocratic or in conflict with local prerogatives. The unions which they created had little control over the volatile nature of their members. Billups, in his study of the shoe industry, stated that the union officials had little control over their Lynn members and that it was not uncommon for the rank and file to go out on strike against the direction of the union. In 1920, the Amalgamated signed a no-strike agreement with the manufacturers, but despite their agreement and similar ones during the following five years, strikes occurred every year. Between 1920 and 1923, there were fifty-seven strikes, nine of which were general strikes.[22]

As can be seen in Table 6, Lynn shoe workers, whether native- or foreign-born, responded to the union movement. The native-born of native stock were only slightly less likely to join the union than were the foreign-born or first- generation workers.[23] Women workers were also a part of the tradition of militant unionism and were not denied participation by male workers. As early as 1860, striking women stitchers shocked the nation by actively taking part in the public demonstrations of the strikers. Women workers continued to play an active role in labor organizations and activity. When the Joint Shoe Council was formed in 1907, the members elected a woman, Ammie T. McCormich, as president. Lynn women stitchers dominated the stitchers' unions. After the strike of 1903, the women maintained a Knights of Labor local separate from the Boot and Shoe Workers Union local 108.[24]

6

ETHNICITY OF LASTERS UNION MEMBERS:
LYNN, 1894-1922
(Percentage Distribution)

Ethnic Group[1]	1894	1908	1910	1920-1922
American-British or British Canadian	49	61	40	20
Irish	22	7	16	—
French Canadian	21	7	12	4
German	1	—	5	1
Scandinavian	3	2	7	5
Jewish	3	13	4	8
Italian	1	4	4	11
Greek	1	2	7	18
Other Eastern Europeans	—	—	5	33
Number in Population[2]	389	46	119	91

1. The ethnicity of the work force was based upon surname, which although a crude measure of ethnicity and only partially accurate in distinguishing between Irish and English, does indicate the arrival rate of the Eastern European nationalities into the work force, and especially their integration into Lynn's powerful and skilled lasters trade.

2. Population for the year 1894 was drawn from the list of dues-paying lasters in the Lasters Union Dues Book, Vol. 10, 1894. A sample of dues payers was used in 1908 and 1910. The population for 1920-1922 is the most suspect since it was drawn from those lasters seeking out-of-work stamps from the union.

SOURCE: Lynn Lasters Union Papers, Vols. 10; 4, 5, and 2, Baker Library, Harvard University.

In 1924, Lynn, "Queen Shoe City," lost her crown. The city's shoe industry went into a precipitous decline, jobs became scarcer, and job competition increased. At the same time, large numbers of immigrants, especially from Eastern Europe, inundated the city. The percentage of foreign-born from Eastern Europe increased from below 1 percent in 1900 to over 10 percent by 1920 (see Table 6 for increased number of foreign workers in Lynn's unions). In the eyes of the city's leading Roman Catholic leader, Father Maley, these immigrants plus the city's strong militant unionism were the cause of the city's depression. Father Maley claimed that "a lot of bolshevick cranks" with support from the city's "foreigners" were destroying the shoe industry in Lynn.[25]

Although few would go as far as Father Maley, in the early years of the 1920s many of the city's leaders picked up the idea that rank-and-file militance, "at times Bolshevistic," as even the local labor paper claimed, had driven out the shoe shops.[26] The Protestant leaders, the Catholic church, local manufacturers, and even the local labor paper joined together in a common chorus denouncing local militance and asking the workers to join the "conservative" Boot and Shoe Workers Union, especially with its compulsory arbitration and opposition to rank-and-file strikes.[27] *The Union Worker* stated that local objections to the AF of L, because it was "reactionary [and] . . . did not uphold the principles of any of the international," reflected a failure to see that in its "conservatism" the AF of L had grown strong. "Opponents of the Boot and Shoe Workers Union deplore the fact that it is controlled by a small and autocratic group of officials. This may be true, but the fact remains that in the quarter of a century of its existence it has prospered tremendously."[28] *The Union Worker* argued that the workers were sacrificing gain and stability for theory: "Democratic control of Labor Unions is beautiful in theory, but does not seem to work out successfully in practice."[29] The paper went on to claim that Lynn's unskilled immigrants, *"unimportant groups of shoe workers"* (emphasis mine), were causing strikes, and holding up production.

The Boot and Shoe Workers Union appealed to many liberals and even to Lynn's labor leaders, for it promised to stabilize labor relations, stop strikes, and, hopefully, retain the city's remaining shoe shops. The city's manufacturers supported it, and most felt that Lynn's skilled workers would soon go over to the union. "It [was] admitted by the Boot and Shoe Workers Union officials, that (under their jurisdiction) the manufacturer pays for his [unskilled labor] just what he wished."[30]

The Union Worker argued that the skilled workers should end their support of the unskilled workers who were "over paid in proportion to amounts received by highly skilled and specialized workers," in order that the city stabilize its economy and labor relations, and to "protect the skilled positions."[31] The skilled workers refused to abandon the unskilled workers or their commitment to militant democratic unionism for the dwindling jobs that remained in the city. They refused to join the Boot and Shoe Workers Union.

The Boot and Shoe Workers Union was rejected for failing to protect not only fellow workers (the unskilled), many of whom were immigrants, but also for what the city's workers felt was a vital issue of self-pride and dignity—job control. Under the union's contract, the workers would have had no control over the job itself. Lynn unions "dictated on the job conditions and protected the individual worker from discharge." The Boot and Shoe Workers Union gave the skilled worker better "bread and butter unionism," but only bread and butter unionism. "Here the question arises [in the eyes of *The Union Worker*] whether the Lynn shoeworker wishes to retain the full measure of independence formally granted him or whether he would prefer to have steadier work and fewer privileges."[32] The shoe workers chose the "full measure of independence," and the pressure to bring the Boot and Shoe Workers Union to Lynn "proved to be a dismal frizzle."[33]

Despite the tremendous pressure brought on by declining jobs, increased job competition, and the encouragement of manufacturers, and even some labor leaders, to join, "shoe workers [of Lynn] would not be led by any civil body or groups of individuals . . . they would continue to look to their own leaders for advice."[34] Bread and butter unionism was rejected by a class-conscious community of workers.

Lynn shoe manufacturers, like most American industrialists, attempted to use job classifications and distinctions to divide the skilled, semiskilled, and unskilled workers. Pay differentials and prestige of the skilled jobs, as well as sex discrimination in keeping women out of the skilled positions, had an effect in Lynn, as in most cities, in dividing workers. Despite the divisions among workers, a compelling sense of the commonality of experience of all shoe workers drove them together. Shoe workers realized the impact of wage reductions on not only the skilled workers but the unskilled as well. In a city dominated by shoe workers and shoe manufacturers, the difference in wealth between workers and manufacturers gave meaning to the arguments of the radicals that workers and employers were in direct conflict. The belief in the conflict between workers and employers, and in the idea that workers were denied what "they were justly entitled" to by the manufacturer provided an ideological base for the militant class-conscious unionism which flourished even during these declining years in Lynn.

All members of the Lynn working-class community shared this sense of militant independence. In the late 1890s, the carpenters left the Brotherhood of Carpenters and Joiners of America because of its conservatism. They felt that the Brotherhood was spending too much time and money on benefits and too little on organizing. The carpenters attempted to form a New England organization that was dedicated to militant unionism, which would be in the vanguard of the eight-hour-day movement in New England.[35] Members of the Machinists Lodge 471 were also a strong independent union in the late nineteenth century. In 1898, they set up meetings to discuss means of broadening their activity beyond "simple trade unionism." They held a special convention to discuss the merits of joining the Socialist Trades and Labor Alliance.[36] The building trades were also well organized in the city and contributed support to the local labor movement, both independently and through the Central Labor Union. The city's union movement was one of the strongest in the state throughout the late nineteenth and twentieth centuries.[37]

In local strikes, the Lynn craftsmen continually supported local union militancy, even when that militancy conflicted with national directives. In 1890, the AF of L carpenters and plumbers supported the Knights of Labor. The nature of Lynn's working-class community explains the militant solidarity of its craft workers. Many of the craft workers had relatives in the shoe industry. During the slack times, shoe workers would pick up jobs in construction and thus work with the craft workers. Many shoe workers stayed on and picked up a craft, while many craftsmen went to work in the shoe shops during the winter rush season when construction jobs were scarce. These workers belonged to the same clubs and lodges. They easily saw the common interests of all workers, especially all Lynn workers.[38]

When the descendants of the shoe workers began to find work in the General Electric plant, they eventually built a militant union movement there as well, but only after several years of struggle against a powerful and sophisticated opponent. The style of work in the General Electric plant was entirely different from that in the shoe shops, and much of the informal work atmosphere which strengthened the bond between the shoe workers could not be duplicated at General Electric.[39]

The General Electric workers were separated from their fellows by loud isolated machines. Their lunch breaks were not informal get-togethers at the local lunchrooms. In 1903, the General Electric River-works (one set of plants in Lynn) equipped a building on its grounds to be used as a restaurant for employees. The restaurant provided the company with a convenient means of keeping the men inside the gates and under the informal supervision of the company during breaks.[40] General Electric itself, unlike local shoe shops, made organizing difficult.

It was not a small company working on a tight budget, but rather a
national corporation with Lynn representing only one of its large factory
complexes. Its management was far more sophisticated in dealing with
its workers than the locally oriented shoe companies. General Electric
practiced the American plan with vigor. Workers were given bonuses
and raises based on merit and company loyalty. Company supervisors
kept a close watch on the personnel to prevent unions from developing,
and following World War I, the company adopted an employee representa-
tion plan, a company union. Despite these tactics, the General Electric
plant did experience attempts at unionization before World War I. In
August 1903, over three hundred Italian laborers struck the plant over
a grievance with the foreman. The strike was thwarted when the workers
were replaced by outsiders. A metal trades council was organized by
employees that same year, but the movement never got off the ground.
Although skilled workers in the plant periodically joined the AF of L
unions of their crafts, they never had a genuine organized union base in
the plant.[41]

During World War I, the National War Labor Board was established
to prevent strikes by acting as an appeal agency for labor grievances. The
Board encouraged the AF of L unions at Lynn's General Electric plant.
Following World War I, the employees at General Electric went out in a
long and bitter strike to solidify the position of their unions and to increase wages which had fallen drastically behind the rapid rise in the cost
of living due to the war. The company locked out the employees and
refused to negotiate with the AF of L unions. Under the leadership of
General Swope, General Electric instead established company unions
made up of management and employees. The workers would have repre-
sentation, and grievances could theoretically be aired. With these Work
Councils, as General Swope called them, the company was able to keep
out of the AF of L.

Just one year after the loss of the bitter strike of 1919, General Electric
workers again walked off the job. Beginning as a spontaneous rank-and-
file protest, the strike soon escalated into a major conflict between workers
and management over the issues of control over the job itself and the hated
"stop-watch system." Richard Carlin, a rank-and-file leader, admitted that
he was "one of the men who refused to work under the time study system";
he claimed that it "would be detrimental to the physical health of the men
and women and also to American ideas." Carlin maintained that time study

was similar to the "Taylor system which was unjust." The metal trades council, which represented both electrical workers and machinists, supported the rank-and-file struggle against time and motion study, but the manager of Lynn's General Electric plant refused to meet with the workers or accept anything which was "a union document."

The power of General Electric in 1920 was too strong for the Lynn rank and file. The manager was able to break the strike and initiate the "stop-watch system," despite continual worker resistance and hostility.[42]

In an attempt to placate the workers and tie them to the company, General Electric also attempted to supply the social functions for their workers that had traditionally been supplied by the Lynn unions. The company sponsored recreational groups, glee clubs, athletic associations, as well as a mutual benefit association.[43]

In 1920, following the strike over Taylorism (scientific management) and foreshadowing the campaigns of General Bowlware at General Electric (after the 1946 strike; see end of Chapter 6), the company began publishing *The Lynn Works News* specifically for "the purpose of breaking up the morale of the Union agitators."[44] General Electric's publicity department followed by issuing statements and company news to local papers in order to focus employee attention away from the working-class community and union news networks and on the company itself.[45] As long as times were relatively good for General Electric and the shoe industry remained unstable but important enough to appear a possible source of employment for General Electric workers, the company's American plan (Swope's paternalistic alternative to unionism) and publicity campaign succeeded in keeping Lynn's militant union tradition out of the gates of the plant.

The Great Depression put an end to this apparent tranquility. By 1933, the shoe industry was clearly dying in Lynn and General Electric became a permanent rather than a temporary source of employment for the workers. The company union fell far short of meeting the real needs of General Electric workers and could not and would not fight the wage cuts, layoffs, and shorter hours which cut into workers' pay envelopes. Wages fell to under thirty-five cents an hour for women. The top rate for a common laborer was thirty-six cents. For an electrician, it was seventy cents, and for tool and die makers, the aristocrats of the electrical workers, it was only eighty cents an hour.[46] In the early 1930s, the AF of L attempted to capitalize on the discontent in the General Electric plant, but the workers, suspicious of the conservative views of the AF of L, refused to accept its craft lines.

In 1933, under the leadership of Alfred Coulthand, an English shipyard worker who entered the country as a veteran unionist (and in 1920 worked at General Electric until he was fired in a labor dispute), the Lynn workers applied to the AF of L on condition that they could maintain an industrial union structure. Coulthand, an experienced trade unionist and a skilled worker, had been a member of the AF of L pattern makers and had experienced the struggles and frustrations of craft unionism. Like many of Lynn's skilled workers, he wanted an industrial union of skilled and unskilled workers at General Electric. The AF of L refused, and the Lynn workers formed an independent industrial union, the Electrical Industrial Employees Union.[47]

General Electric workers were in the tradition of Lynn's militant independent unionism, and from that tradition they learned the weakness of a localized union fighting a powerful national corporation. In August 1933, the Electrical Industrial Employees Union held its first meetings. For the remainder of 1933 and 1934, the union was fighting for company recognition, while at the same time hoping to expand to cover the non-Lynn plants. The company countered the union by pressuring its men to accept the company union. Outside workers were brought in to testify to the benefits of the company union before the workers at work-time auditorium meetings. From the end of 1934 to 1936, the Electrical Industrial Employees Union managed to maintain its foothold in General Electric. In 1935, employees in other plants outside Lynn contacted Lynn for help, and General Electric workers began to organize a national union. In March 1937, the union, now the United Electrical Workers, with the aid of the national CIO, met the company on a national basis.[48]

By 1940, Lynn local 201, with nine thousand members, was the largest local of the United Electrical Workers. By 1941, the local union took its fight for the Lynn working class beyond the boundary of the General Electric plant and fought for housing authority in the city. The local lost this fight by a tie in the city council, partly as a result of the redbaiting of the local Chamber of Commerce.[49]

The Lynn electrical workers continued the tradition of extensive social activity which the shoe workers had in their unions. The local published a weekly paper, the *Electrical Union News,* which helped tie the General Electric workers together. The newspaper combined union news and national news with gossip about members and information on what was happening in the different plants. It propagandized for the local as well. Articles were published on the state of the economy and reasons for the Depression. The paper also carried a column by Upton Sinclair whose attacks on capitalism took in everyone from the millionaire for soaking the poor to the New Deal for subsidizing big business.[50] The union also sponsored a baseball team and held regular sports nights, which involved the union member in a social life independent from the company. It held picnics, dances, and bingo nights, with the proceeds going to needy union families. Thus, it continued the practice of the shoe workers' unions of looking after their own and of encouraging their members to see the union as the source of support in both the plant and the community.[51]

Although the union helped integrate new members into the social structure of the union, the activities themselves were far more formal and structured than in the old shoe workers' unions. The shoe workers' social activity had centered around the informal activity of their union. The workers used the union as a social center because it was not a highly centralized operation. This social functioning of the old shoe workers' union also allowed for greater democracy and more informal rank-and-file interaction than the more efficient United Electrical Workers and the later International Union of Electrical Workers. Because these earlier unions were social centers, the general membership, or at least large segments of it, knew how they functioned and were personally acquainted with their officers.[52] The officers were allowed little monopoly of information or bureaucratic control.

The United Electrical Workers and, later, the International Union of Electrical Workers faced a far better organized and far larger opponent than the shoe manufacturer that the shoe workers confronted. Unlike the shoe factories, General Electric was not located in Lynn. Rather, its headquarters was in Schenectady, New York, and it could utilize the services of innumerable bureaucrats armed with years of legal training to thwart the demands of the Lynn workers. New Deal reforms had not only given labor Section Seven #A of the National Recovery Act and the Wagner Act, but had also increased the complexity of labor-management relations. In fighting a sophisticated and remote enemy, Lynn workers had joined with other electrical workers in other plants in other parts of the country. They built a powerful and highly centralized labor institution to combat a powerful and highly centralized corporation in an increasingly complex and formalized world of labor-management relations.

The union also had a more difficult task than the early shoe workers' unions in keeping the workers together. Shoe workers lived and worked within close proximity of each other; the social life of their union was a natural outgrowth of the work and residential patterns. In contrast, General Electric workers lived outside the city and therefore had little opportunity to socialize within the union hall. Others worked on the night shift or were divided from fellow workers on the job by long distances within the plant as well as by demanding and exacting work which tied them to a particular place. In order to meet the demands of all these workers, the union became more formalized.

When they formalized the social interactions of the union in order to make it function more effectively against the large corporate structure of General Electric, the United Electrical Workers and, later, the International Union of Electrical Workers unwittingly created a bureaucratic distance between the officers and the workers. The workers were not expected to gather at the union hall where officers surrounded the entrance way, well guarded by secretaries. The rank and file lost knowledge of, and thus some control over, the functioning of the union. Success at the bargaining table also contributed to a loss of interest in the day-to-day functioning of the union. Unlike the shoe workers' unions where job actions and grievances were discussed by the membership at weekly meetings, in the electrical workers' union grievance procedures were removed from the day-to-day activity of the rank and file as a result of the contract negotiated by the union and General Electric. The names of the union's leaders dominated the *Electrical Union News* and other official union publications. The workers became divorced from the institution's daily activity, partly because of the increased complexity of its operation. That in turn eliminated one aspect of rank-and-file control and democracy.[53]

5

Community in Struggle

The community and institutions built by the Lynn workers were not simply a response to the conditions of the industrial environment. They were also a product of a historical process which slowly transformed the institutions and community of nonindustrial workers into a new culture which combined some qualities of the pre-industrial society with newly adapted structures.[1] The working-class community was not a passive recipient of the changes in the industrial urban society. Besides providing workers with relief, it helped to alter working conditions and to affirm the worker's dignity. While the unions were in the forefront of this effort and were active agents of the working-class community, they depended upon that community for their strength. Through the cohesion of the community's institutions, the unions were able to focus collective action without danger of fragmentation which would have resulted from ethnic or job divisions. These institutions, from the most informal ritualized gathering at Central Square lunchrooms and Brickyard front steps to the formal Odd Fellows Hall meetings, brought ethnic and craft groups together and welded them into a unified class.

Lynn's working class did not leave behind an extensive record of its community of class consciousness, but it did leave behind a record of its struggle. Hence, during the periods of labor crisis, the extent to which collective action cut across ethnic and craft lines, and the extent to which the actions of isolated and fragmented workers were involved, can be observed. In times of crises, both formal and informal community interactions become visible. A detailed examination of a series of confrontations between labor and capital in Lynn from the workers' strike of 1890 to the declining years of the industry in the 1920s reveals changes in the community and the consciousness and perceptions of its members, and gives a picture of a community reacting to change and changing itself.[2]

THE LEATHER WORKERS' STRIKE OF 1890

Leather manufacturing had always been an important shoe-related industry in Lynn. As early as 1800, firms were manufacturing leather expressly for Lynn's shoe workers, and by 1880, it accounted for about $2 million worth of business. By 1890, Lynn was the second largest national center for the manufacture of morocco leather, which was an important leather for shoe manufacturing. The few families who began the morocco trade in the early nineteenth century continued to dominate the industry into the early twentieth century. One of Lynn's largest firms and a central figure in the strike of 1890 was the Joseph Moulton Company begun by Joseph Moulton in 1835.[3]

Although leather manufacturing was originally connected with the shoe industry (its rise was a result of the demand of Lynn shoe workers), by 1892 only a small portion of the morocco leather was sold to Lynn shoe manufacturers.[4]

The leather workers took great pride in their work. Although the industry mechanized to some extent in the early 1880s, the judgment and experience of the individual workers were the key to the production process. The workers had to be able to judge the hides and the chemical fluids they worked with, so that the hides would not be destroyed by too little or too much time in the processing fluids. A leather worker's misjudgment or carelessness could easily destroy a hide.[5] The workers believed their skill to be indispensable to the manufacturers, and they used that position to build their union.

The leather industry required a relatively high level of skill; hence, leather workers commanded higher wages than shoe workers. The majority of leather workers were foreign-born. As late as 1895, less than 24 percent of Lynn's shoe workers, but over 60 percent of its leather workers, were foreign-born. A larger percentage of foreign-born workers was employed in the leather industry than in any other major manufacturing occupation in Lynn in the late nineteenth century.[6] Although there was little conflict between native- and foreign-born leather workers, and despite the fact that leather workers were better paid, most native-born workers avoided leather work because of the obnoxious odors and

the constant splashing of foul fluids which were part of leather processing.

The leather factories were located next to the shoe shops in Lynn's
downtown area. During lunch breaks and before and after work, leather
workers often mingled with shoe workers in the Central Square area.[7]
When the shoe workers began building powerful Knights of Labor lodges
in the shoe factories, the leather workers also began to organize. By 1890,
almost all of the leather factories were union shops.

Leather workers had been averaging only slightly higher annual wages
than shoe workers in the late 1880s. In 1890, the leather business improved, and the leather workers believed the time had come for a major
confrontation with the manufacturers over hours as well as wages. Leather
workers were skilled operatives and worked in small shops employing between thirty and fifty people who knew each other and could depend
upon union solidarity. They believed that their skilled labor had created
the value of the product and that, by withdrawing their members from
the shops, they could force the manufacturers to terms.

On July 25, 1890, over six hundred workmen from the various branches
of the morocco leather trade crowded into the union hall for a mass meeting to discuss their situation. Their prime demand was for a nine-hour day
which they considered an issue of health and a labor right inasmuch as
they had to work amid the foul toxic fumes given off in leather processing. The leaders of the Knights of Labor, the Leather Workers Union,
under the direction of Master Workman John McCarthy, felt that, because
of the general prosperity of the industry, a strike would be successful.[8]
The men decided to strike on August 12.

On August 22, the leather manufacturers representing Lynn's twenty-
eight leather shops met in a closed meeting to decide how they should
deal with the strike and with what they considered an infringement by
the Knights of Labor on their priorities as manufacturers. They agreed to
fight the union and to bring in the open shop to all the Lynn leather
factories. One manufacturer stated: "if the shops [have] to remain closed
for ten years [we will not let] the men [come] back as Knights of Labor."[9]
The manufacturers were members of the National Association of Leather
Manufacturers (NALM) centered in the Middle Atlantic states.[10] The
NALM was originally organized to protect the manufacturers from union
control of labor and from packers' monopoly of supply. The Lynn companies decided to break the union through the NALM. The national or-

ganization was contacted for support and for information concerning the availability of new men to replace Knights who were shut out. The NALM gave its support, informed the manufacturers that workers were available in Newark, and assured them that orders would not be stolen by other members during the lockout.[11]

Leather manufacturers sold in a highly competitive market; in order to survive, they depended upon cultivating regular buyers. Loss of these regular buyers to other leather manufacturers could cripple the industry in Lynn. The NALM also assured the companies that during the strike they would not lose their regular buyers to competitive members of the NALM.[12]

At the start of the strike, the workmen were convinced of success. Their meetings and rallies were therefore jubilant. On Labor Day of that year, the striking morocco leather workers turned out in strength with banners proclaiming their demand for a nine-hour day.[13] They spent the next few days at the union headquarters on Monroe Street which soon became a social center.[14]

On September 11, after four weeks, the tone of the strike changed. With the backing of the NALM, John T. Moulton, the son of Joseph Moulton, opened his factories to nonunion workers. The Lynn members of the NALM agreed to have "no Knight of Labor work for [them]." Moulton sent his foreman to Montreal to enlist French Canadian operatives who were not affiliated with the Knights.[15] On September 16, the leading newspaper in Lynn reported that the companies were bringing in "foreign labor" to break the union and were advertising in foreign newspapers for workers. A German worker claimed to have seen a notice in a German paper.[16]

With this turn of events the union began to rally the community around the striking workmen. Strikers went around the city trying to enlist the financial support of tradesmen and merchants. In order to maintain their good standing among the workmen, the merchants aligned with the strikers; to do otherwise they would have appeared to be hostile to the union and the working class. Even reluctant merchants went along "in the interests of the city" and hoped for an early settlement.[17] Few refused support.[18] On September 16, the striking leather workers called for a mass meeting to keep the spirit of the strike alive and to explain the new threat to the workingmen and women.[19]

A letter writer to the *Lynn Daily Bee* expressed the feelings of many workmen when he wrote as "a citizen of Lynn":

I feel deeply interested in the contest which is going on between
capital and labor in this city. As a wage-earner . . . I offer my protest to the methods adopted by certain manufacturers to crush
out the manly hopes and inborn liberty of American citizens.

As all wealth is the product of labor, labor should receive its
just reward.[20]

The workingmen felt that Lynn was a city of wage-earners and that an
attack against organized labor was an attack against the whole community.

The concept of "inborn liberty" alluded to in this letter was familiar
to those raised on the ideology of the Declaration of Independence and
Thomas Paine. The writer here was also linking the historically important
struggle for liberty which went back to the Revolutionary period with the
present-day struggle of labor in Lynn. But the struggle for liberty in
Lynn in the 1890s added the concept of the value of labor to the ideology
of the Revolutionary period: "As all wealth is the product of labor, labor
should receive its just reward." In this context, the struggle for liberty
became the struggle of labor for its just reward which it created by its
labor. The writer, like many of Lynn's workers, reflected both an opti-
mism about the future based upon the ideology of freedom and liberty
and a pessimism about the present conditions. Identifying himself with
the working class ("as a wage-earner"), and not with the old order of
the craftsman or the new middle class, he nonetheless maintained that
if the wage-earners were given the wealth that was their "just reward"
for their labor, they could still have "manly hopes" for the future. And
as Jefferson stated in the Declaration of Independence that man was
endowed with certain "unalienable Rights, that among these are Life,
Liberty, and the pursuit of Happiness," this writer believed that those
rights—"inborn liberty"—could be translated in the industrial era as
the right to organize and fight capital, the right to gain the full reward
of labor's product. Liberty itself was brought into question by the
manufacturers who attempted to destroy the equality conjured up by
this writer's reference to the rights of American citizens. The very
concept of liberty and property takes on radical meaning beyond that
which the Founding Fathers articulated in 1776. Like most radicals
and revolutionaries, Lynn workers were calling upon both the traditions of the past—in this case past struggles—and the ideology of the
present which had its origin in the developing manufacturing system.[21]

When the threat of strikebreakers became a reality, the support of the working-class community increased. On October 5, 1890, the Central Labor Union of Lynn, which represented all of Lynn's organized workers as well as the American Federation of Labor, Knights of Labor, and independent unions, held a mass meeting to support the striking leather workers. The Central Labor Union sent out a telegram to labor organizations throughout the nation reading: "Fellow workers: again has a fierce attack by organized capital compelled an appeal from organized labor of this city to its friends throughout the country."[22] A committee was formed to go to the different city agencies to help the strikers and to keep the scabs out of the city. The committee threatened the city hospital with "withholding their [union] patronage of that institution amounting to one thousand dollars yearly if it [the hospital] continued to admit scabs suffering from boarding within the factories."[23]

The strikers went to stores in Federal Square and "ordered [the proprietors] to refuse to supply the special officer employed at the Moulton Factory with any goods under fear of losing the trade of the workmen."[24] Only one merchant refused to accept the demand, and his store was successfully boycotted by the workers.[25] Retailers began placing notices on the front page of the city's leading newspaper attesting to the fact that they were not selling to, or had no connection with, the scabs or struck companies. T. J. Ready denied a "report" in "circulation" that he had sold beds or bedding to any morocco manufacturers.[26] The strikers' success in keeping the merchants and tradesmen in line forced the manufacturers to import food and goods for the strikebreakers from Boston.[27]

Mayor George Newhall of Lynn, concerned about the upcoming election and reflecting the citizens' fear of strikebreakers being brought in from the outside, promised that he would try "to bring about the adoption of some measure which should tend to check the bringing of any further numbers of men into Lynn."[28] The mayor failed to stop the importation of outside labor, however, and he blamed the situation on the NALM "who had taken the situation out of the control of the Lynn manufacturers."[29]

On September 18, 1890, John T. Moulton began operating his factory with scabs. The striking leather workers gathered outside the factory to greet those comrades who had turned their backs on the union. School children congregated around the struck factories after school and threw rocks at the windows and doors, as a result of which the police were

brought in to protect the property.[30] When the whistles of the surrounding shoe factories blew for quitting time, men emptied into the streets
and marched down to Moulton's factory on Marion Street. In one instance,
well over a thousand men gathered: "It seemed that everyone who had
finished their day's work stopped at the factory on their way home."[31]
At quitting time, the crowd began throwing bricks at the building. The
few scabs who finally appeared were met with a barrage of insults and
threats, but not actual violence.[32]

The scabs who were not from Lynn received different treatment from
that accorded the local scabs. For example, a crowd followed one strikebreaker from the door on Marion Street to the train depot, shouting
threats and occasionally throwing bricks at him. At the train depot the
threats became explicit. "Do you want to get out of this town alive? . . .
Well you won't if you come here again!"[33] When the train pulled into
the station, the crowd pushed in closer, and to convince one strikebreaker
of the error of his ways, they kicked and shoved him as he tried to board.
A number of the crowd tried to pull him off the train. When he finally
managed to struggle aboard, a stone crashed through the window.[34]

During the confrontation, the police on duty stood by without interfering, realizing there was little they could do. The police were hesitant
to act against the strikers, not just because the strikers far outnumbered
both the police and the scabs, but also because the strikers were also
citizens and their organization was one of the strongest and most powerful
in Lynn. Ever since the strike of 1878 when the police force had come
under attack by the newly elected workingman's mayor, George Sanderson, the police tried to remain neutral in labor conflicts. Without direct
orders, the officers on duty decided to avoid provoking the strikers by
protecting the scabs.

At the mass meeting of the strikers that night (September 19), the union
called for peaceful picketing at the factory and asked the union men to
stay away, unless they were there to picket. This plea kept the strikers
from the factory door, but not from the train depot. That same evening,
the workmen abused the scabs as they awaited the train to Boston. One
striker told a strikebreaker: "If you choose to remain a scab, you must
accept the consequences and I think your days in that line are numbered."[35]

By Monday, September 22, the mayor's office had issued clear orders
for protection of the strikebreakers.[36] Striker and community hostility
toward the scabs finally brought the community into confrontation with

the local authority when the police read the "Riot Act" that evening.[37]

John Moulton, in the vanguard of the NALM's attack on the Knights, responded to the threat against his new workers by housing them inside the factory. The strikers set up twenty-four pickets, twenty-four hours a day, at all the struck factories.[38]

By September 26, with the coordination of the NALM, other factories began to follow the Moulton example and imported workers from out of town to operate the "free shops." Many of those who worked for the free shops were procured in Newark with the help of the NALM.[39] These companies placed cots inside the factories to house the new workers and petitioned the police for special protection against the working class. John Moulton, again leading in the attack against the Knights, began building a boarding house adjoining his factory, in anticipation of a protracted conflict with local organized labor. His willingness to invest in the boarding house reflected both his commitment to defeating the union and his understanding of the community hostility toward his new workers. He knew that the anger against the scabs would not recede in a few days or even weeks. Accordingly, he had to provide protection for his strikebreakers over a long period of time.[40] The manufacturers stated that the strike would end only with the complete destruction of the Knights of Labor in the morocco leather trade, no matter how long it took. "I don't believe in crowding a man simply because you have the best of him, but when you have a fight I believe in thoroughly whipping the adversary."[41]

The strikers remained confident of victory despite the importation of scabs. They were still convinced that only they had the skills needed to handle the hides correctly and that soon the inefficiency of the new workers would cause the manufacturers to turn to them and to accept their organization. Thus, the men held firm. After six weeks of strike, more than half of the original eight hundred strikers had found jobs elsewhere to hold them over during the strike, and those who were unable to find jobs received aid from brother Knights.[42]

As the strike progressed, the local unions took an increasingly active role in supporting the strikers against what they came to believe was the beginning of an all-out struggle of labor against capital.[43] On October 18, the labor unions decided to boycott leather from the lockout manufacturers, and the shoe cutters promised aid by refusing to work on boycotted leather.[44] On November 14, the boot and shoe unions held a mass support meeting for the morocco leather workers. The unions decided to "canvass the various branches of industry in the city for aid for the morocco workers."[45] The Lynn Lasters Protective Union gave John McCarthy, leader of the strikers, $200 a month until late December when a shrunken treasury cut down their donations to smaller amounts.[46] The Plumbers Protective Union, AF of L, sponsored a band concert and dance for support of the striking Knights of Labor, even though, on the national level, the two organizations were fighting each other for control of organized labor in America.[47] The Lynn workers responded to the local working-class needs rather than to the national directions of organized labor. Even the conservative paper, the *Lynn Daily Item,* noted the determination of Lynn union men in their "well-fought battle against the opposing forces of Capital. . ."[48]

On December 23, after more than four months of strike, the strikers held a mass parade through the streets of Lynn to parallel the massive parades of the famous strike of 1860. Over one thousand marched through the city in preparation for the gigantic rally at the Odd Fellows Hall. The marchers were led by labor leaders from all the trades of Lynn. The men held banners opposing the organization of employers reading: "Employers organize but deny us the same right," "Labor produces all wealth, all wealth should belong to those who produced it," "To labor, to learn, to love is the destiny of mankind," "Our cause is just, public sympathy is with us." The speakers at the rally included the head of the Carpenters Union, AF of L, and the head of the local Knights.[49]

In their parades, banners, and iconography, the marchers emphasized the proud traditions of Lynn workers, their rights as citizens and humans, and, more importantly, their belief in the value of labor in creating wealth. In a city that had been made wealthy by the shoe industry, the shoe workers were aware of their singular role—"labor produces all wealth." Their failure to enjoy that wealth made them militant and produced an ideology which put them in permanent conflict with the manufacturers.

With the start of the new year, a new mayor took over city hall. Mayor E. Knowlton Fogg was himself a member of the Knights of Labor and had campaigned for neutral police protection.[50] Lynn's workmen had a long tradition of "throw the bum out" politics. For example, following the strike of 1860 when police and military units were called in against the strikers, the shoe workers elected one of their own as mayor and completely reorganized the police department. During the Civil War, the manufacturers were able to regain control of the city government through the Republican party and retained that control for the next seventeen years. In the 1878 strike, police were again used against the strikers and to protect scabs. Following the loss of the strike, the workers mobilized and elected labor candidate George Sanderson, an ex-shoe worker and strike leader. The workers continued to dominate the city government throughout the 1880s. Mayor Newhall's use of police against the strikers to protect scabs, and his inability to stop the importation of strikebreakers, gave Fogg an issue which split the labor vote, despite his Republican party identification.

Fogg tried to bring the manufacturers to the conference table to nego-tiate a peace, but the companies refused, particularly on the basis of Fogg's union membership and sympathy. The manufacturers were convinced that they had the men beaten and that it was only a matter of weeks before the strikers would renounce their organization and go back to work as nonunion men. Most of the companies had opened up with imported non-union help, and with the support of the national organization, they felt they could hold out longer than the union.

By the middle of February, six months after the strike began, local men were going against the union and asking for work in the open shops. The companies had been able to open and operate despite the strike in a union town. The men realized that, although they had "public sympathy" and the support of both the labor community and the labor movement, they were not as powerful as the men who owned the shops in which they worked, especially if the manufacturers had the coordinated support of the NALM. The union town could not protect union men against the combined and determined efforts of the national organization. To even the most loyal union supporters, it had become obvious that the com-panies could hold out and that the longer the union fought, the more new people would come into Lynn looking for work in the open shops.

On February 28, 1891, the head of the leather workers, Master Work-man McCarthy, was arrested for conspiracy. His trial drew huge crowds and ended with both sides declaring a victory: McCarthy was found guilty but was given a minor sentence. The trial had created a flurry of activity for a dying cause, however. The crowds which came to support McCarthy could no more protect him than they could prevent the companies from running their shops.

On April 8, after eight months of struggle, the men gave up the strike and went to work in nonunion shops. The support of the community, although crucial in solidifying the ranks for so many long months, had not been enough to defeat the nationally oriented manufacturers who viewed the struggle in Lynn as part of a national plan to break the strength of the Knights of Labor in the leather manufacturing industry.[51]

Ironically, the source of the workers' strength in holding out so long also contributed to their weakness. They perceived themselves as powerful members of a working-class community. Indeed, in Lynn they were powerful: they could elect one of their own if the city government interfered with what they felt were their rights, and all the people around them were union people or supporters.[52] Their belief that all the world was Lynn and that all men were union men with the exception of the "bosses" led them to believe they were unbeatable. On the other hand, the manufacturers' world was wider than Lynn, for they had the support and coordination of a national organization. The workers, too, considered themselves part of a national organization, but they were basically a community movement with a local strategy.[53] As long as the companies were locally oriented and owned and were in competition with other companies, a local union movement could effectively unite its community against the company and last out the strike. When the companies became part of a national organization, they were able to overcome the local community efforts of the union men.

Although Lynn's working-class community failed to defeat the manufacturers, the struggle had a more important result: it demonstrated the success of the working-class community infrastructure. The working-class community saw itself as more than purely craft or ethnic divisions. The AF of L craftsmen put aside craft and national union differences to aid their "fellow workers." Despite the fact that the leather workers were primarily foreign-born, Lynn's native-born shoe workers, under the leadership of socialists Horace Eaton and Frank Cushman, as well as plumbers, carpenters, and the Central Labor Union representing all Lynn workers, joined them in a common struggle "between capital and labor." Despite craft or ethnic divisions, the working-class community united through the intricate infrastructure of formal and informal social institutions and rallied behind the leather workers against outsiders, whether merchants or scabs.

THE SHOE WORKERS' STRIKE OF 1903

In 1888, National Master Workman Henry J. Skeffington, head of the shoe workers of the Knights of Labor, quarreled with Terence Powderly, head of the Knights of Labor, over the establishment of a separate national trade association for shoe workers. Following the quarrel, Skeffington issued a call for the shoe workers to leave the Knights of Labor and join the Boot and Shoe Workers International Union, AF of L. The Boot and Shoe Workers International Union became the Boot and Shoe Workers Union in 1895 and immediately began to organize to bring locals of the Knights of Labor into the new union. The new organization pledged itself to militant unionism in the shoe industry and to a national and thorough organization of all boot and shoe workers. It promised to fight for the eight-hour day, maintain the equality of women workers, and build a strong national organization. The union had great appeal to the Lynn shoe workers who watched the Knights of Labor disintegrate on the national level. The shoe workers, who were particularly receptive to this platform after watching the bitter defeat of the leather workers in 1890 due to the NALM, began affiliating with the new union. The Lasters Union was especially worried by the weakness of the localized union movement. At this point, the lasters were struggling to maintain control over lasting, while the companies were introducing machines to do the work traditionally done by hand. The hand lasters were accepting wage cuts in order to keep the lasting machine out, while the union was desperately attempting to guarantee that the available hand-lasting positions would be given to union members. In this weakened position, the lasters decided to go with the Boot and Shoe Workers Union in late 1895.[54]

Not all of Lynn's workers accepted the new organization as an answer to the weakness of the Knights of Labor. The Lynn cutters refused to leave the Knights of Labor, but they agreed to work with the Boot and Shoe Workers Union on the union label.

In 1899, the Union revised its constitution to create a highly centralized management under President John F. Tobin. The centralized management was explicitly aimed at controlling local militancy, for the local organizations had "sought to force improvements that were so radical as to be inconsistent with both local and general conditions."[55] The new organization was hostile to strikes and militancy. The Lynn shoe workers began to question whether in exchange for a national organization strong enough to fight nationally organized capital, they were losing local autonomy, local militancy, and job control.

This anxiety finally came to a head in the strike of 1903 between the Cutters Association, Knights of Labor, and the Boot and Shoe Workers Union, AF of L. In the strike, many Lynn workers came to recognize that the Boot and Shoe Workers Union was too conservative in its approach to unionism. They began to see that local control, despite its weakness, was preferable to undemocratic, bureaucratic centralism, or to a unionism designed to protect labor peace through accommodation with capital in order to claim a slightly larger share of the limited wealth allocated to labor for its members.

At a special meeting in January 1903, the Knights of Labor Cutters Assembly 3662 repudiated a 1900 agreement with the Boot and Shoe Workers Union over the use of the union stamp. They claimed that the union had violated the agreement by issuing union stamps to factories which paid cutters below the union wage and by interfering with Assembly 3662 members in not recognizing their union cards.

On January 9, ten cutters struck the Walter H. Tuttle Factory to enforce a wage demand. It was the first strike since the repudiation of the agreement, and many considered it a test of the powers of the Boot and Shoe Workers Union. The union immediately began filling the positions of the Knights of Labor strikers with union members. Its officers announced that they would not allow shoe workers to strike against a contract and would fill the places of the strikers in order to maintain the integrity of the union contract with the manufacturers.

The cutters responded by calling a general strike on January 16. The Knights of Labor strike call brought out two hundred cutters and began a long and bitter interunion strike which resulted in a confrontation between Lynn's working-class community and the Boot and Shoe Workers Union. When the union began importing strikebreakers from the outside "to meet their agreements," over four hundred and fifty women stitchers went out in support of the striking cutters. The women stitchers left the union and formed the Knights of Labor Stitchers Assembly 2616. The Lynn Labor Council and AF of L body, although officially giving support to the Boot and Shoe Workers Union, unofficially supported the Knights of Labor cutters.[56] Local 1401 of the Brotherhood of Carpenters and Joiners, AF of L, also supported the cutters and denounced the practice of bringing in outside scabs to take the place of Lynn workers.[57]

Because of local hostility, Lynn restaurants refused to sell food to scab female stitchers brought in from Boston as strikebreakers.[58] The animosity toward the union scabs was so great that, in order to get the stitching done, the union was forced in March to set up a stitching room in Boston. Uppers were sent to Boston, stitched there by Boston stitchers, and sent back to the Lynn manufacturers.

The union brought cutters into Lynn from outside the state. Even though the new workers were union workers, they could not be housed or fed in the city. Restaurants and boarding houses were not open to them. The union was forced to set up cots in their union hall and to bring in food from outside. On January 21, when the union cutters attempted to go to their new jobs, they were met with working-class community hostility. On their way to the factory, they were confronted by an angry crowd of onlookers who booed and shouted at them. As the cutters approached the building of the Watson Shoe Factory, they passed by the factory of U.K. and E. Jones; the operatives of the Jones factory crowded to the open windows and shouted down insults and threats to the union cutters. The crowd gathered in the street began threatening and hurling stones at the new cutters. Finally, the police had to move in and protect the union men. At the door of the Count Shoe Factory, men from other factories located in the same building shouted down to the scabs to go home and not take the jobs of striking Lynn men.[59]

Even within the factory itself, the new cutters were subject to insults and harassment. Women employed in the Harley Brothers Factory hissed and booed the scabbing cutters as they walked through the stitching room to the cutting room. At several factories, the McKay operators left their machines and walked out when the scabs came in. Afterwards, the McKay operators organized with the Socialist Trades and Labor Alliance and supported the striking Knights against the AF of L Boot and Shoe Workers Union.[60] The strikebreakers required police protection on the way back to the union hall. In fact, throughout the remainder of the strike, they were under constant police escort.

All unions independent of the Boot and Shoe Workers Union rallied around the striking cutters and stitchers. The striking stitchers held a three-day fair to raise funds to support the strike, which was widely supported by the Lynn community. The Lynn branches of the Shoe Workers Protective Union assessed members 10 percent of their wages to support the strike. The lasters supported the strike despite their membership in the Boot and Shoe Workers Union. The Grain Counter Workers Union 261 voted to appropriate a hundred dollars a week to support the striking stitchers. The American Labor Union passed a resolution condemning the Boot and Shoe Workers Union action in Lynn. In July, the Lynn lasters broke off from the union, and in August about half joined the Socialist Trades and Labor Alliance, while the rest remained independent as the Lasters Protective Union. Both groups denounced the union. The Goodyear operators and the McKay stitchers went out in support of the cutters, with the Goodyear operators leaving the Boot and Shoe Workers Union to join the Lasters Protective Union.[61]

The strike dragged on six months before finally being called off in June. Both sides claimed a victory. The Knights maintained that they had shown the bankruptcy of the Boot and Shoe Workers Union and had won in five out of the original nine factories that were struck. The union, on the other hand, stated that it had "demonstrated to the employers and the public in general that it could and would maintain the integrity of its contracts."[62]

For many Lynn workers, the Boot and Shoe Workers Union had lost sight of its purpose. They believed that the function of a trade union was to protect labor from capital's attempt to "crush out the . . . inborn liberty of labor, in the short run, and to lay the foundations to recapture the 'wealth produced by labor.'" In this context, unions, they held, should defend the rights of their members against capital. They should accomplish this through the strength of rank-and-file solidarity, and not through accommodations with the employers (through maintaining the integrity of contracts).

Thus, the strike against the Boot and Shoe Workers Union took on larger class-conflict implications. Lynn shoe workers joined the union because they realized the importance of a nationally based labor movement in the struggle against capital. But when the union, in an attempt to establish acceptability with capital and to gain wage compromises, functioned to provide labor stability to capital, it lost its legitimacy for Lynn workers.

The conflict between the cutters and the Boot and Shoe Workers Union became more than a jurisdictional struggle when the union raised the issue of the integrity of the contract with the manufacturers. At this point, the working-class community joined the cutters against the national union. The workers could not accept the union's use of scabs, even if they were union scabs, in order "to meet their agreements" with the manufacturers. Even the Lynn members of the union refused to support the national union in their effort. Shoe workers had to be brought in from Boston locals of the union, for Lynn members refused to break ranks with the cutters even though the cutters were not part of their union.

Many Lynn workers remembered the early struggles to build unionism in the city. Those struggles had centered on defending the rights of labor on the shop floor against the manufacturers. Although many of the early issues concerned wages, they also involved basic conflict between the interests of capital and labor. The early unions fought not only to attain higher wages, but also to defend the shoe workers from speedups (increased production over the same time period) and arbitrary shop bosses, as well as to limit the negative impact of mechanization on the workers. While they did not keep out the machine, they did lay the foundations for a union movement that believed in the opposing interests of labor and capital and fought to defend labor. From this tradition, agreements with the manufacturer were less important than support for fellow workers. This same tradition led Lynn workers to call wildcat strikes without consulting their union—a total of fifty-seven between 1920 and 1923, despite a no-strike agreement—and to reject the Boot and Shoe Workers Union as late as 1924, despite a depression in the trade.

Although it was difficult for the city's workers to reject their union, they did just that. The community rallied around the Knights of Labor against the union's agreements with the manufacturers. The strong community support shown the cutters reflected the community's suspicion not so much of the union itself as of its agreements with the manufacturers. The national union's concern to demonstrate "to the employers . . . the integrity of its contract" turned the struggle against the union into a struggle for worker control and for unionism based on class solidarity, not accommodation.

As a result of the strike, Lynn developed a permanent distrust of centralized unionism and a fear of letting too much control leave the local level. Following the strike, Lynn locals began breaking off from the Boot and Shoe Workers Union. The Lynn lasters local 32 seceded from the union and joined with the machine operators local 260, with other locals soon following. The secessions from the union, which began with the constitutional change of 1899, became endemic with the strike of 1903. Although a minority of Lynn workers remained within the union and its nationally oriented but conservative unionism, the tactics used during the 1903 strike, together with the attitude of the national union, left a bitter residue in Lynn.

The Lynn community reacted to the outside Boot and Shoe Workers Union scabs just as they had to the leather manufacturers' scabs in 1890. The scabs were outsiders taking the jobs of Lynn union men, and in the face of this threat, the working class presented a united front. Local class consciousness and solidarity transcended the issues of the national unions. Although it recognized the importance of national working-class organizations and unity, the community's class solidarity was still very much tied to local consciousness and to the local institutions which welded that community together.

Although the union established itself as a working-class organization, when it failed to maintain its credibility as a militant union and attempted to use the scabs to protect its contract against a segment of the working class not enrolled on its books, it lost its standing within the working-class community. Lynn's workers then united against the Boot and Shoe Workers Union just as it has against the NALM.

THE MANUFACTURERS' LOCKOUT OF 1917

It was evident to everyone in Lynn that the Boot and Shoe Workers Union was more conservative than the local unions, and that fact was not lost to the manufacturers. On April 18, 1917, Lynn's manufacturers tried to take advantage of the split union movement by forcing their employees to join the Boot and Shoe Workers Union. Again the workers refused. The following day, the manufacturers sent out letters to the individual workers asking them to sign up with the union and to leave the local unions.[63]

On September 6, 1917, the manufacturers issued a public statement that they would neither negotiate nor do business with the United Shoe Workers or the Allied Shoe Workers unions. Both unions had grown out of the Lynn desertions from the Boot and Shoe Workers Union. On September 7, the Lynn Chamber of Commerce endorsed the Boot and Shoe Workers Union and attacked the Lynn unions for being too radical and irresponsible. On September 8, the manufacturers asked Samuel Gompers' aid in bringing the Boot and Shoe Workers to Lynn and destroying the local unions.[64]

On September 14, the manufacturers ran a front-page advertisement in the local paper asking the men to join "a single responsible union." It emphasized that the Boot and Shoe Workers Union was affiliated with the A.F. of L. and that it would be best for both the workers and the manufacturers. "Finally and decisively we wish to reiterate our formal statement that the manufacturers will only reopen their factories under the stamp of the Boot and Shoe Workers Union affiliated with the A.F. of L. and in no other way."[65]

The workers responded to these tactics as they had to the manufacturers' other attempts to break their unions. They held daily mass meetings with five hundred to a thousand or more workers which became forums for the local militants to denounce the Boot and Shoe Workers Union as a "sellout" union and the manufacturers as the enemy of the workingman. Local leaders roused the community with marches and parades, and kept the ranks of the shoe workers solid. The manufacturers' approach only heightened the bitterness which the workers already harbored toward the Boot and Shoe Workers Union from the strike of 1903.

In late September, the strikers asked Henry B. Endicott, a respected New England liberal from an old New England family, to mediate between the manufacturers and the unions. On September 20, an agreement was signed allowing for the old wages plus a 10 percent bonus, no discrimination, a local board to settle differences, and no strikes or lockouts for three years.[66] The strike ended on September 22 after five months of lockout. The companies had not been able to introduce the more conservative Boot and Shoe Workers Union.

The men maintained their loyalty and commitment to the militant and radical unionism of the United Shoe Workers and the Allied Shoe Workers unions. That commitment was also to a unionism based upon the principle of the opposing interests of workers and employers. Even though the employers had managed to win a no strike pledge (an agreement which was ignored by the Lynn workers), the unions in Lynn functioned not to accommodate management but to oppose it. Rank-and-file control over the local unions and ideological commitment to that control prevented the local unions from sliding into a position which defended the "integrity of contracts" over the interests of the workers. Although the Boot and Shoe Workers Union had strong socialist leaders at its inception, its day-to-day practice of accommodation with the employers, especially after 1899, meant less control over the job by the workers on the shop floor and the abandonment of the concept of the opposing interests of labor and capital, a concept deeply rooted in the minds of Lynn workers.[67] The workers' insistence on local autonomy was simultaneously a demand for a unionism which recognized the conflict of interests of manufacturers and labor and a belief that the center of that conflict was at the local level in the shop and in the community.

The manufacturers were able to win major concessions from the local unions, even if they were quickly broken by local activity. While they were not able to bring in the Boot and Shoe Workers Union, they got an agreement with a pledge of no strikes for three years and a local board of arbitration. The settlement of the strike and the coming of World War I briefly stabilized the labor situation in Lynn, but as soon as the war ended, the workers again took up the battle against the manufacturers.

As the local shoe industry declined in the 1920s, the tactics of the manufacturers became more aggressive. In 1925, the Wharton Shoe Company contracted with a Boston firm to bring in nonunion strike-breakers. The Boston firm was only able to get twenty men (out of two hundred places) to stay on the job, and the manufacturers submitted to the union. When the settlement was reached, the scabs were sent back to Boston.[68] As economic conditions worsened, it became more difficult for the workers to maintain their tradition of militant unionism. With the constant threat of moving out or shutting down, the shoe manu-facturers were able to keep the shoe workers and their unions on the defensive. The manufacturers began extensive use of the yellow dog contract and other union-busting tactics.[69] In 1936, when the Council of the United Shoe Workers Union (which was to become the CIO Union in 1937) declared a strike against the Lion Shoe Company, the company brought in strikebreakers and functioned under a company union for two years, despite union action and a ruling against the company union by the National Labor Relations Board.[70]

Between 1919 and 1929, Massachusetts' share of national shoe pro-duction dropped from over 40 percent to less than 25 percent, and over-all shoe production in the state declined almost 50 percent. Because the shoe industry leased machinery from the United Shoe Manufacturing Corporation, investment in fixed capital was small. Labor was a major source of differences in costs between companies and sections of the nation: labor costs in Massachusetts were 15 percent higher than in the rest of the country. These facts bore heavily on Lynn shoe workers. Lynn's higher quality of shoes and better skilled labor initially compensated for this wage difference, but by the end of the 1920s, with more and more shoe shops closing down and more and more workers facing unemploy-ment, the rank and file became more cautious in their actions and less successful in their job actions.[71] The Depression of the late 1920s and

1930s further hurt the shoe workers, with the consumer demand for shoes shifting to cheaper shoes. Faced with unemployment, the workers began to look for a compromise between their militance and commitment to industrial unionism and the national condition of the shoe industry. They found that compromise in the CIO Union drive in the late 1930s. Lynn's shoe workers did not abandon their stance of solidarity and militance, but they tempered their militance with the realism of the need for stability in a declining industry.

With the aid of the CIO, labor-management relations stabilized in Lynn just before World War II, but stabilization after a long-term decline only meant a peaceful death for a movement born a violent birth over a hundred years earlier.

THE TORCH PASSES

In the late 1930s, the campaign for militant unionism in Lynn passed from the shoe workers to the electrical workers. Owing to changes in work conditions and the size of the employer, however, the nature of the struggle and much of the tradition itself changed. Electrical workers confronted an opponent whose national power and organization dwarfed anything Lynn shoe workers had had to fight. The electrical workers' style of work and institutions were different, despite their feelings of continuity and comradeship with the shoe workers.[72]

6

The New Era

By the end of World War II, Lynn's structure of work, which affected the evolution of the working-class institutions, had changed. In turn, the institutions modified the community structure which they helped sustain and which helped maintain them. The transformation in the community was gradual, both because the change in the structure of work was gradual and because the interaction between community, institutions, and structure of work muted the effects of each individually. Although the old-timers held on to the old institutions, the younger members of the work force did not. Retired shoe workers still gathered at the union hall on Washington Street to gossip, exchange information, and play cards, but they were coming together out of habit. The younger shoe workers no longer looked upon the union as a social institution.[1]

The shoe workers who kept the Pioneer A. A. Club alive were mostly retired workers. The local union still had almost two thousand members, but these members no longer felt a sense of community with each other or the city: "Shoe workers are not together the way they used to be."[2] Many of the younger workers did not live in Lynn but rather in the surrounding towns and suburbs.

The city itself did not offer the younger members a community or even the functions of a community. At one time Lynn had five "motion picture houses"; in 1973, there were none. By the 1970s, most of the old cafes, lunchrooms, and pool halls had closed down.[3]

Many of these changes reflected a change in the economy of the city. The older shoe workers who lamented the loss of the community had been socialized before the decline of the shoe industry in Lynn in the late 1920s, when there were over twelve thousand, and not two thousand, shoe workers. These older workers were socialized into the working-class community dominated by shoe workers when these workers' institutions were strong enough to define the city and the community. Even electrical workers defined the pre-1930 city as a shoe worker city, where all of one's friends would be shoe workers and one went to the shoe workers' cafes and lunchrooms for talk and entertainment.

The younger workers of the 1970s saw none of that strength and community. As one retired shoe worker stated in 1972, " [We] were a lot closer than they are now."[4] New members of the work force saw a dying industry and a depressed city; few of their friends were shoe workers; General Electric, not shoes, dominated the city. The old institutions did not seem relevant to the reality the younger workers saw around them. Because shoe workers' institutions were no longer strong enough to define the culture or community, the younger workers identified with other forces. They were much more part of the mass culture of cars, bikes, and popular music than of cafes, union halls, and Labor Day parades.

The retired shoe and electrical workers interviewed in 1972-1973 blamed the automobile for destroying the community they had known: "It [the car] has killed the living in the city itself."[5] Retired shoe workers felt little continuity with the younger workers and maintained that the younger workers had no continuity with the past.

The passage of time has mellowed past reality for the retired workers, however. Their depression must be seen to some extent as a reflection of the shoe industry's depression; hence, their sense of a loss of community must be viewed with some suspicion.[6] "The people . . . will never really know how people of my day lived. It was good and it was bad, bad in so far as there wasn't any money, you know what I mean; and the good part, that the home life was there."[7] Home life for these retired shoe workers did not signify the nuclear family, but rather a whole network of community institutions which integrated the worker's leisure time with his work and family life. It involved activity with fellow workers after work, as well as taking the family down to Central Square for a leisurely walk. Involvement in the total community was what the retired shoe workers meant by "good living" and "home life." It was the loss of that integrated community which the shoe workers lamented and which they blamed the car for destroying.

The automobile was an appropriate symbol in what was in fact a community structure that changed as a result of the decline of the shoe industry, the development of the mass-production General Electric plant, and the patterns of urban dispersal encouraged by the availability of government loans for new housing and rising real wages following World War II. Particularly in the expansion years of the mid-nineteenth century, to be sure, many workers commuted into Lynn on the railroads or walked in from neighboring towns. By the end of the nineteenth century, however, the constant demand to find employment within walking distance of home brought most of Lynn's workers into the city. Indeed, it tended to centralize them in the working-class neighborhoods which bordered the factory district. When the shoe workers who were retired by the 1970s first entered the labor force, their community was a walking community. As mentioned earlier, they could walk to the shops and to their entertainment. On Saturday evenings, they would go downtown and just walk around the central city, or go to cafes and meet with friends.[8] If they went on an outing, they took the Narrow Gauge to the beach. Today the area in which these workers grew up has been leveled. High-rise office buildings and vacant lots now occupy the Brickyard. The Narrow Gauge was discontinued before World War II, and cars are now required to reach the beach from most areas of Lynn. The concentrated working-class areas were scattered after the war. Young families bought small homes outside the city with VA and FHA loans. As the downtown shops closed down, cars were needed to go to new jobs outside the city, many of which were in the developing electronics industry growing up on the beltline which surrounds the Boston metropolitan area. The car symbolized the death of the downtown city and the community of Lynn for these workers because it transported people outside the community.

The retired workers of Lynn looked on the few remaining shoe workers with distrust. The younger workers did not appear to share the class and community solidarity which they had felt upon entering the shoe shops. The very distrust of the older workers contributed to the lack of continuity between the younger and older generations. The older workers were particularly resentful that many of the younger workers did not live in the city and thus were outside the circle from which the old institutions grew and maintained their strength.[9] They blamed the younger workers for the failure of both the industry and the institutions. They cited the "poor workmanship" of the younger workers as the major cause of the decline of the shoe industry in Lynn, even though the industry had been dying long before the present generation of workers entered the shops.

The disappearance of the shoe workers and the slow disintegration of their institutions and activities also affected the electrical workers. During the early part of the twentieth century, electrical workers joined in the activities of the shoe workers, socializing with them in the cafes and lunch-rooms.[10] All they did was dominated by the shoe workers' activities.[11]

As the city became less of a shoe center, the electrical workers began to socialize elsewhere. In many cases, as with the Odd Fellows, the electrical workers took over the institutions and redefined them in terms of their own needs.[12] However, many of the informal institutions of the shoe workers were not appropriate for the General Electric workers. The down-town cafes and lunchrooms had been convenient and useful for the shoe workers, but not for the electrical workers. The General Electric plant was located at the far western edge of the city—too far to walk to the center of town.

The very structure of work was different for the electrical worker. Forced to work in a massive complex which required a long and tedious walk to free themselves from its walls, these workers took their lunch breaks within the company's cafeterias or in the lunch spaces provided. The complex was oppressive and constricted. Again and again, workers who left the shoe shops to work for General Electric described the ex-perience in terms of confinement: "I felt like I was in prison."[13]

With the exception of depression layoffs, General Electric provided its employees with year-round work. Even during the Great Depression, the company recalled employees through its own formal channels rather than through informal contacts as had been done by the shoe industry. Al-though in the early part of the century the older methods of job procure-ment, such as connections with friends or membership in the Odd Fellows, predominated at General Electric, by the post-World War I period, these informal patterns had been eliminated through rigid personal policies. In the modern General Electric plant, the institutions which the older shoe workers had used for job placement and security had no function.

The nature of the work also discouraged the informality and comrade-ship which spilled over into off-the-job social activity. Beginning in the 1920s, work became "Taylorized" and intensified with time and motion studies. The workers, pressed with speedups and highly intense on-the-job pressures, had little time or energy to socialize with their fellow workers.

General Electric sought to eliminate any unnecessary delays or idle periods on the job which the shoe workers had used for socializing, first with speedups under the Badeau system, and later with time and motion studies. Despite worker resistance, the stopwatch procedure was adopted at General Electric. It so increased the intensity factor of labor that the laborer felt isolated from his co-workers and considered his very labor debased.[14] One retired worker expressed the impact of Taylorism on the worker as follows:

> The most vicious thing they brought in the G.E. was that motion-time study! Now that, that was vicious! They had the Badeau system, and you could make a decent living on it, and then they brought this motion-time study in. The actual time to do the work was not timed, it was just the motions. You had something to do with the right hand and something to do with the left hand. The motions were timed, the actual working was not timed. Oh, it was vicious![15]

The informal social structure of the community was a victim not only of the increased intensity of work, but also of the General Electric Corporation itself, which in 1946 began an active campaign to replace the informal structure with a General Electric structure. Although the union was withdrawing from active participation in the community as a result of its concern for national efficiency and effectiveness, much of its support still came from the integration on the local community level of job concerns, attitudes, and informal social interactions. Even though the workers no longer used the union as an informal social center, they still depended upon it and, even more importantly, upon union friends and officials for information.

In the late 1930s, Lynn electrical workers, in the city's tradition of militant independence, became dissatisfied with the leadership of James Carey, the United Electrical Workers Union president, because they felt he had not given proper attention to local rank-and-file demands within the union. The Lynn local contended that their local president, Albert Fitzgerald, was not allowed enough input into union affairs. In September 1941, the Lynn members of the United Electrical Workers went to the national convention and elected Fitzgerald president of the national union over Carey.

Despite the workers' radical posture, the union continued to have peaceful relations with General Electric before and during the war. At the end of the war, this cooperative mood changed rapidly. The Lynn workers were no longer willing to settle for a negotiated agreement. Their wages had been frozen and prices had skyrocketed. They turned down an offer of a 10 percent increase which would not cover continuing inflation. The local voted to send its delegates to the union conference board to demand a strike vote. With the common laborer earning less than eighty-eight cents an hour, Lynn workers demanded at least a two dollar a day raise. The local voted 12,391 to 1,860 for a strike. On January 11, 1946, the strike began, the largest single strike in the city's history.

The strikers were part of a national union effort to bring the General Electric Corporation to terms. They held local rallies and maintained a strong picket line throughout the strike. Finally, the General Electric Corporation agreed to meet the union's demand of an 18.5 cents an hour raise for all workers, including women, and so the strike was settled. The strike was successful because the national union was able to coordinate the militancy of thousands of locals across the nation. To defeat or even confront such a power as General Electric, the United Workers also had to mount an effectively organized national strike.

The strength of the union also lay in the local informal support for unionism, such as the working-class community's grapevine and union spirit. This spirit turned out the large numbers of workers in support of the strike and carried the workers' militancy into the second half of the twentieth century. In addition, General Electric ultimately realized that it must undermine this community strength in order to weaken the union.

With the settlement of the 1946 strike, the company realized the importance of the informal communications and socializing networks in keeping the union ranks solid. Hoping to weaken union influence over the members, the company attempted to replace many of the informal networks with its own.

Following the strike, General Electric, under Lemuel R. Bowlware, undertook to break down the informal community "grapevine" which functioned both on and off the job. It activated every available resource—from personal contact with each employee and letters to the home, to advertisements, stories, and articles in the local papers. It consciously attempted to become an active force in the life of the worker after he left the job. The company established and revamped in-plant papers, bulletins, and various types of written and oral communications media. It established a special group of talented writers and experts to make sure that its views dominated the community.[16]

Convinced that effective union and worker communication was responsible for managerial loss of control over the shop, the company sought to undermine that interaction. It attempted to actively reshape the worker's community and life patterns, not only by altering the structure of the work, but also by reaching out to its "community neighbors" and creating new ties and institutions upon which the worker would depend for information and aid. The United Electrical Workers' leadership correctly noted in their history of the union that other factors such as internal raiding and redbaiting helped the company break down union solidarity. However, while Bowlware's campaign, like the company's earlier campaign following the 1919 and 1920 strikes, did not take a direct toll on the workers' solidarity, it did reflect the importance of the working-class community infrastructure in class solidarity and collective action.[17]

Without strong supporting institutions, General Electric workers no longer felt they were part of a working-class community. Their participation in the social institutions of the Lynn community diminished, and the less they participated, the less the institutions functioned and the more the community became atomized. Rather, they increasingly looked outside the community to fulfill their needs. Following World War II, the workers turned to consumerism for that fulfillment.

The rise of consumerism, coupled with industry's attempt to channel discontent into patterns of consumption, dates back to the 1920s.[18] Its impact on working-class culture was minimized by low wages and by the intricate system of matured working-class institutions and the culture they reinforced. The scarcity of the Depression years further dramatized the failure of advertising to deliver on its promise of the better life. These years also augmented the workers' sense of economic insecurity and deprivation, and traumatized many workers. Wage-earners were unable not only to gain the "benefits" of the frills projected to them on billboards and in magazines but also to maintain the basic needs of survival. With the war boom of the 1940s and the continued government-supported economy of the late 1940s and 1950s, many workers (especially with overtime) had financial access to the suburban homes offered by VA and FHA loans, as well as to the goods projected as part of the suburban life-style. Although studies of the working-class suburbs have shown that a distinct working-class culture has been maintained there, the memory of deprivation during the Depression, together with the availability of goods in the 1940s and 1950s, increased the working-class's participation in the consumer culture of the postwar period.[19] Lacking the strong class institutions which were rooted in the central city, workers now sought economic security and the goods which symbolized that security. It was only in the 1960s, after a generation of attempting to substitute consumer goods for the community of the late nineteenth and early twentieth centuries that disillusionment with that means of dealing with the alienating and demeaning labor began to appear. Absenteeism, labor turnovers, and disinterest in work are beginning to plague General Electric as well as other mass-production industries.

Today, Lynn's working class retains a sense of tradition, but it is confined to the older workers who remembered how it used to be. The younger workers, while militant as Lynn workers always were, are not directing this force into community solidarity. Nor is the militancy an outgrowth of community solidarity and traditions, based upon an understanding of the role of the producers and owners of production in society. Rather, it is a result of frustration with meaningless work and discontent over working conditions, with no effective institutional outlets. Workers often blame the union, which traditionally functioned as that outlet, for the unpleasant conditions and lump it together with the company as the source of work place discontent.[20] In the future, this discontent may become more directed, and new community institutions may arise to give focus and analysis to the dissatisfaction. Such institutions could work to alleviate the alienation of these younger workers, give them the means of understanding their past, and enable them to direct actions in terms of past experience and analysis.

7

Fall River: Dizzying Heights to Depths of Depression

In 1924, *The New Republic* began an article on Fall River with the following paragraphs:

> For more than a century any mention of the city of Fall River, Massachusetts has almost invariably called to mind but one thing—the cotton industry. Throughout the nineteenth century that New England community grew with such rapidity that shortly after the Civil War she had attained such perfection in her chosen field that she was known as the "Manchester of America," "Queen City of the Cotton Industry in the United States."
>
> Her scores of mills gave employment to more than half a hundred thousand people and more than double that number of individuals looked to her busy spindles and looms for their daily bread. Her mills poured millions of dollars into the pockets of families connected with the industry. They produced over 2,000 miles of cotton cloth every day, and they brought from Europe and Canada many thousands of immigrants seeking opportunity and treasure on the golden shores of the Western Hemisphere.
>
> But having risen to such dizzying heights in the nineteenth century she was, during the twentieth, to fathom depths of depression such as she had never known. Today Fall River is a city of misery, want, unemployment, hunger, and hopelessness. The

cloud that shadows her seems to have no silver lining, and she
lies almost dormant, while stark wants stalks her streets and her
workers wonder what the end is to be, hanging on desperately—
God knows how—waiting for they know not what.[1]

This chapter is the story of the rise of the "Queen City of the Cotton Industry" and its fall to "misery, want, unemployment, hunger, and hopelessness."

Fall River, a city settled on a minuscule but rapidly falling river flowing
into Mt. Hope Bay, was like Lynn, an industrial city. Like Lynn, too, it
grew rapidly because of its major industry, and it experienced a major depression in that industry. Unlike Lynn, where local merchants took control
over an artisan craft, from the very beginning Fall River's industry was
organized by merchant capitalists bent upon becoming industrial capitalists.
They brought in machines and the workers to use them. They found no
resistant artisan culture deeply rooted in the community. From the outset,
it was their community, and whatever resistance they encountered came in
with the workers who confronted the machines of industrial capitalism.
Fall River's experience as an industrial city was both similar to and different from Lynn's. In both cities, the majority of the population depended
upon wage labor for survival, and the working class looked to their communities and institutions for support. However, the topography and the
nature of the work performed in Fall River differed from Lynn's, and its
work force had different origins and traditions. All of these factors affected
Fall River's working-class community and its response to the conditions it
faced in the community and in the mill.

In 1800, when Lynn merchants were traveling deep into the hinterland
making contacts for the shoes being crafted on the banks of the Saugus
River, Fall River lay dormant inside the southern part of the community
of Freetown. It was located fifty miles south of Boston on high ground
rising from a narrow bay which opens to the sea between Long Island
and Cape Cod. Its early community of eighteen interrelated families made
their living by farming. This early nineteenth-century farming village did
not realize the importance of the precipitous fall of the Quequechan River,
127 feet in less than half a mile, its even flow and granite base, the highly
humid climate, and the easy access to markets. In only a few decades
these advantages, together with the effective utilization of opportunities
by local entrepreneurs, transformed this hamlet into the center of the
American textile industry. In 1900, Fall River was as well known for

textiles as Pittsburgh was for steel. Today the city has slipped back into relative obscurity, known chiefly as the hometown of Lizzie Borden who "with an ax gave her father forty whacks."[2]

Like most mill towns, Fall River developed through a combination of local geographic advantages and the initial investment of outside capital. Once involved in the textile production, the city rose quickly to a position of national predominance, with local entrepreneurs directing its career.

The Quequechan River provided the early manufacturers with ample water power and a secure foundation to build the early water-powered mills. The moist atmosphere of Fall River, likened by many to that of Lancashire, England, kept the cotton in good condition and lessened the possibility of thread breaks and slowdowns in production. The coastal location allowed for cheap and easy delivery of raw cotton. Boats up from southern ports could deliver bales of cotton almost to the doors of its mills. In the second half of the nineteenth century as the mills switched from water to steam power, the coastal location provided quick and easy access to tidewater coal. Fall River's location as a port town and its close proximity to Boston and New York markets gave its manufacturers an edge over other New England mill owners.

Most of the original inhabitants were yeoman farmers, some of whom had valuable land and water privileges, and only few had liquid capital. Of the original eighteen families, nine were Bordens and most of the others were closely related. In 1811, one of the early settlers, Joseph Durfee, attempted to put Fall River's geographic advantages to work with a small mill, but lack of funds for expansion forced his mill to close in 1829. During this period, capitalists from Providence became interested in the city for textile production. Olive Chace and David Anthony formed the Troy Cotton and Woolen Manufacturing Company, giving the Borden family, who controlled the water privileges of the upper Quequechan River, a substantial interest. In this pre-Civil War era, the mill workers in Fall River, which was a homogeneous community, came from the neighboring towns and countryside, and most of them were sons or daughters of local farmers. The mill owners either were members of the original families of Fall River or settled there from Providence. The families that owned the mills also owned the stores and the land on which the population settled. These leading families controlled the city itself, its mills, banks, and commerce, from the early nineteenth century down to the twentieth.

The Fall River Iron Works, established by Richard Borden and Bradford Durfee in 1821 with $18,000 capital and associated with Jefferson Borden, Holden Borden, David Anthony, William Valentine, Joseph Butler, and Abraham and Isaac Wilkinson, reflected the control and entrepreneurial vision of these early resident capitalists. In 1825, the Iron Works was incorporated with $200,000 worth of assets; this sum increased to $960,000 by 1845. From the very beginning, the company was involved in operating not only a rolling mill, a nail mill, and an iron foundry, but also cotton textile and printing factories. It held large tracts of land and important water rights. It soon owned the Wattupa Reservation Company, the Annaman Mill, the American Print Works, the Metacomet Mill, the Fall River Railroad, and the Bay State Steam Boat Line, and was part-owner of the Troy Cotton and Woolen Company and the Fall River Manufacturing Company. In 1889, the Fall River Iron Works under M.C.D. Borden built the first great Iron Works Cotton Mill, which dwarfed its earlier mills. Others were erected in 1892, 1893, and 1895, and a fifth, sixth, and seventh soon after the turn of the century.[3]

Fall River boasted a population of two thousand in 1825, with seven hundred people in the cotton mills, two print shops, and related iron works. By 1837, the town had ten cotton mills with 31,000 spindles turning out 7,767,614 yards of cotton yearly, and two print works turning out 12 million yards. The cotton mills employed 357 males and 648 females, and the print works another 500 males.[4] By 1854, Fall River had over 12,700 inhabitants.

There was little labor unrest among the early mechanics. Although the local Mechanics Association put up three workers and a sympathetic lawyer for the state legislature under their Mechanic Farmer party, the association waned after a short period. The upper class attempted to keep labor relations quiet by busying itself with paternal supervision of the workers' lives. Various attempts to instill temperance into the habits of the new work force by means of controlling wages through the store pay system and periodic appeals to curb intemperance, along with the alms-giving by the leading "Christian" women of the city, kept alive the image of a concerned ownership class, despite the obvious self-interest of this concern.[5]

The upper class kept close control over both their workers and their own wealth and status. By an intricate pattern of intermarriage, the leading families were all related to each other throughout the nineteenth century. Marriages among the Fall River elites were arranged to further economic interests as well as social status. Through this pattern of intermarriage and tight control over capital, the mill families were closely tied to the banking and transportation families, the judges, and the owners of the local newspapers. Occasionally, some members of the new merchant class, such as the Osbornes or Slades, or outsiders such as the Dryers, challenged the older families, but they were simply integrated into the older structure after they had proved their permanence. This sytem of control was so successful that even into the late nineteenth century the families that dominated the Fall River mills could trace their background to the city's original families.[6]

Textiles, unlike shoes, required large capital investment. Although a shoe manufacturer had to have credit and contacts in order to set up shop, and these were usually well beyond the means of even the most skilled shoe worker, compared to a textile corporation, the requirements were quite modest. Most of the shoemaking machines were leased. Thus, although there was continuity among the shoe manufacturers, there was also a certain fluidity, especially from merchant or tradesman to manufacturer. This was not the case for Fall River's elites. The large initial capital investment required to build the mill and purchase the machinery meant that only those with access to large amounts of capital, banking connections, and influence to float stock in the corporation could set up a textile company. This requirement greatly limited the fluidity of Fall River's upper class and accounted for the dominance of a few families. It also created both a distance and familiarity between workers and owners. For many older workers the names of the mill owners were household words; their parents may well have worked in the mills owned by the same families. At the same time it reinforced class division. The wealthy were an impenetrable class living as if in another world in the mansions of the Highlands where the working class went only as servants, delivery boys, or beggars. The wealth of the elites came from the mills down below where the workers had their homes and their jobs—and were exploited. If the manufacturers believed that their wealth was a product of hard work and upward mobility, that belief was not shared by the workers who worked hard but had no hopes or illusions about becoming owners themselves.

ECOLOGY OF AN EARLY MILL TOWN

The early mills that Fall River operatives entered at daylight each day were small compared to the later nineteenth-century structures. They were usually only two or three stories high, and most were built of wood or stone, 100 by 45 feet at their base. The workers in these small mills worked in groups of less than a hundred operatives per mill.

In the late 1840s, the mills began to take on the appearance of the large nineteenth-century textile factories familiar to those who drive through rural New England. Many of the newer mills employed between 200 and 400 or more workers. The Metacomet Mill, built in 1846, was 247 by 90 feet and five stories high. It housed over 21,000 spindles alone, and by 1854 employed 130 males and 164 females. Although most of the workers in these early mills were native Americans, with local women and children doing the unskilled labor, as the mills grew larger and the machinery more sophisticated, English, Scottish, and Irish workers began filling the more skilled positions.

Despite the peaceful relationship between the worker and the manufacturer in the pre-Civil War period, the long hours and exhausting labor with low pay took their toll on the social peace of the community. A typical day for an early nineteenth-century worker such as Fall River's Hannah Borden began at 4:00 A.M. By 5:00 A.M. she had her two looms running; she broke for breakfast from 7:30 to 8:00 and worked from then until her half-hour lunch break at noon. Hannah would not be home until 7:30 P.M., and many nights she would fall asleep at the dinner table. These conditions finally sparked a losing strike in 1840. In May and June of that year, workers in two mills, the American and the Fall River Print Works, struck.[8]

Many of the early workers resented the paternal attitudes of the employers. In 1833, the Fall River Mechanics Association set up a co-operative store for the workers in order to break out of the pattern of dependence upon the mill stores. In 1844, they published their own paper, *The Mechanic,* which argued that the "mills are ruled by a most despotic system of government. The autocracy of Russia is not more despotic than the management of the factories in New England. It is a despotism without a spark of humanity in it. Its one and only object is to enrich the few and impoverish the many."[9] The paper pushed for the end of the store pay system (the company store) and the requirement of living in company housing. In 1850, workers struck for six months, only to be defeated by the importation of outside laborers. But the class activity of these early workers was erratic even to their own leaders. In 1844, *The Mechanic* complained that class solidarity had waned.[10] It was not until after the

Civil War that Fall River's working class built up a defined community consciousness of its own self-interest which had any lasting effect.

In the 1860s and 1870s, when Lynn merchants, having already taken control of shoe production from the artisans, began to introduce the factory system on a large scale and utilize the machine, Fall River, already having firmly established the factory system, began building huge granite mills. The number of spindles jumped from 117,636 in 1854 to over a million by the middle of the 1870s. Between 1859 and 1874, the population increased from 12,534 to 43,289. The geographic advantages of Fall River which had originally encouraged the textile industry in the city before the Civil War gave it dominance over the northern Massachusetts textile centers in the late nineteenth century. Following the Civil War, textile production shifted from water power, with its limited expansion potential, to steam. Because of the city's easy access to tidewater coal, costs were low compared to those in the less accessible inland centers. Fall River also had abundant supplies of water located in several areas around the city. Mill construction expanded throughout the city wherever these sources of water were located. The level land near the waterfront in central Fall River was quickly built up with large five-story granite structures. Mills were also built in the area along both sides of the pond, portions of the Quequechan River, and in the southern part of town around Cook's Pond. Around each of these mill clusters residential areas sprung up, many actually built by the companies themselves (see Photograph 7).[11]

The city encouraged this growth by giving the mill owners tax benefits. Between 1865 and 1874, the mills paid only twenty-four cents per spindle of city taxes, while comparable towns such as Lowell taxed their mills twenty-nine cents or more per spindle. Throughout the nineteenth century, the Fall River mills paid less in taxes than other New England towns.[12] The effects of the low taxes were borne by the poorer workers in terms of inadequate city services and improvements.

The tremendous growth of the Fall River mills in the 1860s and 1870s put great demands on its working-class population, especially women and children. Operatives under twenty-one years of age formed over 55 percent of the work force, as opposed to 40 percent in other New England towns. A quarter of all workers were under fifteen in Fall River as compared to an eighth in the other textile cities. In 1879, Jonathan Baxter Harrison was shocked by the number of women and children in the mills: "more than one-half the [Fall River] operatives were women and girls."[13]

7. Mid-Nineteenth-Century Company Housing and Borden Mills

Notice the compactness of this mid-nineteenth-century housing. Most of the workers and their families would find work across the street in the mill. On their way to and from work, on doorsteps and front porches they would share their experiences and learn important lessons of class solidarity.

Mill owners sent out recruiters to bring workers to Fall River. These hiring agents actively recruited Lancashire workers, and as the 1870s progressed, they began moving into Canada to entice French Canadians to work in the less skilled jobs. As these immigrants poured in, they disrupted the city's life to such an extent that the Massachusetts Bureau of Statistics of Labor claimed at the end of the 1870s that "they caused a regression from which Fall River is now (just) recovering." According to the bureau, during this initial growth period, Fall River "was full of the outpourings of the poorhouses of England."[14]

Although there were plenty of jobs when the immigrants first began arriving in Fall River, their numbers put a demand upon the housing market that the normal commercial real estate development could not meet. The textile companies themselves, following the pattern of other New England mill towns, filled the gap by building company housing near and around the new mills. These tenements went up in a great hurry with little concern "for the comfort of life."[15]

Fall River textile companies built over twelve thousand dwelling units during the late 1860s and 1870s which were mostly barracks-style multi-family frame buildings. Some twenty-one of thirty-three corporations owned these units, and they were so pervasive in the industrial parts of the city that company houses became the general rule in Fall River throughout the nineteenth century, more so than in any other Massachusetts textile center. Clustered around each mill were row upon row of poorly built units. Although they relieved some of the pressure on the already existing housing, their close quarters and high-density structure contributed to the overcrowding and congestion of the working-class neighborhoods.[16]

At first, these crowded company houses were packed in the central part of the city where the early mills were situated. Later, when the mills began to scatter toward the edge of the city, the crowded housing spread in clumps around the various mills. Thus, Fall River, unlike Lynn, did not have one or two fairly centralized working-class communities, but rather several dispersed communities. The first immigrants who resided in these communities had a smiliar ethnic tradition, but as later immigrant groups came into the city and began to settle into one or another of these dispersed communities, there was no centralized working-class residential area, such as the Brickyard in Lynn, to bring together the various ethnic groups employed in the shops.

The early company houses were built to supply the influx of immigrants with homes near the mills in which they worked. In the early years following the Civil War, company housing rented at a lower rate than what was available privately. Although cheaper, these company housing units were in far worse condition and far more densely built than private working-class housing. By the late 1870s, when the workers began organizing, the companies used their housing as a means of keeping the workers in line: "The mill-owned houses served as a means of control over employees and was frequently a source of profit."[17] As late as 1886, the Metacomet Mill was still deducting rent from the wages of a number of their operatives; an average of $2.66, or 31 percent of their gross weekly earnings, was deducted each week.[18]

By the 1870s, many mill workers were *required* to live in company houses. A spinner stated in 1875 that he was forced to live in a company house despite the wretched conditions there. The sink in the dwelling was in the corner of the room used as a living room, dining room, and kitchen. The outhouse was stopped up and gave off noxious odors. The hydrant in the yard was the only source of water, and when the mills let out there were long lines to get to the water.[19] Workers who refused to live in company houses were discharged regardless of the condition of the tenements. Once the workers were in the company houses, it became difficult to procure housing during strikes, when the companies would evict strikers.[20]

Almost nine thousand of Fall River's population in 1875 were from England, mostly Lancashire County. Over nine thousand were Irish-born, but many migrated from Lancashire where they spent several years in the Lancashire textile mills.[21] The traditional literature on the Irish in Lowell and Lawrence argues that they came to these cities from Ireland via Boston. They were brought to the textile centers as construction workers, building the canals, mills, and, later, railroads. After finishing the construction work, the Irish, especially their wives and children, moved into the less skilled positions within the mills. In the 1840s and 1850s, Fall River had a small Irish population which had its origin in the Irish construction workers who helped build the original mills, laid the tracks for the Fall River Railroad, and did the city's heavy labor. These Irish immigrants, like the Irish of Boston or New York, were poor peasants and had little to offer but their brawn and backs. This group was greatly augmented by another influx of Irish into Fall River in the

1860s, 1870s, and 1880s. These immigrants came with different experiences and different skills.[22] They migrated from Ireland to the textile mills of Lancashire, where they were thoroughly apprenticed in the English trade union movement and class consciousness. With the English, they then left Lancashire for Fall River because of blacklisting strikes or depressions in the textile towns of Oldham, Blackburn, or Manchester. Of the individuals who received funds from Lancashire trade unions to migrate to America because they had become "victims" of the class struggle in England, a large number were Irish.[23] By 1875, almost thirteen thousand of Fall River's population came from Lancashire County, England. Next to this English-Irish group were five thousand Canadians, mostly French, who began migrating to work in the least skilled jobs when farming was depressed in Canada.

In January 1858, the early arrivals from England formed the Mule Spinners Association and elected Patrick Carroll as president and John McKeowen as secretary. Both were Lancashire Irish.[24] Another Fall River leader, Robert Howard, a Lancashire Irishman, came to Fall River in 1860; in Lancashire, he was president of the local Spinners and Twiners Association.[25] In 1893, James Tansey, later secretary of the Fall River Carders, came over from Rochdale, Lancashire, where he had been both a carder and a union member.[26] These Lancashire mill hands formed the Fall River Workingmen's Cooperative Association in the late nineteenth century.

By the middle of the 1870s, for Lancashire workers the name Fall River had become synonymous with America. On a voyage from Liverpool in the 1880s, Bin Brierley, a writer from Lancashire, recorded this conversation with textile workers coming over in steerage:

"Where dun yo' come fro'?"
"Oldham, an' Mossley."
"Where are yo' goin' to?"
"To Fall River."
"Hav' yo' shops to go to?"
"Nawe, but we'n friends there."[27]

Of the 6,354 English operatives working in the three largest textile communities, Fall River, Lowell, and Lawrence, in 1878, Fall River was the home and work place of 4,237.[28] As late as 1903, it was stated that Fall

River "in the early morning is but a gateway into workaday Lancashire. Fall River is Lancashire in epitome."[29]

The constant contact between Lancashire and Fall River produced an environment which encouraged working-class ties and organizations. These workers attempted to re-create in Fall River the working-class community and institutions which they had left. In the process, they helped to transform the city, almost as dramatically as the mills in which they worked were transforming the ecological structure of the city.

THE CITY IN 1880

By 1880, Fall River was no longer the quiet farming community it had been in 1810. Its early members' success in introducing and organizing the textile industry guaranteed the demise of that pastoral community. The Fall River of 1880 was not the small mill town of 1840 either. It no longer supported a small community of native workers drawn from neighboring towns and farms to work two or four primitive looms. Its quiet community with workers identified with and even related to the entrepreneurs, had been disrupted by the massive growth and success of Fall River's textiles.

The huge granite mills which rose up from the center of the city not only were monuments to the success and vision of the city's leading families, but they also housed hundreds of thousands of spindles which demanded the attention of thousands of workers. (For two views of the typical Fall River mills, see Photographs 8 and 9.) These workers brought with them skills, labor, and a consciousness of their own role in the success of the city and its trade. They built a community which was centered in institutions that the workers developed for themselves. So distant were these workers from the quiet community of the early nineteenth century that an observer noted in 1879 that the working class had been "allowed to be so alien and separate from the influence and spirit of our national life."[30]

Fall River was proud of its development, despite the change it forced upon itself. In 1895, Jonathan Lincoln, a speaker at a banquet to honor the Borden family and the new mill of the Fall River Iron Works, commented that Boston and New York considered Fall River a culturally backward and unsophisticated place because all its energy was put to "the single task of prosperity and industry."[31] The business community felt that their success in building not only the huge mills but also the granite

8. Typical Rear of Fall River Mill

Each floor of the massive textile mills was usually reserved for one aspect of the production process. The cotton would generally enter in raw form, be sent to the top floor for cleaning and carding, go to the next floor down for spinning, then down to the weaving floor, and finally to the first floor for folding. Weavers had little time to communicate with each other and were physically separated from other workers.

9. Fall River Mill, Rodman Village, 1872

This center shot of the Borden Mills shows the multiple levels of a typical textile mill. The raw cotton would be brought to the center shaft, moved to the top floor, begin its movement down each floor, and finally come out the bottom as folded finished cotton cloth.

7

AVERAGE NUMBER OF CORPORATIONS
AND
WORKERS IN FALL RIVER,
1880-1930

Year	Number of Corporations	Number of Workers
1880	33	14,127
1890	41	19,476
1895	41	23,476
1900	42	26,371
1905	39	21,604
1915	—	32,000
1920	—	32,300
1925	—	26,800
1930	—	13,700

SOURCE: Thomas Smith, *The Cotton Textile Industry of Fall River* (New York: King's Crown, 1944); *Twenty-fourth Annual Report of Massachusetts Bureau of Statistics of Labor, 1910* (Boston: 1911).

8

POPULATION OF FALL RIVER, 1860-1960

Year	Population	Year	Population
1860	14,026	1915	124,791
1865	17,481	1920	120,485
1870	26,766	1925	129,000
1875	45,340	1930	115,300
1880	48,901	1935	117,414
1885	56,870	1940	115,428
1890	74,398	1945	115,062
1900	104,863	1950	111,963
1905	105,762	1960	99,942
1910	119,292		

SOURCE: United States Decennial Census, 1860-, for each decade; Massachusetts State Census, 1865-, for odd years.

churches, libraries, and schools reflected the value and worth of their city. The cultural snobs of New York and Boston may not have thought much of Fall River's culture, but its wealth created great things, unmatched in any city its size.

Fall River's population continued to grow as the number of spindles the workers operated increased (see Tables 7 and 8). Between 1870 and 1880, the number of spindles doubled, and the population almost doubled. Between 1880 and 1890, the city added another 352,054 spindles, and its population jumped almost ten thousand.[32]

The mills were scattered around the city, in groups near the different water supplies (see Map 2). Dense urban residential areas or "villages" gathered around these scattered clumps of mills. This process created a series of high-density villages within the city, but they were separated from the center city. This is reflected by the general high level of density experienced in all nine wards (see Tables 9 and 10).

Thus, there emerged in the late nineteenth century, especially in the 1890s, Globe Village to the south, Flint Village to the east, Mechanicsville and Bowenville both in the north, "Petit Canada" (Little Canada) south of the river, and Border City to the extreme north.[33] The tenements that grew up in these villages were "constructed to accommodate two families on a floor. The exteriors [were] indicative of poverty and hopelessness." Garbage was not collected, and it "piled up and scattered around doors, decaying."[34]

A local newspaper reporter described Globe Village which gathered around the King Philip Mills as "clustering, like chickens under their brooding mother's wings, [King Philip Mills were] long lines and scattered groups of one, two, and three story wooden tenements where the [operatives lived.] Some of these homes [had] fifty tenants under one roof, others [had] but two or three."[35]

A late nineteenth-century description of Fall River by William Bayard Hale, a churchman concerned by the church's lack of a role in industrial settings, vividly captured the mean conditions of its operatives. Hale began his survey of Fall River at the tenements of the Borden Mills on Rodman Street. There were sixteen blocks of houses around a court, each block containing six tenements. The court was built on low ground and was filled with pools of standing water most of the year.

Operatives live in bedrooms and kitchens. They pay seven dollars a month; this means to the corporation a rental of $8,000.00 annually at five percent interest. Four to a room is perhaps an unusual number. . . . They are not often willing to tell how many share a tenement; it will average perhaps ten, though the

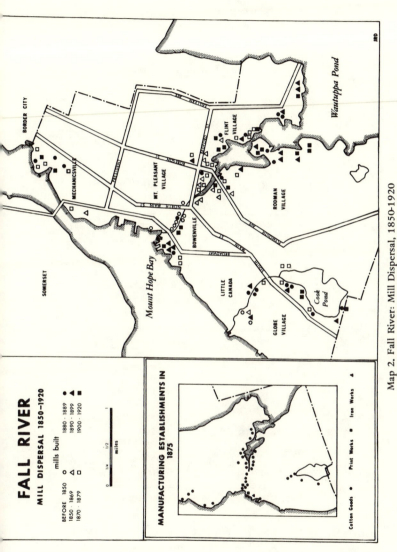

Map 2. Fall River: Mill Dispersal, 1850–1920

Adapted from Thomas Smith, *The Cotton Textile Industry of Fall River* (New York: King's Crown, 1944).

9

DENSITY PER WARD:
FALL RIVER, 1885

Ward	Persons per Dwelling
1	9.47
2	10.59
3	12.21
4	12.22
5	12.59
6	11.19
7	9.98
8	6.40
9	11.81

SOURCE: Massachusetts State Census, 1885,
Vol. 1, p. 160.

10

POPULATION PER WARD:
FALL RIVER, 1885

Ward	Persons per Dwelling
1	7,547
2	6,004
3	6,557
4	6,809
5	6,255
6	8,720
7	5,059
8	2,559
9	7,360

SOURCE: Massachusetts State Census, 1885,
Vol. 1, p. 160.

patrolman thinks more. The population of the court is about one thousand. The buildings have been painted a cheap color which might have been selected for its dinginess; the court, however, is always gay with hundreds of fluttering garments of many colors; clotheslines cross it in every direction. Looking in at entries, the plastering of the walls is seen to be discolored and broken and the stairs bare and dilapidated. The court is littered with refuse; one threads one's way among unsavory heaps. Along under the eaves of every block is a ridge composed of potato parings, egg shells, and garbage; the universal rule is to pour the kitchen emptyings out the window.

The court is the playground for the children and the thorough-fare for all. In certain details of filth, it is probably not matched outside of Fall River anywhere in what we call civilization. And in the center stands a pump. The air is pestilential and the place revolting to every sense. The heart sickens at the sight of the crowds who sit on stoops and hang out windows and gaze at their misery. The saloon is a retreat [for the] . . . men. For the women there is no refuge but the streets. . . . Among them all, hatred of the rich, and rage against life [are] inevitable. In such a place what can men do but sit on steps and curse their employers; what can women do but nurse their crippled babies and wish them dead.

Leaving this place, you pass a block where a dozen families draw water from a single faucet, the condition of which may be judged from the statement of the patrolman; that to fill a pail from it required several minutes. You see many blocks worse than those of the Borden Mills. "Little Canada," the property of the American Linen Mills Company, is unspeakable. The Slade Mill tenements stand in a swamp . . .[36]

Despite these wretched conditions, rents for these company houses were not low. In hard times, the tenants had to cut into their food and clothing money to pay the rent. As one tenant put it: "There's no money coming in now, so there's none to go out. But they've got it down against us. Lower the rent when we are out of work? No, Sir. They're too busy cutting wages. They've no time to cut rents."[37]

The interior of these units was no better than the exterior. One had "three cots, two supported on soap boxes, the third being made up on the floor." Fifteen men occupied the room at night, including a boy dying of typhoid.[38] Although this report probably suffers from the nineteenth-century reformer's tendency to exaggerate the conditions of filth and degradation, the conditions must indeed have been wretched, as is demonstrated by Fall River's high death rate.[39]

LIVES OF THE OPERATIVES, 1880-1900

Fall River's mill workers in the 1870s, when wages in general were relatively high, were burdened by low wages, pressure toward whole-family employment, and congested high-density living—the same problems textile workers have suffered from the nineteenth century to the present.

Even the more successful textile workers had to withdraw children from school and place them in the mills. For textile workers there was not a single bread winner, but rather a collective family economic unit. Survival meant that every family member contributed to the family's budget. Children were expected to make their contribution to the household at the earliest possible age. A sample of the Massachusetts Bureau of Statistic of Labor survey in 1875 reveals that a typical Fall River weaver whose daughter, age sixteen, also worked in the mill, earned $524 a year. With the daughter's income of $448 the family of six lived comfortably in a six-room tenement situated near the mill, with good surroundings and sanitary arrangements. The house was also well furnished. The family was able to save $32 a year and still eat meat, eggs, and cheese regularly. Even in this relative comfort, however, the bureau noted that "run[ning] too many looms" left the weavers "without energy for anything else after work" except home and sleep.[40]

For the unskilled, even with children at work life was a much greater struggle. An unskilled English laborer's earnings of $395.20 forced him to send his twelve-year-old daughter into the mills. Nonetheless, the family of seven lived in a five-room tenement: the ceiling leaked and the sink drainage was so bad that it caused an almost unbearable stench in bad weather. Moreover, the tenement was poorly furnished, and the family was in debt and behind on the store bill. The next youngest child was to be sent into the mill that summer when the family hoped to pull out of debt. But with doctor's bills of $32.75 because of poor diet and living conditions, household expenses were over the income notwithstanding all the frugality.[41]

The annual income of individual textile operatives was three-fifths that of shoe workers; thus, the textile workers were much more likely to have some family members employed in the mill. With several children working a textile worker's family could enjoy a moderate amount of comfort, but conditions were mean indeed for those with offspring too small or too sickly to enter the mill.

In 1879, Jonathan Harrison felt that the dense living and the "foulness of the air in the rooms in which the operatives eat and sleep" gave the Fall River operatives a pale, "peculiar look." The cooking in most of their homes was done in the "sitting room," where the members of the household not only ate but also "pass[ed] the evening together."[42] Population density led the *Monitor,* an 1872 Fall River weekly, to note that it was impossible for newcomers to find shelter, and the "most miserable accommodations yet find ready takers at exorbitant prices."[43]

A newspaperman in 1889 described the homes of these nineteenth-century workers much as they had been a decade earlier:

> The places were . . . not in the best of repairs. Some of the places had rugs, a few had carpets, but the majority were bare and as clean as soap and water could make them. . . . The only real homelike appliances about the room were large comfortable stoves which sent out a cheerful glow to tender the cold blasts that swept about the place and knocked and rattled at every door.[44]

The worker's day began early. Even when there was a strike, as at the time of the above report, the workers kept the hours dictated by their work.

> The occupants, long used to mill hours, rise about 5:00 in the morning. . . . The breakfast in two of the houses consisted . . . of pea soup, coffee, and bread. Another family in the same house had butter, another had milk to garnish the coffee. The meal though frugal was substantial and served to supply the demands of nature. At dinner . . . three families ate pea soup, another had a boiled dinner of salt beef and cabbage, and still another was eating oatmeal. . . . A black T.D. pipe [*sic*] was the only dessert furnished to the men, and the women were too busy even for this solace.[45]

The workers who came to Fall River during the expansion years of the 1870s saw few evidences of progress in either their homes or their meals. Although those years had brought immense wealth to the residents of the "Hill" and progress to the city, the workers who created the cotton cloth which brought in such wealth did not share in it. For the individual operative, the passing decade brought only deteriorating conditions, lower wages, higher costs, and less control over his or her labor.[46] The only "progress" the workers could expect was dependent on their children's coming of age when they could be sent to work and supplement the family income.

This pressure to send children into the mills in order to lift the family above the poverty level continued into the twentieth century. In 1900, Clare DeGraffenried testified before the Industrial Commission that the "lowest standard is found with the man with the large family whose children are not able to work. He may live in one room or he may live in two rooms, but seldom more than two. One is called the front room, they have a bed in it, the other is the kitchen and workroom."[47] This pressure was also reflected in the large family size of Fall River's operatives as compared to that of Lynn's working class. In Lynn, the wages of the main breadwinner averaged two-fifths higher than those of a Fall River textile worker. In Fall River, where wages were so low and child labor usually contributed over 33 percent of the family's income, larger families were not a financial drain but a collective asset.[48]

THE FRENCH CANADIANS

The English, Irish, and native Americans were not the only residents of Fall River to suffer under the yoke of low wages and excessively demanding work (see Table 11). In the 1870s, economic conditions in Quebec were not favorable, and agents from the American Linen Mills of Fall River began recruiting employees among French-speaking Canadians for the unskilled positions in the mills.[49]

Frustrated by the militant unionism of the English and Irish workers, employers began recruiting more and more French Canadians on a permanent basis as the century wore on. In 1879, in one of Fall River's most bitter strikes, which lasted thirteen weeks and broke all but the Spinners Union, the mill agents brought in large numbers of French Canadians to break the strike. The "knobsticks," as the strikebreakers were called, were housed in the mills and in special adjoining houses built for them. Hostility toward the scabs ran high in Fall River, and many Canadians felt the blows of militant working-class violence.

With the defeat of the strike, many of the French Canadians settled in Fall River, despite the suspicion and hostility of the trade unionists.[50]

11

ETHNICITY OF WORKERS
IN THE FALL RIVER MILLS
(Percentage Distribution)*

Ethnic Group	1886	1896	1897	1902	1907
English	51	41	36	40	37
Irish	49	16	21	16	16
French Canadian	1	42	35	43	25
Portuguese		1	6	8	17
Polish			1	1	4
Italian			1	1	
Other					1
Major Occupations:[1]	41	77	56	66	75
Number in Sample:	152	171	206	305	139

*Percentages have been rounded off to the nearest percent.
1. Major occupations indicate the cumulative percentages of those occupations within the mill which represented over 10 percent of the sample.

SOURCE: Stratified samples of operatives from the payroll records of the Fall River Iron Works, 1886, are based on the records of the Metacomet Mill; 1887 on the Metacomet Mill's payroll records; 1895 and 1896 on the Iron Works Mill Number 4; 1897 on Mill Number 2 of the Iron Works; 1902 on Mill Number 4; and 1907 on Mill Number 5. The ethnicity of the work force was based upon surname, which although a crude measure of ethnicity, particularly in distinguishing between Irish and English operatives, does offer a good distinction between Irish-English and French Canadian, Portuguese, Polish, and Italian ethnic workers. Papers of the Fall River Iron Works, Baker Library, Harvard University.

By 1885, 8,219 Fall River residents were born of French-speaking parents from Canada.[51]

The first company to use French Canadians in large numbers, the American Linen Mills, used its tenements on Broadway, Division, and Bay streets to house the French Canadians who came down to work in the mills. This settlement soon became known as "Petit Canada," or French Village. It was to this section that French Canadians first came when they arrived from Canada. As the population grew, it spread out and settled a new colony around the King Philip Mills being built in Globe Village to the south and Flint Village to the east. The French Canadians' pattern of living in their own districts of the city persisted throughout the nineteenth and early twentieth centuries.[52]

Although the number of French Canadians working in the mills grew steadily from the late 1870s on, their impact on the work force was selective. Outside the American Linen Mills, the French Canadians did not begin showing up in the payroll records of the major Fall River mills until well into the 1880s.[53] When they did begin moving into the mills, they first concentrated in the least skilled positions, frequently migrating back to Canada during the harvest season.[54] Their early ties were much closer to agrarian Canada than to industrial Fall River, and in the early years of migration, they were often motivated to gain enough capital to return to Quebec and buy a farm.

The largest influx of French Canadians occurred between 1885 and 1905. Over 8,200 French Canadian immigrants came between 1885 and 1895, and almost 9,000 more between 1895 and 1905, bringing their population up to 28,357. After 1905, this population held steady, decreasing slightly after the strike of 1905.[55] By 1903, the French Canadians outnumbered all other foreign-born populations and almost equaled the combined Irish and English population.

The French Canadian population differed from the Irish and English immigrants as well as from the later Eastern and Southern European immigrants. Like the "new immigrants" from Eastern and Southern Europe, the French Canadians were farmers or agricultural laborers. Large families, poor soil, and limited land drove them from their traditional occupations and communities. Unlike the majority of "new immigrants," however, the French Canadians had a strong culture, they were already familiar with English and English-dominated society, and for over a hundred years, they had waged a successful struggle against that Anglo culture.[56]

When the French Canadians first began to migrate southward from Quebec to the industrial centers of New England, they did so through a process which anthropologists call a stem-family (or stem-community) system.[57] As pressure on the main family became acute as a result of financial and spatial difficulties, the main branch of the family or community in Quebec would send down branch families into the industrial cities of New England where they would work seasonally or for a short time and return to Quebec. As the pressure in Quebec increased and the jobs in New England became more attractive, the branch families would settle in the new communities on a more permanent basis. The main community in Quebec would continue to send down its surplus population, particularly its young males, to the branch community. During times of depression in the destination community, the immigrants could flow back through the stem system to the main community, either to remain or to wait out the depression in the city below the border. With time, the branch communities in Fall River became a main branch, but for years, and sometimes generations, a main-branch community relationship with Quebec continued. Through this process, thousands of French Canadians who migrated to Fall River looked to their branch contacts for support upon arrival and found a means of integrating themselves into the new industrial community. This integrating process went on within families and among friends and provided the infrastructure which held the community together. Although the recruiting agents of the mills helped facilitate the migration process, the employment of whole families encouraged not only individuals but also whole families to flow through the stem-community migration process. This system of migration through the stem family gave the ethnic community a certain amount of independence from the mills.[58]

Because of their poverty and their traditional preference for having all family members at work, the French Canadian population did not consider labor in the textile mills disruptive to the family. The textile industry traditionally employed large numbers of women and children. The mill agents in Canada recruited not single individuals but whole families, and the company houses were given out according to the ability of the whole family to work in the mill.[59] As late as 1909, almost 30 percent of a sample of French Canadian textile workers had their wives at work, compared to under 12 percent for native and English workers and just over 12 percent for the Irish. Only the Portuguese workers who began to migrate to Fall River at the turn of the century were as likely to send their wives to work, with just over 28 percent of the families having the wife at work.[60]

When the French Canadians took over Little Canada, their social life centered in this neighborhood. They maintained their distinct ethnic culture throughout the nineteenth century and the early part of the twentieth.[61] They retained their religion, their language, and, to a large extent, their social customs despite the pressure to "Americanize." They built an extensive parochial system unparalleled by any the Fall River Irish or Portuguese Catholics developed.[62]

The French Canadians held themselves apart primarily out of fear of the school system itself. Not only did they distrust the "Protestant" anglicizing aspect of the schools, which they had already experienced in Canada, but they also saw the schools as adversaries to the economic advancement of the family. The schools kept their children out of work and were seen as the enforcers of the child labor laws.[63] George Gunton, a leader of Fall River's workers and a follower of Ira Steward in the eight-hour-day movement, stated that

> parents of all Fall River operatives, but especially the French
> Canadians, avoided the law on employment of children even as
> early as the 1880's. I myself know parents who actually changed
> the age of all their children in the registry in their family Bible in
> order to evade the law and get their children in the mill two years
> earlier.[64]

The French Canadians were divided from the English and Irish workers both residentially and in terms of job skills. Unlike the English, the French Canadians who filled the unskilled positions did not enter the textile industry as experienced industrial workers. Based upon a sample taken during the early twentieth century, slightly less than 1 percent can be assumed to have been textile operatives before entering the United States. Just under 15 percent were general laborers, with most of the remaining working on the land in some capacity.[65] The English and Irish dominated the skilled positions within the mills and were also the most organized. The French Canadians filled the least skilled positions and were the least organized. The French Canadians first concentrated in the doffing room, the weaving room, in the unskilled jobs of warper, drawing-tender, stripper, and scrubber, and in the spinning room after the introduction of the ring spinner (which required little skill). These were the least paying and least skilled jobs in the mill. In 1897, the mean wage for a warper in the mills of the Fall River Iron Works was $7.09 weekly; this wage compared to $11.05 for a slasher tender. The mean wage for drawing-tender was $4.56 and strippers earned only $6.54. Unskilled ring spinners earned a mean wage of $5.05 compared to the English and Irish grinders who made almost $9.00. Doffers, another job category often filled by French Canadians, took home an average of $4.45 a week. These occupations with the greatest number of French Canadians also had the greatest variance in wages (standard deviation from the mean wage of ring spinners earning only an average of $5.05 was $1.67, for a coefficient of variation of 0.33, and for scrubbers it was as high as $2.29) and thus the least stable income.[66]

Although there was much suspicion of the French Canadians, they were not excluded from either the union or the general working-class activities. However, the beginning of stress on the working-class community clearly could be seen in the response of the English and Irish workers to the French Canadians and in the residential segregation by ethnic group, which began with the settlement of Little Canada.

OTHER ETHNIC GROUPS

At the turn of the century, Fall River's population again underwent a dramatic change. In 1899, a member of the Borden family and a leading manufacturer claimed that "the nationality of the operatives has undergone radical changes."[67] (He was referring especially to the Portuguese.) The Massachusetts Bureau of Statistics of Labor reported in 1905 that "the nationality of the operatives is changing [see Tables 11 and 12]. . . . Some time since the textile foreign population in Massachusetts was largely English, but we find them supplanted by the French Canadians who in turn gave way largely to the Portuguese."[68] By 1905, 7,020 Fall River residents were born in Portugal.[69]

The Portuguese, like the French Canadians before them, began to settle in particular sections of the city, so that by 1900 the fifteen blocks bounded by Broadway, Hunter, Columbia, and Division streets were already beginning to be associated with the Portuguese.[70] The Massachusetts Bureau of Statistics of Labor emphasized this segregation of the Portuguese: "one of the most recent large additions to the foreign-born population congregated together [so] that certain quarters of the city have become identified with them."[71] In 1885, there were only 300 Portuguese in Fall River; by 1895, there were over 1,700 and by 1909, 10,000.[72] Despite their numbers, the Portuguese had difficulty obtaining employment in the mills. As late as 1902, they represented only 8 percent of the textile work force in the Iron Works. Most of the workers were concentrated in the doffing room, the spinning room (after the introduction of the ring spinners), and in the unskilled positions of spooler, drawing-tender, and stripper. In these unskilled jobs, the Portuguese found the mean weekly wages to be only $5.17 (doffer), $6.66

(spooler), $6.07 (drawing-tender), and $6.69 (stripper) in 1902. In
contrast, the weavers were earning an average weekly wage of $10.43,
grinders $8.40, intermediates $9.39, and slashers $13.14 (occupations
with few, if any, Portuguese at this time).[73]

A few Polish families came to Fall River from Chicopee in the late
1880s, but it was not until the early 1900s that the Poles began to come
directly from Europe to work in the city's mills. In 1895, there were
109 Poles in Fall River, a smaller number even than the city's 762 Russians.
By 1905, there were over 400 Poles, still less than the 1,366 Russians or
806 Austrians.[74] Between 1905 and 1913, Poles and Russians began
settling in the strip of land by the river, around the older mills, and by
1910, the high density contributed to making that area one of the worst
in the city.[75] A small number of Syrians and Lebanese added to the
foreign-born population and settled in Flint Village during the early
twentieth century.[76] In 1895, 49.91 percent of the population was
foreign-born, and by 1900, the U.S. Census showed Fall River to have
the highest percentage of foreign-born of any large U.S. city.

As each ethnic group settled in its own distinct area, the villages
took on ethnic characteristics. Hence, by 1919, the National Conference
Board reported that "the people . . . settled in neighborhood groups
of a single nationality rather than around the particular mills in which
they were employed. There were, in fact, ten different villages into which
Fall River outside of the center may be said to be divided."[77] The residential structure of the city, the encouragement and manipulation of the
different ethnic groups, and the structure of the work itself facilitated
this division of the city into separate ethnic enclaves which began with
the French Canadians.

Because the mills were scattered about the city, it did not form the
normal urban divisions of business, manufacturing, and residential areas.
Except for the center of Fall River where the commercial enterprises
were located and the Highlands or "Hill" where mill owners lived, there
were no specific residential or manufacturing districts. Scattered about
in all parts of the city were the huge mills that gave employment to
the city's workers, and clustered about these mills were the houses
and tenements of the operatives. The density of Fall River's wards reflect
this scattering of working-class communities. By the mid-1880s, all but
three of Fall River's nine wards showed an average of more than ten
persons per dwelling, and two of the remaining three averaged more

than nine. Only one of the nine wards averaged less than six and a half persons per dwelling. In contrast, Lynn showed much higher variations between the central working-class wards and the outer wards. Even Lynn's condensed working-class wards did not average over eight persons per room, and except for the central three wards, that city's remaining wards averaged less than six persons per dwelling.[78]

These residential districts, often located far from the downtown area, developed their own neighborhood institutions and services. Each area took on the characteristics of a self-contained village—hence names such as Border City, Flint Village, Globe Village, Mechanicsville, and Bowenville. The residents of these districts had their own saloons, taverns, restaurants, and clubs (see Photograph 10). Although many, especially single women, spent Saturday afternoons window shopping in the downtown, socializing was generally conducted within the different villages for convenience, if for no other reason. It was a long walk to the center of Fall River. Thus, when the American Linen Mills began using French Canadians, the very structure of the city facilitated ethnic segregation.[79]

Work within the mills, especially as the nineteenth century progressed, also discouraged socializing and the development of friendships off the job. The noise of the machines, along with the extreme pressure of piece work on eight or more looms and low wages, discouraged social intercourse (see Photograph 11). Workmen had little enough time to finish basic chores, such as cleaning and preparing their machines, let alone socialize. Weavers and spinners were expected to clean their machines during their breaks, and they continually complained that they had no time to finish their meals or talk to their friends.[80]

The effect of piece work and the operation of several looms at low wages created a type of ongoing time-motion pressure; rather than competition with a hypothetical model, the workers were in competition with time itself. Although working on piece work, the workers could not set their own pace; the pace was set by the company. The operators had but one choice, "on or off," and at low wages, "off" meant starvation. The impact of piece-time, stretchout pressure, and the constant shutting off and on of the looms or other textile machinery was reflected not only in the worker, but also on his take-home wages. The textile workers could not expect a standard take-home pay. In 1896, for example, a sample of weavers with a mean wage of only $7.60 a week had a standard deviation of $1.72 from that mean.[81] The pressure of uncon-

10. Working-Class Club in Border City, Fall River

These clubs were important social centers for working-class residents of Fall River. In Border City and other isolated areas, the local club and taverns provided the main source of activity for the residents. The club above was originally a Portuguese club which between 1910 and 1930 had become a general working-class club.

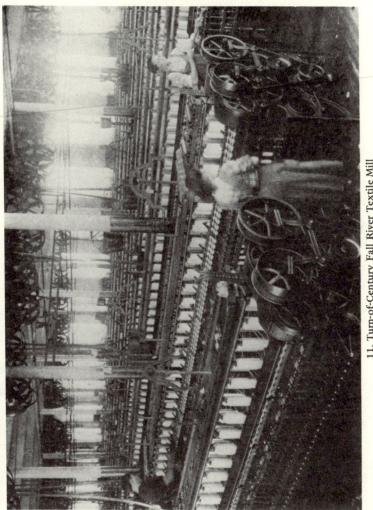

11. Turn-of-Century Fall River Textile Mill

By the end of the nineteenth century, workers in Fall River mills were isolated in large rooms. The noise and the isolation prevented much on-the-job socializing.

12

NATIVITY OF
FALL RIVER OPERATIVES, 1879

Area of Birth	Number of Operatives
Massachusetts	2,072
Other, United States	1,065
England	4,237
Ireland	2,591
Scotland	273
Canada	2,159
Portugal	39
Wales	16

trolled speedups, stretchouts (by which workers were expected to handle more machines or do more work per hour), and low wages left the workers with little time and energy for socializing on the job. Informal patterns of interaction which integrated the world of work with the world of leisure so important for the Lynn shoe workers were thus not possible for the textile workers.

The textile workers were further isolated and segregated when the manufacturers placed them in different departments. French Canadians were usually put on ring frames;[82] the English and Irish on the mules; and the later arrivals, the Portuguese and Poles, in the blowing, carding, and doffing rooms. Although no single ethnic group dominated the weaving room, it was the weaving room which was the loudest, required the most concentration, and suffered the most from speedups and stretchouts.[83]

All of these factors isolated the newcomer. He was isolated on the job because of the excessive noise, speed, and pressure, and when he left the job, there was no central meeting place such as Central Square offered to the Lynn shoe workers. These workers walked back into their own neighborhoods and socialized with area residents at the local pubs and taverns.[84] Residential isolation off the job within ethnic ghettos also encouraged ethnic segregation. It discouraged workers from sharing their experiences with workers of other ethnic groups and from understanding their role in the industrial system.

THE CITY AND A NEW CENTURY

At the turn of the century, Fall River had forty cotton-manufacturing corporations with a total capital of $25 million, 3.3 million spindles, 83,000 looms, and 32,000 operatives to tend the machines. The Fall River Iron Works, the most important city corporation since its founding in 1821, alone employed over 4,500 workers. The migration of foreign-born workers into the city continued in great numbers. By 1905, over 36 percent of the foreign-born were Canadians, with over 90 percent of them French-speaking; 26 percent English; 13 percent Irish; over 15 percent Portuguese; and almost 3 percent Russian.[85]

Fall River led the nation in cotton production, but the wages of its workers fell far below "a fair standard of living as measured by the customs of the country."[86] A study by the U.S. Bureau of Labor in 1909 reported that over 70 percent of cotton operatives' families in Fall River suffered from this low standard. It required the labor of the husband, children, and sometimes the wife (especially if there were no younger children at home) to secure even this inadequate income.[87]

The low wages of the central wage-earner forced other members of the family to work, a situation that was encouraged by the manufacturers, not only by their low wages but by their very hiring policies as well. Many workers claimed that an employer would only hire a man if other members of his family also worked.[88] The report of the Commission on Minimum Wage in Massachusetts found that "women in general are working because of dire necessity and in most cases the combined income of the family is not more than adequate to meet the family's cost of living."[89] Unmarried women over sixteen years of age who lived at home contributed over 43 percent of the family income.[90] In interviewing over 486 women, a 1909 commission on women and children wage-earners found that over 95 percent turned their earnings in to the family budget (see Tables 13 and 14). In fact, women were carrying a "crushing family burden."[91] In 1905, over 38 percent of women in Fall River over nine years of age were gainfully employed, and almost 30 percent, or nearly thirteen thousand, were employed in cotton mills.[92]

Children as well as mothers were required to work in order to maintain the family (see Photograph 12). As late as 1909, various studies revealed that from 20 percent to over 40 percent of the family income came

13

PERCENTAGE OF FAMILY INCOME FROM VARIOUS FAMILY SOURCES, FALL RIVER

Ethnic Group	Husband	Wife	Child	Lodger	Other
French Canadian	52.0	7.4	33.3	6.0	1.2
English	56.1	3.9	35.6	1.5	2.8
Irish	43.2	3.7	45.3	4.2	3.6
Portuguese	50.9	9.0	21.6	15.6	2.9
Polish	75.3	8.3	6.5	6.0	3.9

SOURCE: Immigration Commission, *Immigrants in Industry*, p. 114.

14

PERCENTAGE OF ETHNIC GROUP WITH WORKING WIVES, FALL RIVER

Ethnic Group	Average Family Income	Percent Working Wives
Native-born	$825	11.9
French Canadian	$846	22.9
English	$901	11.9
Irish	$915	12.4
Portuguese	$673	28.1

SOURCE: U. S. Bureau of Labor Statistics, Senate Doc. 645, 1907, 1908, Part III, p. 976.

from the children.[93] To be sure, Massachusetts prohibited child labor under fourteen and required a certificate between the ages of fourteen and sixteen certifying that the child had completed a minimal amount of schooling, but low wages placed great pressures on the parents to lie about their children's ages and to pull them out of school and into the mills at the earliest time possible. In 1917, a child labor investigation estimated that over 40 percent of Fall River's children left school in the fourth or fifth grade.[94]

Parents considered schooling to be a luxury they could not afford. As one parent said, "it's only gentlemen's sons that have time for learning

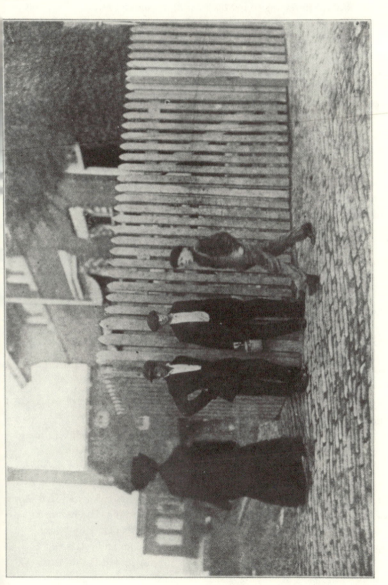

12. Entering Fall River Mill

A woman and young child are entering the mill.

from books." Referring to her own child, the mother noted, "he's only a poor boy and ought to earn his own living."[95]

The children of many textile workers went into the mills two to four years before the legal age. A retired textile worker, whose own wife entered the mills four years before she was legally able, stated that many Portuguese families showed phony documents in Portuguese claiming the child's age to be over fourteen. Overburdened officials, not reading Portuguese, were more than willing to cooperate, especially since Fall River elites opposed child labor laws anyway.[96] In the city of Fall River which produced almost two thousand miles of cotton a day in 1895, over 10 percent of its cotton operatives were illiterate, and twenty-two years later it still claimed the highest percentage of illiteracy in the country.[97] Textiles took both an educational and a physical toll on the children. The cotton mill child had just half the chance of reaching the age of twenty as the child outside the mills.[98]

The children who worked in the mills were not the only members of the family who faced increased risk of death and disease. The conditions of work and life in the mill towns were harshest for the smallest and newest members of the community. Textile centers were conspicuous for high mortality at all ages, especially for those under one year of age.[99] Fall River had a high rate even for textile communities. It had the highest infant mortality rate of any North American city, averaging over twenty deaths per thousand between 1900 and 1909. Over 38 percent of all deaths were children under one.[100]

In the early years of the twentieth century, Fall River's infant mortality climbed. In 1910, it was 186 per thousand births, and in 1913, 202.3 per thousand. Most of these infant deaths were caused by diarrhea, enteritis, and gastritis, all of which were related to the unsanitary conditions in which the workers were forced to live.[101]

Employment of mothers and children was not the only way the working-class families maintained themselves. Many families hired out rooms to boarders or relatives in order to sustain the family on substandard wages. In the hard times between 1903 and 1904, the working class reduced by over six hundred the number of occupied tenements partly by "doubling up." Whole families moved into tenements of friends and relatives.[102]

As late as 1912, a survey of Fall River housing recorded the large number of lodgers occupying space in the homes of working-class families. In most cases, beds were set up in the kitchen for boarders. The kitchen for these families would function as a dining room, cooking room, sitting room, and, in the evening, as a bedroom. The process of taking in boarders, although relieving financial pressure, overcrowded the family itself. An average family, the survey found, lived in a two or three room flat. Even though the survey has been described as biased because it represented the more congested areas as average, the conditions it reported still indicate tremendous overcrowding for at least a significant element within the community.[103] In the poorer working-class areas, almost 25 percent of the families took in nonrelated boarders, with the most recent arrivals being the most crowded.[104]

The high density and overcrowding within each household also took its toll on the conditions of the unit itself. Most of the tenement buildings were made of wood, many of them left over from the quickly built factory tenements which were built following the Civil War. Many were rear tenements (almost 10 percent in some working-class areas) or court tenements, two-and-a-half to three stories high. In some cases, the basements were used for saloons where the sale of cheap alcohol muted the misery of the life above. In the cellars which were not used for living and even in some inhabited ones, garbage filled the empty spaces and gave off odors which permeated the building.[105]

In areas of high density and inadequate city services, the practice of dumping garbage in backyards and cellars could not be avoided. The garbage which the Bowler Street dump did remove from the neighborhood came back to the residents in the streams of water which drained through the dump and came to rest in the muddy swamps in the yards of the tenements built on low ground.[106]

Not all of Fall River's housing was as bad as that surveyed in 1912. A 1910 study of Fall River conducted by the Massachusetts Bureau of Statistics of Labor found that, although there were areas of excessive squalor and congestion, especially in the Russian and Polish districts near the river, the newer tenement houses built as separate detached blocks "secure[d] in most instances, of a sufficiency of light, and air, though among some of the immigrant classes it is probable that even in dwellings which are themselves satisfactory from a hygienic point of view, a certain amount of overcrowding exists."[107]

In the 1910 survey, as in the earlier and later studies of Fall River's working-class families, the kitchen was found to be the center of the living unit. In the center of the kitchen would be the family stove, the most important and most valuable piece of furniture in the tenement. The stove served not only for cooking but also for heating and, just as important, it was a source of great family pride.[108]

Over half the living units studied in 1912 lacked a decent water supply. The tenants of these units had to go into the cellar for water, and in many cases these sinks were inoperative or polluted. In winter, many tenants found their water supply turned off by owners fearing pipe breakage.[109] The toilets, often located in the basements or halls, suffered from broken or missing seats, leaking pipes, and overflowing or clogged bowls.[110] These conditions were most severe in the company housing and in the older, more congested areas, the very areas in which the newer immigrants found housing.

CRACK IN THE PROSPERITY, 1900-1925

Fall River continued to dominate textiles throughout the first decade of the twentieth century.[111] Between 1904 and 1910 the city added another 400,000 spindles, so that by 1910 it housed one-seventh of all the nation's spindles. Despite these signs of prosperity and growth, in 1910 the city also showed signs of the weakness which would quickly drop it from that leading position (see Table 15).

15
PROFITS OF
FALL RIVER CORPORATIONS, 1886-1920

Year	Percent of Average Yearly Profits	Year	Percent of Average Yearly Profits
1886	6.50	1900	8.85
1888	9.63	1903	6.47
1889	9.97	1904	5.44
1890	7.62	1905	3.19
1891	4.93	1906	6.83
1894	5.25	1907	11.00
1895	8.12	1910	6.85
1897	3.39	1915	3.73
1898	2.41	1918	18.27
1899	5.99	1920	29.46

SOURCE: E. Gordon Keith, "A Financial History of Two Textile Cities," Ph.D. dissertation, Harvard University, 1936.

In 1895, the Northrop loom was introduced to textiles. It greatly increased production per loom and it was more self-regulating than the traditional looms. It replaced the bobbin in the shuttle while the loom remained in motion, thus eliminating some costly steps. The Northrop also stopped automatically when the warp thread was broken. All of these advantages allowed the weaver to handle more looms and to do so more efficiently. Fall River failed to take full advantage of this technological advancement. Local textile owners had invested heavily in local loom manufacturing enterprises which still produced the traditional looms. The interlocking directorships which had fared reasonably well for most of the nineteenth century now helped to topple Fall River from its leadership position in textiles.[112] The treasurers of the mills continued to buy the less automatic looms rather than switch to the Northrops or the later developed and even more efficient Draper looms.

Tradition was another reason which prevented Fall River from adopting new technology in the industry. The head official in its mills was the company treasurer. Traditionally, the treasurer had maintained his position by his ability to keep wages down and buy cotton at its cheapest price. Thus, in the difficult years of the turn of the century, this official concentrated on speculating on cotton rather than investing in technological improvements. Many mill superintendents favored the Northrop looms but could not change over because of opposition from the company treasurer.[113] Although the Bourne Mills installed over two thousand Northrop looms by 1900, by 1917 only 4 percent of Fall River's total looms were automatic.[114]

In order to meet competition from the South and rural New England, Fall River began to further exploit the work force. The treasurers ordered the weavers to work more of the older looms, in many cases without making any technological improvements. Between 1900 and 1905, the already overburdened weavers were asked to work ten to twelve looms rather than six to eight. On many looms, larger and more cumbersome bobbins were introduced to increase production. Unfortunately, with the larger bobbins there was greater risk of breakage. They also put additional pressure on the weaver by posing the possibility of lost wages and by creating a greater chance of faulting the material by missing a breakage.

Although many of the older looms were rebuilt with stop motions to stop the machine if a thread broke, these additions did little to relieve the tension on the weavers.[115] Nor did these rebuilt looms represent a serious technological challenge to the more sophisticated Northrop and Draper looms which were being used so widely in the newer developing areas of the South.

Despite Fall River's failure to capitalize on the technological improvements in the industry, competition from the South did not seriously hurt its profits during most of the first two decades of the twentieth century. The city had traditionally concentrated on finer and printed cloth. (That was what originally brought the English to Fall River rather than to the other New England textile centers.) The early textile industry in the South concentrated mostly on coarse cloth and did not compete directly with Fall River.

Failing to realize this advantage, the city responded to the long and crippling strike of 1904 by switching over to ring spinners and coarser cloth production.[116] Between 1910 and 1914, its industry stagnated, and production and wages fell. The effects of southern competition, coupled with the failure to invest in technological improvements, finally began to be seen in "Spindle City."

In 1915, war demands began to pour into the city. The war market demand was for coarse cotton cloth, and Fall River, along with other New England textile centers, provided it. The war created new peaks in production, employment, and wages.

Profits were well above 20 percent a year, and the mill owners living on the Hill enjoyed a return on their investment unknown in most industries. The first few years after the war continued to be good years. In 1920, profits averaged 33 percent on a capital investment of $33 million.[117] Production and employment even surpassed the wartime peaks. But the weakness of Fall River's position (and for that matter, that of all the older centers), together with the steady decline of prices in the 1920s, finally caused its decline as a leading textile center in America. From June to September 1920, prices for print cloth dropped from seventeen and a half cents to seven cents. The years 1921 to 1922 saw a slight improvement in prices, but prices began to decline again in late 1922. The following year, sales dropped off for all cotton cloth. The owners continued to try to soak the mills for profits, but cheaper cloth from the South soon brought total collapse. On top of technological improvements, wages were from one-third to one-half lower in the South than in Massachusetts, and Fall River's wages were among the highest in Massachusetts.[118]

In 1924, Fall River had 4,072,123 spindles in operation; four years later that number had dropped to 2,920,632 (see Table 16). Mills unable to

16

NUMBER OF SPINDLES IN FALL RIVER, 1865-1928

Year	Spindles		Year	Spindles
1865	265,328		1900	3,042,472
1870	544,600		1905	3,246,468
1875	1,269,048		1910	3,931,464
1880	1,390,830		1914	4,001,429
1885	1,742,882		1924	4,072,123
1890	2,164,664		1928	2,920,632
1895	2,833,691			

Spindles in U. S., 1929	15,463,054
Spindles in Massachusetts	9,349,994
Spindles in Fall River, 1928	2,920,632

SOURCE: *Fall River and Its Manufacturers, 1803-1914* (Fall River, 1915), p. 34; J. Herbert Burgy, *The New England Cotton Textile Industry* (Baltimore, 1932), p. 30.

meet the southern competition began liquidating. By 1918, Fall River had fallen behind New Bedford as New England's leading textile center, and New England itself was lagging behind the South as the chief supplier of the nation's cloth. The process of decline in profits, production, and wages which began in the 1920s continued and was never reversed. Between 1923 and 1950, thirty of the city's mills liquidated.[119] In 1920, Fall River boasted 111 cotton mills; in 1961, there were only 4, and in 1965, there were none. The population fell from its peak of 130,000 in 1922 to 112,000 in 1950. Between 1923 and 1930, thirteen of forty-six corporations closed. Between 1926 and 1930, the city lost over 1.5 million spindles, 33,405 looms, and 11,210 jobs. In 1930, only forty mills were in full production, thirty-eight employing 12,700 workers were stopped, and another 3,210 workers were on part time; almost half of the work force was unemployed.[120]

Unemployment crippled the city during its decline and Depression years. When one mill reopened to make yarns for tires, the crowd outside the gates seeking employment rioted to get the few jobs offered.[121] Unemployment soared to over thirty thousand. In 1920, the city spent $750,000 on unemployment relief.[122] A writer for *The New Republic* described the pitiful condition of the workers: "On street corners stand knots of unemployed, silhouetted against the silent mills towering behind closed gates. . . . Unemployed girls stand on the streets—the girls who will sell their souls and bodies for a square meal."[123]

By the late 1920s, taxpayers were unable to pay taxes, and collection fell off over 60 percent. In 1931, the city went bankrupt, and the state took over municipal finances for the next ten years.[124] The city responded by trying to attract new industry. Unfortunately, the Depression years and Fall River's peripheral location prevented the city from gaining any new heavy industry. The city instead became the center for "runaway" garment shops, "gypsy shops," and other low-investment industries.

"THE POWER MACHINE" REPLACES THE LOOM

The garment industry was also hit by the Depression. Since labor was the largest item of cost in this industry, the owners saw reduction of wages as the easiest means of cutting costs, especially during hard times. The high degree of unionization and politicization among garment workers in New York, the major garment center, made wage reduction difficult there. The industry therefore looked outside the city for cheap, mostly female, labor and for space to set up the "power machines" to turn out clothes, without unionism. Fall River had both. In the 1930s, Fall River's city fathers were desperate for any type of industry to relieve unemployment and eventually supply badly needed city revenue.[125] They were willing to offer empty mills rent-free to garment manufacturers and tax breaks as well. The city had a surplus of space and female labor. Used to the textile industry which required large numbers of female laborers, Fall River families were more than willing to send their daughters and wives into the garment shops moving up to the city from New York. The depressed condition of the city with its large number of unemployed guaranteed the garment manufacturer the low wages he wanted.[126]

Once in Fall River, the garment industry leaders employed every means available to keep wages down. The "gypsy factory" was the most notorious approach to cutting costs. The "gypsy" sweatshop owner would load cut shirts, underwear, coats, or dresses, ready for sewing into a few trucks, drive up to Fall River, move into an abandoned mill, set up his sewing machines, and hire unemployed women as "learners," at no or pitifully low wages. After the orders had been completed, he would pack up his trucks and drive away, leaving behind the women whose labor he used for nothing or next to nothing.[127] In this fashion, New York garment manufacturers could avoid both the unions and the newly enacted minimum wage law. In many cases, they also were given free use of the floor space in the old mills as encouragement to move to Fall River.[128]

The garment factories which made Fall River their permanent home avoided paying full wages by firing their workers once they had "learned" the trade and could no longer be paid learners' wages. Some shops required their new workers to attend their garment industry school, where prospective employees paid three dollars for the privilege of learning the trade. The schools supplied a constant flow of new workers and kept the old ones in line.[129]

Typical of this new industry in Fall River was the Har Lee Manufacturing Company, incorporated as the Wentworth Manufacturing Company. Har Lee moved to Fall River in 1938 from Chicago, where it had experienced continual labor trouble. Har Lee became one of Fall River's largest garment shops and employed between 1,500 and 1,700 workers, mostly young Portuguese and French Canadian women. This prosperous industry was a great catch for the city fathers, but it paid wages well below the minimum for women workers. The practice of hiring "learners" and firing experienced workers was so extensive at Har Lee that over two hundred a year were fired and hired. The company ran a school which gave it a continual supply of new learners. Guards were hired to watch over the employees to prevent in-shop associating. Floor-ladies were assigned the punchcard area to prevent the women from learning each others' names and becoming friendly. To add to the company treasury, money was deducted from the employees' paychecks for the company "social club." When Har Lee workers reached the top of their pay level, they were fired.[130]

By 1946, Fall River's garment industry employed over ten thousand workers, and by 1953, it accounted for 37 percent of the total manufacturing employment in the city.

The workers blamed the textile owners for their predicament. A common myth among them was that Henry Ford wanted to build his factory in Fall River, but the mill owners, afraid of the competition of higher wages, kept him out.[131] At a public hearing held in 1930 to investigate unemployment, Martin Welsh, "a private citizen," held the capitalist accountable for the workers' situation because he had lost touch with his workers and had thus become indifferent to their plight. Romanticizing the old-time corporate leader, Welsh claimed that the older boss knew "that the workingman was his fellow man." In 1930, the employer did "not come in personal contact with the other human beings, and [did] not regard them as such, therefore he consider[ed] them as kind of chattel, nothing more or less than machinery."[132] Other workers blamed the union for the loss of the textile mills. "The union became too powerful. The workers got away with murder. . . . Unions have forced the mills out with their demands."[133] Although nineteenth-century textile workers would have argued with Welsh's description of the old-time boss, his description of the 1930s employer reflected later workers' opinions of the cause of Fall River's depression.

The textile workers in Fall River responded to the loss of jobs much as the shoe workers had in Lynn. Older workers remained in the industry, while their children and the younger workers left. Layoffs or promotions after the establishment of the Textile Workers of America Union were made according to seniority. Thus, the older workers were retained, while the younger ones moved out as jobs became tighter and wages remained low. The older textile worker also had a strong attachment to his trade, which in many cases had been the trade of his father or grandfather.[134]

The remaining skilled and semiskilled textile workers especially resented having to take unskilled, degrading jobs outside of textiles.[135] Although women did not have as much opportunity to find new jobs in textiles, they had greater employment choice once they left the industry. However, they, too, resented their new jobs and the lowering of their wages and skill status.[136]

Fall River's unemployed were trapped in the city by the very mechanisms that had evolved to protect them. In some cases, they had been textile workers in the city for generations and did not see geographic mobility as a logical option. The community they lived in offered them what little security they had. Friends and relatives were their main sources of jobs, as well as financial assistance during hard times.[137] Few of these workers had knowledge of labor, wage, or working conditions outside the city or trade. The local newspapers' policy of not printing job information outside the city, even in the severely depressed period of the 1920s, contributed to their lack of knowledge of outside conditions.[138] This policy, as well as the workers' ties to local institutions and community, mitigated against the push out of the city.[139]

In the middle of the twentieth century, "Spindle City" found few of its spindles active and many of its repositories housing "power machines" which made clothes from cloth produced several hundred miles to the south. The city of the dinner pail no longer woke at 6:00 A.M. or rang with the sounds of the army of industrial workers. Fall River had receded into obscurity. Its workers, who had once created a proud community of operatives and the strongest union movement in textiles, now fought desperately for the few remaining jobs and blamed their unions for the situation.

8

Fall River: Workers, Ethnicity, and Community

Textile workers, from the early days of the Lowell girls through to the tenders of the multiple looms, have shared certain common conditions (and these promoted the classical critique of early industrialism); namely, a machine-tending technology, low skill level, predominance of unskilled, especially women and children workers, and lack of job interactions.[1] The accompanying job insecurity and lack of control over the work increased alienation for the operatives. The textile workers in turn looked to friends, community, and social institutions for stability and direction. Despite Fall River's dominance in the production of cotton cloth in the late nineteenth and early twentieth centuries, it was no exception to this pattern. The work was degrading and insecure and, where they could, the workers used their community, fraternal organizations, and institutions to mitigate that insecurity. These institutions, especially for the most recent immigrants—first those from England and Ireland and later the French Canadians, followed by the Portuguese—were brought from the Old World and adapted to the New, or were based upon common ethnic identification. They helped integrate the textile workers into the urban industrial world or served as a buffer against those forces which newcomers felt bearing down upon them. When the working-class community and class institutions were receptive, the textile workers' common condition of exploitation led them to transcend ethnic divisions in a common labor struggle against capital. When the class and community institutions failed to function as integrating institutions, ethnic divisions and hostility emerged.

Nineteenth-century textile workers in Fall River rose daily in the early dawn to face exhausting, intensive labor, long hours, and low pay. This condition of low pay and long hours of exhausting labor was shared by their children and grandchildren in the twentieth century. The system itself was insidious: low wages forced the children of mill families into the textile factories, and, once inside, low wages kept them there. In order to survive, the workers were dependent upon the labor of the family. After entering the mill, each worker eventually mastered a skill, which although paying little, tied the worker and ultimately his children to the mills. They were also tied by their very familiarity with the mill. The family history of one mill child, forced to leave the mills because of the strike of 1904, illustrates the cycle which trapped the mill worker. The girl's mother had worked in the mills in England since she was nine, and, after migrating to Fall River, she sent her twelve-year-old daughter into the mills as a spooler. "I must have been about fourteen when I got to take over some looms. I liked the mill better than workin' at home." Working in the mills permanently deafened the girl and destroyed her health. She described to a social worker how "you got so tired 'drivin' at eight looms, and when they gave us twelve looms I didn't see that we could make out to live at all. . . . It makes you crazy watchin' 'em." Despite the horror of her experience, this child of Fall River lamented, "I kind of hate to leave the mills. I worked there all my life."[2]

In 1883, when testifying before a U.S. Senate investigating committee, Thomas O'Donnell, who went to work in the mills at eight years of age and had worked eleven years as a Fall River spinner, was asked, "Do you see any way out of your troubles [low wages and brutal work]—or do you expect to have to stay right there [as a Fall River textile worker]?"

He answered, "No, Sir; I have no means nor anything; so I am obliged to remain there [Fall River] and try and pick up something as I can."

The senator asked again in desperation, "You do not know anything but mule spinning, I suppose?"

The man answered, "That is what I have been doing; I am looking for work in the mill."

Thomas O'Donnell was caught in the vicious cycle of the textile operatives. He was "looking for work in the mill," despite the fact that he could barely feed his family on that work's wages and only then because he went down to the beach and scavenged for clams. He continued to work at his trade, knowing, as he stated, that "they [the owners] are doing everything of that kind that they possibly can to crush down the poor people—the poor operatives there [Fall River]."[3]

The workers responded to this condition from the battery of experiences they brought to the mill. The English and Irish workers set up benefit organizations, friendly societies, cooperatives, unions, and other less formal institutions to help them cope with the strains of industrial life. Many of these institutions were brought over from England. As new members of the work force entered the city, they brought with them traditions that interacted with both the industrial structure and the existing community and community institutions. In some cases, the new immigrants built parallel institutions and community structures; in others, they integrated into the existing patterns. But all the workers, new and old, had the conditions of labor in common.

The constant pressure of work affected the structure and visibility of the workers' community institutions. According to a nineteenth-century observer, the workers were "dejected, tired, worn-out, discouraged," and generally unhealthy, "growing out of the bad influences of long hours of labor, the close confinement of mills, the din of machinery [and] their exclusion from social intercourse." They were not continually looking to the institutions for social interaction, but rather, as the pressure of work increased, they were increasingly withdrawing from interaction.[4]

A textile worker could not control his machine; it either ran or did not run. His job, to quote a long-time spinner, was "a constant race from morning to night *after* this machinery."[5] Unlike the Lynn shoe worker, the textile worker did not have two to four months of seasonal unemployment to revitalize and reinforce the formal and informal institutions of the community. He did not have the continual interaction between other workers during lunch breaks, before or after work, or during the seasonal slack periods. His job isolated him to one department. Lunch breaks were taken in the mill, with the time used to clean and prepare the machines so that work could commence the instant the break ended.[6] The noise of the machines and the pressures of constant attention which they required prevented on-the-job conversation.

The nineteenth-century textile workers faced continual speedups and stretchouts, so that by 1904 a weaver would be working as many as twelve to fourteen looms at a piece rate lower than in 1885. The other crafts inside the trade were also "stretched out." The pressure so exhausted the Fall River workers that even as early as 1875, when the weavers were only working six to eight looms, they were too tired for any socializing after work. That pressure did not reach extreme proportions, however, until the end of the century. Although there was a social life for the city's textile workers, by the end of the century the sapping of the workers' energy level and the increased industrial discipline had reduced that activity.[7] The "drive" which weavers complained about affected other textile workers as well. In 1882, a spinner testified before the Massachusetts Bureau of Statistics of Labor that he

> had been frequently unable to secure his breakfast before
> time for dinner, which was owing to the drive as much as
> the poor quality of cotton he was requested to spin. He
> was tied to his work owing to the fact that the production
> of the looms had been so increased that the production of the
> spinning room was not sufficient to keep the looms running and
> if the spinners stopped their mules to eat their breakfasts, the
> looms would have to stop also.[8]

CLASS STRUCTURE OF THE CITY

The ecology of Fall River was that of a mill town. The top level of the class structure lived on the Hill, as they had for generations. The middle classes lived scattered about the city and neighboring small towns. The rest of the city, which lay below the Hill, was the city of workers, mostly textile workers. Before the end of the Civil War, they had come to dominate the city; by the end of the 1870s, they stamped it with their institutions and culture. Fall River was the city of the dinner pail. In the late nineteenth century, it was said that

> a great line divides the population of Fall River into two classes.
> This is a vastly more apparent division than is usually to be found
> because there is here but one industry—that of clothmaking. Every
> man, woman, and child in the city either is or is not an operative.
> If he or she is an operative, he or she not only works, but goes
> to church, buys, finds companions, dresses and lives as an operative. The designation is fastened upon each one and is laid
> off neither day or night. . . . The attitude of [Fall River's two
> classes, operatives against the owners] is one of mutual suspicion,

hatred, and war. The unquestioned assumption is that their interests are necessarily opposed; their dealings with each other proceed upon that assumption. Each is eager for chances to take advantage of the other.[9]

The workers were conscious of their role as workers. In 1879, they were said to feel a "distrust, suspicion, and hostility regarding all who [did] not belong to their class."[10]

FALL RIVER BECOMES THE OLDHAM OF AMERICA

As mentioned earlier, the working-class community of Fall River, separate and hostile to the ownership class and its supporters, was dominated by the English and Irish immigrants from Lancashire County, England. The community they built and the institutions they supported had a distinctive Lancashire flavor. In order to understand this community in the late nineteenth century, it is important to know the history of the Lancashire textile workers before they emigrated.

Textile workers in Lancashire in order to protect themselves from wage fluctuations and layoffs (both of which were endemic to the textile industry), repression against unions, and sickness or death developed a whole system of institutions—from the most informal pub activity to the more formal workingmen's clubs, lodges, benefit societies, and unions. In the early nineteenth century, in hopes of avoiding the combination laws (Rose Act of 1795), Lancashire textile workers met and planned collective action under the guise of friendly societies and community clubs, meeting in local pubs. The informal "mill clubs," organized for higher pay, used local taverns for group consciousness-raising sessions and strategy meetings.[11] The Parliamentary Committee of 1825, appointed to investigate friendly societies, reported:

These clubs were in very many instances composed of persons working at the same trade; the habit and opportunities of association which the Friendly Societies gave them doubtless afforded facilities of combination for raising wages and other purposes, all of which were unlawful. . . . In the manufacturing districts, dangerous meetings have been held under the disguise of Benefit Clubs for the relief of sick workers.[12]

Throughout the first half of the nineteenth century, "every decent public house" of Lancashire's working-class areas had organizations which discussed "the state of the trade and any differences that had taken place between manufacturers and operatives."[13] Even after the English worker won the rights of law for his trade unions, he still maintained much of the informal club activity from which the unions had sprung.

The loss of several strikes in the late 1820s and 1830s, and periodic depressions during this period, caused the collapse of many of Lancashire's unions. During these lean years, the operatives fell back upon the old clubs and societies which kept the union spirit alive. In the 1860s and 1870s, when many Lancashire workers were migrating to Fall River, the Lancashire unions were again emerging from the informal organizations into formal activity and structure.[14]

The combination of clubs, societies, and unions provided the English worker with a network of institutions which protected him from the insecurity of his industrial position. The Industrial Renumeration Conference Report of 1885 stated: "The workmen of Lancashire were tied into a whole system of unions, cooperatives, building and benefit societies."[15]

When the Lancashire workmen came to Fall River, they began establishing branches of their home institutions there. The first unions in Fall River were direct outgrowths of Manchester unions.

The Odd Fellows lodges were important Lancashire institutions in the working-class communities, providing sickness benefits and comradeship for textile workers. Once the workers crossed the Atlantic, they quickly established a local Manchester United Lodge, as a branch of the Lancashire, Manchester United Odd Fellows, and soon followed this with other lodges. In the Fall River Manchester Unity Lodge, all but one of the officers were textile workers or temporarily unemployed textile workers, with most being weavers. The Lancashire workers also brought with them the Ancient Order of Foresters, which like the Odd Fellows was dominated by textile workers. Many of them were Irish, which reflected the interaction between the English and Irish within the institutional support systems that both groups looked to while still textile workers.[16]

The English workers also duplicated their earlier social activity in Fall River. Pubs became important social centers, acting as focal points for class unity. The operators of these pubs, in the tradition of Lancashire publicans, encouraged trade union discussion and activity, and courted class solidarity within their taverns. They themselves were often discharged operatives, many having been blacklisted for supporting union or strike activity.

An officer of a Fall River labor union stated in 1880 that "men who have been discharged from one mill and are unable to obtain work in any other, have to go into some other business. It was only the other day we gave a spinner one hundred dollars to go into another business, and he will probably open a liquor store."[17]

The three councilmen on the late nineteenth-century Fall River City Council who consistently voted for the workers and their causes were all tavern owners. Although the survey of Massachusetts textile towns in the 1870s, undertaken to explain Fall River's militant unionism, obviously reflected a middle-class bias in attributing the city's labor troubles in part to the drinking habits of the city's English workmen, it is true that the city's taverns were often centers of working-class agitation over job issues.[18] Despite the fact that many late nineteenth-century labor leaders were also temperance advocates, the patterns of working-class socializing in pubs were deeply rooted in the culture which the city's workers brought from Europe. As one wage-earner claimed, the drinking habits of Fall River's operatives stemmed from "the work we have to do, combined with the national tendencies of the English and Irish races."[19]

The workers also set up a workingmen's club which served as an informal working-class center much as the taverns did, except without the high cost of alcohol. This club was a gathering place for workers interested in discussing politics, unionism, or other issues important to the working class. Charles Evens, a local "agitator" and blacklisted organizer of the weavers union, often used the club as a forum for discussing social issues.[20] The club was much like the Lancashire workingmen's clubs, which also provided temperance centers (although some served beer) for working-class politics.[21]

The taverns, clubs, lodges, and unions helped transform Fall River from the quiet community of the pre-Civil War period into a mill town with two distinct communities—one of mill owners and another of workers.

Lancashire unions began setting aside funds for the emigration of workers as early as 1837, but it was not until the second half of the nineteenth century that these funds affected emigration to the United States. Through out the 1870s and 1880s and continuing into the twentieth century, Lancashire textile unions provided money for blacklisted or "victimized" members to emigrate. Many chose to come to Fall River where they had both friends and a chance to take up their old trade. Since those most actively involved in labor disputes were the most likely to be "victims," and the emigration grants were given out according to union seniority, Fall River was the gathering point of workers steeped in the traditions of unionism and class consciousness.

Robert Howard, leader of the Fall River spinners in the 1870s and later elected to the Massachusetts legislature, typified this pattern. He left Lancashire, where he had been president of his local spinners union, for Fall River in 1860 after he had been blacklisted for his activities in the nine-hour day movement.[22]

The English workers' unions and related societies were centers for class comradeship and strength. They not only provided a means of controlling wages, but also, according to a nineteenth-century source, gave the workers an opportunity

> to participate in the progress of culture, increase their wages, insure them against sickness, old age, and death, provide them with cheap and wholesome food (through the various food co-operatives), ensure to adults the means of continuing their education after leaving school, and also a certain amount of social life.[23]

By the 1870s and 1880s, Lancashire workers in England saw Fall River as another textile town in Lancashire. The major newspaper of the Lancashire operatives, *The Cotton Factory Times,* published continual reports on the city. The paper had a local correspondent in Fall River who kept those at home informed on the activities there, from the scores and players of the Fall River Cricket Club to the more important reports on union meetings and the state of the trade.[24] Lancashire men elected to union offices in Fall River were publicized in the paper, and the rank and file were urged not to forget the lessons of Lancashire, "join some organization in the interests of labour. Organization is strength, trade unions are schools of true civilization, and the discussion of great social questions. . . ."[25] Many Fall River operatives received *The Cotton Factory Times* and corresponded with the editors, describing the conditions and progress of the union movement in the city.

In Lancashire, the workers had created a strong self-contained community.[26] In Fall River, these Lancashire workers formed the vanguard of the union movement. In 1879, an Englishman observed that American manufacturers were particularly hostile to Lancashire operatives because of their "Old World ideas on the benefits of trade unions and profitableness of strikes."[27]

As late as the turn of the century, Lancashire workers maintained their reputation for militant unionism. Thomas Young, an English observer of the American textile industry, reported on a visit to Fall River:

> I was told that the most skilled weavers here [Fall River]
> were from England, but that the Englishman gets himself into
> trouble by "pulling the chestnuts out of the fire" for the other
> working people. English weavers are therefore not regarded by
> the employers with that degree of favor which their excellence
> as workmen would otherwise command.[28]

Fall River's working-class community was dominated by those "unliked" Lancashire workmen. Because they spoke to the experiences of the textile workers in Fall River and because their militant unionism spoke to the needs and frustrations of the class, they were the leaders of the community. Their institutions drew together the community around shared values and experiences, and helped define its world view.

In 1884, an operative wrote to the *Fall River Herald* about the injustice suffered by the workingmen of Fall River. He asked that the readers excuse his simple language, for it was the language of the working class: "If I lack language to clothe my thoughts in proper form you must excuse me, as I am only a spinner and may never trouble you again, yet all my sympathies, all that I am, or even hope to be are with the laboring class."[29] This worker did not share the great American myth of mobility and individualism; he accepted and was proud of his position as a worker. He saw the interests of the working class as his interests and viewed advancement in terms of collective advancement. The pattern of life he observed around him reinforced that attitude. The people he knew were workers, and the activities he participated in were the activities of textile workers. The social clubs he and his friends belonged to were clubs of mill workers, and the information he received was filtered through a communication system dominated by textile workers. In short, his world was a world of operatives, and the "others" were viewed with hostility and suspicion. The textile worker was born into that world, and from his earliest years he was integrated into the life of the working-class community.

FROM CRADLE TO LOOM: THE INTEGRATION OF NEW MEMBERS INTO THE WORK FORCE

Before the child of the textile community was able to function on his own, he was thrown into the collective care of the community. With so many mothers working, child care became the responsibility of relatives and neighbors. A nonworking mother in the area would assume responsibility for several children. Grandparents too old to work or other kin would help watch children during working hours.[30] As the children reached the age where they could fend for themselves, they were sent out to the peer group. Before they entered school, the children picked the dump or "spent their time on the streets."[31]

Even in school, the mill culture was preeminent in the lives of children born to textile workers. These children were given time off during their parents' lunch breaks so that they could take lunch pails to their parents or relatives in the mill. Once inside, the children were put to work cleaning and preparing the machines.[32] F. K. Brown, in his autobiography as a mill child, explained that he was introduced to the mill by bringing lunch to his uncle. The uncle gave Brown chores to do during the break. The child learned to run a mule, clean and take out rollers, pinch broken threads, and replace bobbins.[33] The mill became a thoroughly familiar environment for the children of mill workers.[34]

At school, the children talked constantly of the mills and of their desire to enter them and the adulthood that entrance symbolized.[35] The school committee itself was ruled by the idea that school should not interfere with integrating the mill child into the work force: "An exclusively bookish education has created in the minds of many of the [mill children] a radically wrong attitude toward life which would make the child look upon working at cotton manufacturing . . . [as] an evil."[36]

The arbitrary discipline of the school contributed to the children's desire to enter the mills. Fall River's school system, with its excessive discipline, was especially hard on working-class children. Moreover, the mills at least offered wages which gave mill children a certain respect at home and the dignity of the adult role.[37] When Massachusetts passed a new child labor law in 1912, which forced some of the young children out of the mills and back into school, many of the children interviewed by the Massachusetts Child Labor Committee claimed that they would rather work in the mills because of the school's meaningless discipline and the degradation they experienced there, especially for those with language problems.[38]

Once out of school, the child entered the mill as a sweeper or bobbin boy. Some children were given training for a skilled job, but at a lower pay rate; hence, most spent years at the least paying jobs because their parents were not willing to sacrifice their wages.[39] Young workers depended upon information from their parents, relatives, or parents' friends about job openings at the mill. The father would usually find out about a position in his or a friend's mill and would talk to the overseer about placing the child.[40] This employment pattern is reflected in the large percentage of relatives working in each room of the Iron Works Mills, which ran as high as 34 percent, or forty-three of the ring spinners in a single room of Iron Works Mill Number 4.[41]

The peer group activity of the younger children broadened once the child entered the mill. In the mill, the young workers would usually join the groups of children who worked in the mill and lived in their neighborhood.[42] In good weather the children, not pressured by piece work, would leave the mill at noon and gather outside in groups, "talking and smoking cigarettes."[43] After work, the younger workers would gather in poolrooms and vacant lots, smoking cigarettes and dreaming of the day when they could spend their spare time in the taverns and clubs of their parents.

Although many young girls did gather downtown on Saturday afternoons after work, most were far more tightly controlled by their parents than were boys. The French Canadian and Portuguese girl workers were expected home to help prepare meals and wash clothes. Parents were suspicious of any time spent outside the home because it took time away from housework, and, even more vital to the family survival, it opened options which might lead to an early marriage and deprive the family of important funds. Several times in interviews, retired female workers in Fall River mentioned that their parents discouraged social interactions with males because they feared losing the family income. Mary Felix, whose mother was a spinner and father a weaver, was taken out of school at fourteen by her mother: "you've got to go and work like I'm working, in the mill." When Mary told her mother that she was planning to get married after going with her husband for five years, her mother refused: "You're not getting married till Doris (the younger sister) goes to work."[44]

Although women could be found in taverns and clubs, the social life of most female textile workers was very much a home-centered life, even if she worked.[45] If the wife was "a drinker," she would do her drinking at home, sending out a child or male acquaintance for a pail of beer.[46] Fall River did not have cafes and lunchrooms as Lynn did. Although the women were very conscious of the impact of working conditions and wages, not only personally but also on their budgets and their families, and were active participants in the early union battles, they did not have access to the social institutions of tavern or cafe as in Lynn.

After the worker was old enough to go to the bars and saloons, he entered an important social institution which integrated him into the society of the male textile worker. The saloon, which played a key role in both the community and the trade, was Fall River's equivalent to Lynn's cafes and lunchrooms. Here the men aired their grievances, discussed their problems, escaped their homes, and defined their enemies.

The importance of the saloon or tavern as a social center goes back to many of the traditions brought over by the Lancashire operatives. The tavern or saloon was the workingman's institution and was beyond the meddling and control of the "bosses" and "tyrants"—the Hill people. Jonathan Baxter Harrison stated in 1879 that the taverns were often run by mill operatives who had been discharged for union activity and had set up a saloon in a corner of a store or in a basement of his tenement building, "starting with a small stock—a keg of beer or a few gallons of low-grade whiskey."[47]

In various neighborhoods of the city, the more prosperous taverns displayed signs such as "Harmony Hall" or the "Avon Arms." In the 1870s and 1880s, the patrons of these taverns (usually fifty feet long by twenty feet wide, with a bar, eight to ten tables, and a piano for singing) were operatives.[48] Other taverns such as Coleman's in Bowenville, although not as fancy, nonetheless gave the workers an escape from the home and a center for social interaction within the village.[49]

When funds were low or the tavern was too far off, the doorstep substituted as the worker's social arena. After dinner, those workers who were too tired, poor, or temperate "congregated in groups on the leeside of some house" and talked about the conditions of the trade, wages, and the union.[50]

THE WORKERS DEFINE THE ENEMY

Workers in all parts of the city shared certain experiences and beliefs. Although their work and social life centered in the semi-isolated villages of Bowenville, Globe Village, Mechanicsville, Flint Village, Border City, or Little Canada, they all understood that they had a common enemy—the man on the Hill—and a common experience—life in the mills. Even if they "accepted their lot," the nineteenth-century workers still felt what they deemed the heel of tyranny and oppression on the part of the "mill owners and capitalists of the city [as] thoroughly selfish and heartless," caring only for the exploitation of the laborer. Factory life in Fall River "almost reached serfdom," according to George Gunton, a local labor leader and editor of the labor paper.[51] The paper was a common denominator among "many hundreds of the older operatives, especially foreigners of two or three nationalities."[52] In 1879, the paper ran a special utopian story of how the "working people [in America] rise up in arms under the direction of a nameless leader . . . a man of huge build and brawn." According to the paper, the workers of the new revolutionary army were instructed to supply their own needs from the abundant stores of their neighbors, giving them receipts in the name of the revolution.[53] A nineteenth-century observer of Fall River expressed great concern about the widespread reading and interest which this apocalyptic vision received in the working-class community.[54]

Information, news, events of the trade, conditions of work, and the importance of unionism were passed on to the worker through a communications network controlled by operatives. Through the saloon, tavern, the neighborhood club, labor paper, and front porch, the textile worker developed a world view. Any information that came from the middle-class networks was distrusted. A Fall River operative testifying before the Industrial Commission of 1901 stated that he did not believe the statistics and facts of the "moneyed men or capitalists," for he knew the contrary "as an *absolute* fact, as a party told me who lives in the same block as I do."[55] For the Fall River workers, facts were heard from fellow workers;

lies were the claims of the other classes.

The union hall, although a long walk for many operatives, did offer the worker a wide variety of social activity during the nineteenth century. In the Weavers Building, where several small craft unions had their offices, workers gathered to play cards, talk, or pick up information. In 1889, the Weavers Union, which was beginning to gain some organizational strength and was entering into its first major strike, bought athletic equipment and set aside room in its hall for workouts. During the strike itself, the union held dances and rallies while the officers were negotiating for higher wages.[56]

Besides the unions and pubs, the workers created and participated in several other community-wide social institutions during the nineteenth century. In the 1870s and 1880s, through the Labor Campaign Club, they gathered together for political discussions and activity. In 1879, the club supported the Greenback Labor party and elected Thomas Webb, one of the "communistic labor reformers that had cursed Fall River with their destruction and pestilential influence," to the State senate.[57] The following year, the club helped elect the local president of the spinners, Robert Howard, to the state legislature.[58]

In the tradition of their Lancashire brethren, the Fall River operatives also belonged to benefit organizations or lodges. By the end of the nineteenth century, there were over eighty-eight lodges in the city, distributed among the Odd Fellows (the largest and most important for the working class), the Knights of Foresters, the Ancient Order of the United Workmen, and the Masons. The workmen formed the first Odd Fellows lodge in the 1840s. In the 1870s and 1880s, several additional lodges were formed.[59] The Odd Fellows lodges were particularly important, especially for workers from Lancashire of both English and Irish extraction. Manchester, the heart of the English textile district, had the largest Odd Fellows membership during the nineteenth century. Moreover, the Odd Fellows were supportive of textile workers migrating from mill to mill and location to location. They even assisted brothers in cities across the ocean and provided companionship, conversation, and information about jobs and wages in other mills. A textile worker from Lancashire coming to Fall River could expect support, company, and job information from the local Odd Fellows lodge.[60]

Fall River's immigrants, like all immigrant groups, established ethnic clubs and benefit organizations in order to take care of needs which arose in the new country and to maintain ties back home. English operatives, besides forming local branches of the Odd Fellows, also established the Livington Lodge, the U. S. Grant Lodge, and the Bonnie Red Rose Lodge of the Sons of Saint George. The Irish, although united with the English on issues of unions and working-class unity, were sensitive to Irish nationalism as well and built up five divisions of the Ancient Order of Hibernia and a Thrum de Lauve Club.[61]

Resenting the Irish and English attacks against them as strikebreakers and sensitive to their minority status in an English-speaking world, the French Canadians actively attempted to keep their language, religion, and cultural identity separate from the English and Irish through ethnic clubs and lodges. They established several clubs, including the Ligue des Patriotes, the Grade Napoleon, the Societe de St. Jean Baptiste, the Societe Laurier, the Societe La Boucane, and the Cercle Montcalm. They also developed an elaborate parochial school system and a strong independent church in opposition to the Irish-dominated Catholic church.[62]

Like the clubs of all ethnic groups, these clubs provided the immigrants with community institutions which held them together and preserved ethnic beliefs and culture. But the French Canadians, like the Irish and the English, were also textile workers; hence, their role in these clubs and organizations must also be evaluated in terms of their role as workers. Unlike the Odd Fellows, apparently the French Canadian clubs openly opposed unionization.

Through their ethnic organizations, the leaders of the French Canadian community spoke out loudly against unions and strikes. Hugo Dubuque, a lawyer and a leader in the local church, was a major politicial spokesman for the French Canadians. He was supported by Father J. B. Bedard, Fall River's most antilabor priest, and Pierre Peloquin, the music director of the French Canadian band. All three were militantly antiunion. Although they dominated the formal ethnic community, they did not control the working-class members of that community. Forty percent of the male population of the French Canadian community found employment in the textile mills, but only 11 percent of the members of the Societe de St. Jean Baptiste who held any position within the fraternal order throughout its initial decade of existence were mill workers. Only 22 percent of the organization's members were working class, while over 92 percent of the French Canadian community were working class. Although one would expect middle-class members to predominate in the fraternal organizations

of the ethnic community, the Societe, supposedly designed to care for
and support the ethnic community, had little in common with the community it "represented." What was true of the Societe de St. Jean Baptiste
was also true of other ethnic organizations within the French Canadian
community. In the Ligue des Patriotes with over two hundred members,
only one of a total of thirty-three persons who held any leadership position
was working class. L'Union Canadienne St. Jean Baptiste de Bowenville
had no working class or textile workers in any leadership position. Although these organizations were ostensibly benevolent organizations,
they were organized and run primarily for the French Canadian's small
but significant white collar members. The heavy domination of these
organizations by middle-class ethnic leaders reinforces the idea that working-class members may not have looked within their ethnic community
for leadership. Rather, the ethnic community itself may have been divided,
with the small middle class controlling the ethnic organizations, while the
working class may have looked elsewhere for support and fellowship. In
this context, working-class French Canadians were actively involved in
strikes and other union activity.[63]

ETHNIC TENSIONS: THE COMMUNITY DIVIDES

The ethnic segregation of the French Canadians, the dominant English
and Irish workers' hostility toward them as strikebreakers, and the French
Canadians' initial distrust of the union movement—which they saw as
depriving them of their chance to labor—put severe strains on the working-
class community.[64] It tested the strength of the institutions and their
ability to integrate new members.

Although Fall River's community was fragmented residentially and
many of the older working-class institutions became the preserve of the
English and Irish workers, the young and still-growing union movement
was able to integrate the French Canadians and keep alive the informal
social activity which helped hold the community together. The unions
had not yet formalized much of their interactions, and they continued to
depend heavily upon rank-and-file participation and activity. No clear line
could be drawn between the unions and the community at large, or between the union and nonunion members. The unions were still elastic

enough to integrate the newly arriving French Canadians, although that integrating process, as will be seen in Chapter 9, was very difficult. Ultimately, through their participation in the union struggles, the French Canadians became good union brothers in the eyes of the English and Irish workers. The unions continued to speak for all operatives, French Canadian as well as English and Irish. Despite the influx of the French-speaking workers, the unions still saw themselves as the instruments of the general working-class struggle against capital, and craft divisions were seen as practical conveniences, not ideological commitments.[65]

When the Portuguese began to emigrate to Fall River in the late 1890s and early twentieth century, they were confronted by the prejudices of the English, Irish, and French Canadian work force. The Portuguese responded by creating their own formal and informal social institutions to support their community, which was developing in the enclave of south Fall River. The Portuguese established sickness and death benefit organizations even before they set up their own church. Unlike the French Canadians or Irish whose backgrounds were charged with ethnic, national, and religious antagonism, the Portuguese upon their arrival were not as concerned about independent churches and schools. Rather, they concentrated on immediate relief and help in dealing with the industrial environment which they encountered when they first entered Fall River and its mills.

In 1884, the early Portuguese settlers formed the St. Joseph Portuguese Benefit Society, and in the 1890s, the St. Michael Benefit Society. They also set up fraternal societies, such as the Portuguese Fraternity of the U.S.A., which served as both a social center and a benefit organization. In addition to these more formal organizations, they also built up a network of social clubs and athletic organizations within their village.[66]

The Portuguese who settled in Fall River came from the Azores, the most traditional and conservative section of Portugal. The church and the clergy, for example, were more deeply imbedded on the islands than on the mainland itself. Most of the islanders found work as agricultural workers or small subsistence farmers in the Azores or fished when they did not farm. Coming from a highly traditional peasant society, they brought to Fall River many of these traditional beliefs and customs. But the Portuguese population which migrated to Fall River was a youthful one. Many had made the move across the ocean more than once before finally settling in Fall River. The institutions they developed, although rooted in their culture and traditional experiences, were not parochial. These newcomers even encouraged those outside the ethnic community to join. Marriages with other ethnic groups were regarded with pride rather than hostility. The Portuguese were quick to shed the image of "greenhorn," a term most often used by older members of an ethnic community to refer to recent arrivals.

The working class of Fall River cut the Portuguese off from the existing social institutions. Although not officially prevented from joining the unions, the unskilled positions which the Portuguese filled in the mills, as well as their concentration in doffing and carding, discouraged their participation. The unions themselves responded to the tremendous influx of Portuguese workers, who were even more alien and darker than the French Canadians, by further curtailing the informal social activity which had heretofore been so important as integrating forces.

Because of Fall River's residential segregation, the Portuguese did not participate in the tavern and pub activity which had served an important socializing function for the older workers. Concentrated in their own village in south Fall River, they built their own social institutions which, although relieving the isolation and loneliness of the new immigrant, did not help integrate him into the larger class community. At the turn of the century, Portuguese immigrants formed the Portuguese American Athletic Club, which was much like a tavern, providing recreation and fellowship for the younger workers within the community. In 1911, they formed the Republiano Alphonis Castor Club, named after a famous Portuguese anticleric and revolutionary. It provided a bar where the men could talk, "hang out," shoot pool, and play cards.[67]

Social and residential segregation broke down later in the century, and the Portuguese workers became involved in the new union movement of the 1930s. They intermingled and socialized on the job, and their ethnic clubs, although retaining ethnic names, were slowly transformed into working-class neighborhood clubs with a mixed ethnic makeup. Some had a Portuguese president and a French Canadian or Irish vice-president.[68]

Although the Poles represented only a very small percentage of Fall River's work force when they began to immigrate to Fall River in about 1900, they confronted the same hostility which the Portuguese had faced. The peasant communities from which the Poles migrated were not substantially different from those of the Portuguese. Life was governed by familial obligations and concern over the land. Perhaps even more than the Portuguese, the Poles were obsessed with a desire for stability and, although concerned with money, at the same time distrusted excessive materialism. Polish peasant families were fiercely paternalistic and hierarchical, with the strongest control being exerted over the oldest children.[69] The choice to move to America tended to be made by those with the least traditional bonds. Once in Fall River, these same Poles tended to select from their traditions those values and behaviors which were most suited to their success or survival in the new industrial setting and, at the same time, adjusted those that were not. The bias toward innovative, young, and adventurous migrants helped the adjustment process.[70]

Like the Portuguese, the Poles built up their own independent institutions. In 1906, for instance, the Polish community formed the Children of Poland Club, renaming it the Julius Slowacki Lodge of the Polish National Alliance a few years later. The Poles were also excluded from much of the informal activity of the unions and other social activity of the English, Irish, and French Canadians. Hence, the Polish community created its own informal interactions in the crowded enclave developing along the river.[71]

Besides taverns and ethnic clubs, the working class had access to a wide variety of mass-culture entertainment forms, among which were the twentieth-century movies which appealed mostly to the younger workers. Dance halls, bowling alleys, and poolrooms also offered the young textile worker a place to spend his off-hours and the allowance given him from his take-home pay (see Photograph 13).[72]

Notwithstanding the availability of these entertainments, the workers tended to look within the community for recreation. They spent less on entertainment in the early twentieth century than workers in any other major city in Massachusetts.[73] Immigrant families, in particular, saved money by eating at home and socializing among friends or at neighborhood ethnic clubs.[74]

During a period when the general public was supposedly integrated into a popular, if not middle-class, culture through the medium of popular entertainment, the Fall River working class was relatively immune or isolated from that popular entertainment form. They spent their time and energy within their class and ethnic community, reinforcing ethnic and community bonds and culture rather than diffusing them through interaction with mass culture forms.

THE MIDDLE-CLASS RESPONSE TO THE WORKERS

The middle and upper classes of Fall River, like the middle and upper classes of Lynn, were concerned about the alien and independent class

13. The Hub Recreational Center, 1925

Most patrons were likely to be young male textile workers. Although most of their earnings would go to the family, the young male textile workers would keep more of their earnings than would their sisters. Their sisters were most probably helping at home, while they were socializing at clubs or taverns.

of operatives who lived below them. In 1888, following an inspiring speech by philanthropist Robert Paine of Boston in which he pointed out the need for moral guidance to the poor and working classes of Fall River, the middle- and upper-class women of Fall River set up the Associated Charities. This organization went into the very homes of the working class to demonstrate the superior quality of the middle-class virtues of temperance, frugality, housekeeping, hard work, and moral and social order within the family.[75] The male leaders of the elite families officiated over the organization, while the wives and daughters of that same upper class were its rank and file.

In the late nineteenth and early twentieth centuries, the middle and upper classes began to reach out to organize and formalize the recreational activity of the city's working class. Through the Boy Scouts, YMCA, Boys Clubs, and other social and recreational activities, the middle class hoped to uplift and direct the young and "uncorrupted" members of the working class. The working class itself responded to this attempt to direct its activities by withdrawing from participation and switching to spectator activity. Although Fall River had over six hundred Boy Scouts by 1922, there were almost no working-class members. An observer in the early 1920s expressed disappointment that, since recreational activity had become more organized, "for rather than by the mill operatives," the "people preferred watching sports to actively participating in them." This tendency was "of their own choosing and [was] regretted by recreational leaders in the community."[76]

The working class, whether recent migrants or sons and daughters of textile workers, shared the conditions of low wages and alienating labor. To mitigate these conditions, they looked to friends, neighbors, and community institutions for support. As new immigrants came into Fall River and filled up the lower levels of the work force, they naturally fell back upon established support systems. Initially, this set a pattern of ethnic divisions, but the working class, although separated into ethnic enclaves, was bound together by its distrust of the Hill people. The workers' shared opposition to the mill owners and management eventually led to the breakdown of ethnic divisions and ethnic communities and to the building up of class-wide community institutions. The division of the community along ethnic lines, and later the slow process of rebuilding the community, can best be seen through the struggles of the workers and their attempts to build and maintain a union movement.[77]

9

Conflict and Cohesion

As the Fall River corporations became larger and more mechanized, labor became more organized. During the pre-Civil War period, the workers agitated against the thirteen-hour day, for less woman and child labor in the mills, and for higher wages through their paper, *The Mechanic,* and a primitive union structure. In 1850, the spinners struck the Metacomet Mill to obtain these demands. The owner, Colonel Borden, proclaimed that he had watched the walls, floors, and machines go up and would watch them all fall to the ground before he would recognize the workers or their demands. After six months of bitter struggle, the strike ended in defeat. Union spinners were forced to leave the city, while remaining workers swallowed their pride and returned to work. This defeat marked the coming of age of the Fall River operatives. Although it would be several decades before they would have a more permanent union structure, the age of harmony was over in the city which would soon become known throughout New England for the radical activities of its operatives.[1]

In 1858, the spinners reorganized under Patrick Carroll and John McKeowen, both Lancashire Irish, to form the Benevolent and Protective Association of United Mule Spinners of New England. The union agitated for reduced hours for women and children and increased wages. The owners met many of the initial demands, but this progress was dissipated during the war when the leaders joined the Union Army. In 1866, a strike crippled the union which was already weakened by the wartime disruption.

In the 1860s and 1870s, when Fall River manufacturers expanded their mills and the city itself doubled in size, the workers built a trade union movement. The movement engaged the manufacturers in a struggle which lasted the remainder of the century and left the city in divided camps. The community supported these struggles, just as it supported the idea of unionism when the unions themselves were destroyed.

In the 1870s, most of the workers lived in a compact area near the mills which lined the river. (The villages to the extreme north, Border City, to the east, Flint Village, and to the south, Globe Village, had not yet been fully settled.) English and Irish workers dominated the community, and their institutions held the community together. Many of the operatives were union leaders and members before they came over, and in the words of Robert Howard, secretary of the Fall River Spinners Union and ex-president of the Stockport Spinners and Twiners Association in England, they were anxious "to follow the example of the English in the matter of labor reforming."[2] His statement was echoed by a Blackburn paper which, after pointing to the success of the unions in Blackburn, Lancashire, stated, "there would seem to be no reason why the Fall River Association should not be equally prosperous as its sister association of weavers in Blackburn."[3]

Thomas O'Donnell, who followed Howard as the Spinners Union secretary, also learned his trade in Lancashire. He came to Fall River at age twenty-one in 1873. He was forced to leave the city for five years as a result of blacklisting following the strike of 1879, but returned a few years later to make use of his trade union experience. Both James Whitehead, secretary of the Weavers Protective Association, and James Tansey, a Lancashire Irishman, secretary of the Carders and later president of the Fall River Textile Council, learned their trade and their trade unionism in Lancashire.

The workers' unionism was tied up in a whole series of interlocking formal and informal organizations, all of which were dedicated to protecting the workingman.[4] These organizations, however, were subsidiary to the main thrust of the workingman's politics of unionism. And unions were what the Fall River workers created. In 1867, the workers struck for the ten-hour day and succeeded, thereby gaining confidence in their solidarity and in their ability to influence the manufacturers by collective action.[5] This confidence was encouraged by the expanded ranks of veteran union men from Lancashire who were coming to work in the city's growing mills. Their next major test came in the summer of 1870, when the manufacturers, competing against the lower wages and longer hours of mills outside Fall River, posted a notice of wage reductions and the Spinners Union voted to strike.

Although the spinners initiated the strike, workers from almost all departments opposed the reduction and supported the spinners' action. In late August, the mills attempted to open up with the use of knobsticks. A large crowd of operatives representing all the branches of the trade gathered at the Durfee Mills to prevent any "backsliding." The local police and fire departments were called in to break up the crowd. The fire department hoses temporarily quieted the crowd, but it soon became necessary to bring in two local militia companies to disperse the crowds which gathered daily. Resistance to the scabs and support for the strike were shared by union members and nonunionists alike, for there was widespread community support not only of the strike but also unionism itself.

Despite the popularity of the cause, the spinners did not have the financial reserves or organizational strength to sustain a long strike. The workers were poor and their alternatives were few. With militia to protect the strikebreakers, and hunger and threatened evictions to drive the strikers back, the mills began operations and the strike collapsed in September.[6]

THE LESSONS OF UNIONISM

The strike of 1870, although crippling the Spinners Union, did not destroy unionism in the city. The wages were reduced and the sixty-two and a half hour week was reinstituted, but the manufacturers were unable to eradicate the sympathetic and ideological support for the union movement. Having lost one battle, the strikers began to build for the next one.

The building process took four short years, and the struggle which ensued reflected the informal nature of the movement. The first few years following the 1870 strike were good ones for Fall River mill owners. Eleven new mills were built in 1873 alone, but by the end of that year depression hit the city and the mills began running on short time. In December, the owners decided to reduce wages. The 1874 ten-hour day which cut 1.5 to 2 hours a day, coupled with the threat of reduced wages, meant a severe reduction in take-home pay for families barely able to pay bills under the old system.

Membership in the unions, which had been mere skeleton organizations before 1874, grew from a few hundred to three to four thousand by that year. Old unionists who had let their membership lapse paid up, and new workers who had not bothered to join now took out membership cards.

Mass rallies and protest meetings were held, and the working-class community boiled over with militant agitation. At a mass meeting to determine their course of action, Harry Servey, editor of the local labor journal, together with the leadership of the Weavers Committee, advised union members not to strike. The weavers agreed, and it appeared that Fall River would make a peaceful transition to shorter hours and less pay.

But the women weavers decided not to accept the position of the male-dominated union. On January 16, 1875, they met separately, refused admittance to males, elected their own chairwoman, and argued for an independent women's position. The women argued that the strength of the workers lay in their solidarity and that putting off the strike would give the companies more time to prepare countertactics. The women voted to strike three mills, which were the "ringleaders" in the reduction movement, and to protest the reduction in the other mills. They decided to tax all working looms and distribute the funds of the working weavers to strikers. All strikers would be treated equally, regardless of official union membership.

Following the women's announcement, the Weavers Committee, representing the Weavers Union, endorsed the action. The other branches of the trade soon voted to support the women, and on January 30 and February 1, the workers in the selected mills went out on strike. In the words of a contemporary weaver, "all nationalities were sunk under the name of fellow operatives."[7] All strikers were automatically added to the union books, whether or not they had belonged to the union.

The strikers found some support among the general community but most of it came from the working class.[8] Workers who did not support the strike and attempted to work in the struck mills were greeted with stones, bricks, and mud, along with an assortment of invectives. The union and strike committees made feeble attempts to keep crowds away from the mills, "but the huge crowds assembled, consisting of the help from the other mills and the workmen of various trades throughout the city."[9] The town called up the militia but had continual trouble controlling the crowds. Mills that interfered with the raising of funds for the strike or supported the struck mills were added to the list. On March 18, the mills agreed to rescind the reduction and the workers went back to work.

The workers ended the strike by pledging themselves to class solidarity:

We . . . pledge ourselves that we will not be unmindful of our brethren and sisters in other places who are struggling against the domination of capital, but will put forth our united effort and purpose for the emancipation of downtrodden and oppressed labor. . . . The working classes will not always be as successful as the Fall River operatives have been during the strike of 1875, but by uniting together and husbanding their strengths, they will find it of great service in the time of need. . . . So long as capital shall make itself the greatest enemy of labor, so long shall trade unions be required to protect labor.[10]

The strike of 1875 demonstrated not only the unity of "all nationalities" and crafts, but also the close relationship between nonformal class action—in this case that of the female textile workers—and class solidarity. The women and the working-class community behind them demonstrated the flexibility and inclusiveness of the union movement at this stage in Fall River's history.[11]

The victory of early 1875 was shortlived, and the warning of the strikers that "working classes will not always be successful" came home to these very operatives in August of the same year. Just as the women had feared, the corporations prepared for the next strike. In early August 1875, the owners posted another reduction in wages. The operatives, under the leadership of George Gunton, voted to go on a four-week vacation rather than accept it. At the end of the four weeks, the workers found the mills shut tight. The owners, under the direction of the Board of Trade, which they had formed to coordinate the efforts against strikes, had decided to lock out the workers until the unions were broken. After four more weeks of idleness, the mills opened their doors to those who could prove no union connection and would sign a contract pledging not to belong to the union. The signing of this "yellow dog" contract caused such bitterness among the operatives that fifteen years later, during the strike of 1889, a popular song was sung about how the workers had had to sign their freedom away:

Kind friends give me your attention
A few words I will say
It seems too bad to have to fight
To get a little more pay,
But stand by one another
We will show that we are game
We'll show them we've not forgotten
The day we signed our name.

Chorus:

Then join the Weaver's Union
Yes, join it right away
And till you do, my shopmates,
We'll never get fair play.
We'll make our numbers thousands
The child, the woman, the man,
And the day will never come again
When we must sign our hand.

How they talk of the cruel South, boys, and
How they talk of slavery days,
And point to poor old England,
And the wages that she pays;
But I don't believe in either place
There ever was a man
Before he ever went to his daily toil
Was forced to sign his name.

Chorus:

How they boast of proud America
And praise this land so free
And say we are on a level
That rich and poor agree.

I should think the proud American
Would hang his head in shame
When he remembered long ago
The day he signed his name.

Chorus:

But we've got one friend in heaven
Who looks down on the poor,
And all our little troubles
He will help us to endure.
He will guide us in our actions
To do the thing that's right.
So join the Weavers Union,
Yes, join this very night.[12]

The yellow dog contract and blacklisting not only left a residue of hatred and bitterness which lasted for fourteen years, but also caused massive demonstrations and violence. Workers stoned those who signed and went in, and they smashed mill windows and doors. Strikers staged a massive parade in which operatives from Mechanicsville, Mt. Pleasant, Bowenville, and Rodman Village gathered in their local villages and marched into the city center in groups. Villages were the local centers for the union movement, especially in the 1870s and 1880s when the villages were still located near the center of the city. Solidarity was built at the village level and then linked to the city-wide movement. Pride in the solidarity and militance of the local village was an important part in building the community-wide solidarity, especially since most of the informal class institutions, such as taverns and neighborhood gathering places, were located at the village level. Over fifteen thousand workers participated in these rallies and demonstrations, reflecting general community-wide support for the labor movement, as well as the bitterness against the manufacturers.

Despite these gestures of defiance and solidarity, the mills were able to run with the yellow dog contract and union leadership blacklisting, and a show of strength in the form of the state militia. The Weavers, Carders, and Loomfixers unions were destroyed. Only the spinners were able to keep their union alive. The union leaders left town, changed their names, or depended upon the aid of friends or relatives to stay alive. The union movement went underground and prepared for the next battle.[13]

The workers spent the next four years (1875-1879) building and preparing their community. Their formal organizations were destroyed or crippled, but the community's support and ideological commitment remained strong. Although it was an indignity for the workers to sign a pledge against unionism, it could not destroy their attitudes and sympathies, which were reinforced in the daily after-work talk on the doorsteps and in tavern rooms of the local villages.

The workers in Fall River, whether the skilled spinners or the semi-skilled weavers, were tied to a machine whose speed and profits were controlled by the owners who lived on the Hill. Those owners ruled the community and the mills, and the workers were well aware of that domination. They viewed themselves as "downtrodden and oppressed" not only because their wages were low, but also because the machine and its owner controlled so much of their lives. Their emancipation involved their liberation from that owner and his machine. They saw themselves as opponents of capital, and as long as that opposition existed "trade unions [were] required to protect labor." That lesson came both from the defeat of the strike of 1875 and from their daily experience on the job where, as a song writer of the 1880s stated, the "master takes all the meat," or productive surplus of the machine itself.

The symbol of labor's dependent relationship to capital was the signing of the yellow dog contract. For not only were the workers enduring low wages and degrading working conditions, but they also had to sign away their liberty to give their loyalty voluntarily. In the minds of Fall River textile workers, this made mockery of the concept that the "rich and poor" are "on a level." It challenged their conception of what freedom meant and reduced industrial toil to "slavery days."

In 1878, the spirit of unionism began to rekindle the flame of discontent, and the unions again began to stir. Weavers began organizing secretly, while the spinners joined the International Labor Union and sent organizers to Lowell and Lawrence in order to gain state-wide cooperation in keeping wages up.[14] In May 1878, two thousand operatives demonstrated in front of the house of William Jennings, the treasurer of the Merchant Mills, who was considered particularly severe on the workers. Inasmuch as the Merchant Mills employed only 850 workers, most of those who demonstrated did so in sympathy and support of their brothers and sisters. The size and spontaneity of the rally reflected the strength of class loyalty within the community of workers in Fall River, despite the weakened state of the unions.[15]

In May 1879, the spinners began to agitate for a strike to restore wages to a higher rate; their leader was Robert Howard, who was elected full-time secretary of their union in 1878. Howard, who was tempered by militant unionism, having been blacklisted in England when he was a union president and having been arrested in Bowenville as a labor agitator and ringleader in fomenting trouble, cautioned the spinners not to strike too soon.[16] The spinners did decide against striking but asked for a restoration of lost wages.

The manufacturers, meeting under the direction of the Board of Trade, met this request by proposing to take out four mules in each mill and to replace them with ring spinners. This move, they argued, would cause a surplus of 125 spinners and disrupt the power of the union.[17]

On June 14, the spinners called for a general strike to begin the following day. The workers held rallies daily through the end of June, with more spinners voting to go out in support of the strikers.

In July, the companies, especially the American Linen Mills, began an active campaign to bring in strikebreakers from Canada. These workers were housed in the company tenements of the evicted strikers and in many cases inside the mills themselves.[18] The strikers responded with violence, the only successful tool they had against the use of scabs. Scabs were attacked, stoned, and shot at. Strikers gathered at the company gates in massive picketing to prevent workers from entering. Crowds stoned the mills and threatened those workers who took their jobs. Riots occurred continually at the company gates, and by the middle of September, 114 spinners had been arrested.[19]

By the end of September, the companies were beginning to operate with imported Canadian labor. Workers at the newly built Border City Mills (located in the extreme northern section of Fall River two miles from the central city section and cut off from the center of union activity) began returning to work. By October 26, the strike was called off.[20] Strikers were blacklisted and unionists were rooted out of the mills. The community rallied around the blacklisted workers by aiding them in their search for work. One method they used was for spinners to claim sickness on the job, leaving their positions to blacklisted spinners waiting outside the gates. This system provided for those blacklisted spinners and kept the spirit of unionism alive. In addition, the continual rotation of the militant unionists helped prevent backsliding in the more isolated mills.[21]

The spinners learned the lesson of the weakness of craft unionism. They had the support of the weavers but did not attempt to coordinate an industry-wide strike. Consequently, weavers in struck mills were weaving from yarn spun by scab spinners. By 1884, the spinners were no longer appealing to their own craft. In leaflets passed out to nonunion workers, they appealed to the common brotherhood and interests of all workers and asked: "Are we not all one family?" To the weavers particularly, they called for unity: "Weavers, our fight is yours, victory for us is victory for you. Our cause is one and the same."[22]

The four years between late 1879 and 1884 were used to educate the community to the need for collective pan-craft unionism. Robert Howard expressed the attitude of the workers when he stated in 1884 that "unity of thought and action in industrial warfare is the stepping stone to victory."[23] Trapped by the tradition of craft unions, the spinners were unable to organize all workers into a single industrial union, but they did begin the process of organizing community support by building on the informal ties already existing within the community. By 1884, a local paper felt that a strike vote by the Spinners Union would turn out the whole community.[24]

THE FRENCH CANADIANS BECOME UNIONISTS

The process of organizing the community was complicated between 1879 and 1884 by the changed makeup of the population. No longer did the organizers face Lancashire-trained industrial workers. Now they had to deal with a mixed work force of trained English and Irish workers, and unskilled or recently skilled French Canadian farmers and agricultural workers. As mentioned earlier, many of these French Canadians had entered the mills as knobsticks in the strikes of 1875 and 1879. These workers held the jobs and homes of good union men, and the resentment towards them ran high among the English-speaking operatives.

For their part, the French Canadians were just as suspicious of the unions. In February 1884, French Canadian weavers employed in the Stafford Mill (in Flint Village in the far eastern section of the city) met, and, under the influence of their violently antiunion priest, Bedard, they voted to have nothing to do with the newly formed Weavers Union.[25]

The union men needed the support of the French Canadian workers if they were to be successful in pulling out all the operatives. The strike of 1884 represented the union's first attempt to pull together the community which had begun to segment into ethnic enclaves and to spread into more villages which were even further isolated from the central city area.

Although the English workers were hostile toward the French Canadians, they realized the importance of spreading the message of unionism and class solidarity to them. As Thomas O'Donnell, the secretary of the spinners, testified to the Industrial Commission in 1901, the union workers depended upon all operatives "following one another out. The unorganized follow[ing] the organized out."[26] George McNeill stated before the same commission that, as nonunion workers, the "French Canadian labor in the cotton mills . . . reduce[d] the wages, but after some years the genius of unions took hold upon them."[27] The unionists realized that their struggle could not be successful without interethnic unity.

The strike of 1884 tested the ability of the spirit of class-wide community solidarity to overcome what an English trade unionist recognized as the fragmented labor force in Fall River: "Different nationalities, although working together in harmony had little in common and were indifferent to anything around them except in those of their own nationalities."[28]

In 1884, the workers began a struggle to hold the community together in the face of company hostility and internal ethnic differences. It was a struggle that was lost by the end of 1904. The differences between 1884 and 1904 are apparent in the behavior of the workers during the strikes that rocked the city during that period.

Between 1884 and 1894, Fall River operatives went out on three major strikes. The approach and the functioning of the community differed little between the strikes. The unions grew in great numbers during this period and had the support of unionist and nonunionist alike. The ranks were kept solid and spirits high by continual rallies, parades, demonstrations, dances, and even clambakes. The union hall functioned, much as it had for the Lynn strikers, as an important social center. Those who lived close enough to the hall spent their time socializing with friends, picking up news about the strike, volunteering for picket duty, or just playing cards or talking. In the various villages of the city, some several miles from one another, similar centers developed either in taverns such as Coleman's in Bowenville or on doorsteps or in corner stores.

Through these informal and formal activities, recent arrivals to the work force, and especially the French Canadians, were integrated into the community of trade unionists, even if that community did not extend to religious and political party comradeship. The Immigration Commission in 1909 explained that Fall River's union strength among the French Canadians came about through continual association with fellow workmen, especially during strikes. The French Canadians learned "to stand by the unions, though previously they may not have been members."[29]

The immigrants' unionism was rooted in the community sympathy for unionism rather than in actual membership. Membership at any one time measured only a fraction of those operatives who had at one time or another been members and whose sympathies remained, but whose membership, especially during financially hard times, had lapsed.[30]

The process of assimilation into the trade union movement, although eased by the social activity and interaction of the unions, was difficult for the newly arrived workers who looked to the mill for their livelihood and their escape from rural poverty. For the immigrants, "the boss was king."[31] Even the immigrants themselves were divided. On February 13, 1884, weavers claiming to represent the French Canadian population denounced the union. Less than a week later, however, other French Canadian weavers announced that the French Canadians were joining the unions in large numbers. Even workers of the Stafford Mill, the source of the antiunion statement, were ignoring the actions of the "submissive" French Canadians who would not support the unions.[32]

In the immigrant villages, priests and shopkeepers led the attack on unionism. Eager to please the larger commercial figures of the city upon whom they depended, they urged the workers to abandon the unions. Strikers were denied credit, and scabbing was encouraged. The French Canadian textile workers who had been exposed to unionism and whose loyalty was to the community of operatives they associated with at work and at the union hall denounced the sellouts within the French Canadian village. They passed out circulars protesting the shopkeepers' position and calling for the French Canadian union supporters to encourage their comrades to abandon the false prophecy of the shopkeepers.[33]

The conflict between union supporters and union detractors often involved older French Canadians who did not participate in the class-wide institutions or socialize with unionists, and the younger French Canadians who were more likely to support the unions and not accept the mills as their savior from rural poverty. In 1884, when the mills tried to use young French Canadian workers as scabs, the youngsters refused and joined the strikers. The following day, many of these same workers were forced back into the mills by their fathers who did not support the union.[34]

Following the strike of 1884, French Canadians had achieved greater assimilation into the institutions and activities of the Fall River operatives. By the early twentieth century, they, along with the Irish and English, were considered "strong trade unionists" and, according to an Immigration Commission study, were second only to the English in percentage of union affiliation.[35]

The workers accepted the French Canadians into the ranks of the unions because they saw the importance of solidifying the whole community. They brought the French Canadians not only into the formal union movement, but into the informal activity and social center as well.

French Canadian weavers, like English and Irish weavers, experienced the terrible pressures of the looms which they were tending at increasing speeds and in greater numbers. As an anonymous Fall River weaver wrote in 1889 (and as was sung during many of the strikes), "Once you furnished good vitals to eat, and I loved your clickity-clack," "your speed they increased each day . . . but they never increased my pay," and to this the machine answered back, "it is not my fault if you don't get good vitals to eat. I'll yet furnish both meat and salt, but your master takes all the meat." These workers realized that although they worked hard at the machine, it was the owners who profited and took all "the meat." They also understood that it was not the machine which overworked them, but the owners: "You run me ten hours each day / common sense would run me six." For workers under these conditions, it was not the factory or the machine, but the overworking at the machines which generated their anger.[36] They continually experienced more and more work, yet the profits from that work seemed only to be reaped on the Hill. They were tied to machines by the bosses who cared nothing for their health or freedom. Many weavers embraced the solution proposed by a striker during the weavers' meeting of 1884: "the clearing of all the bosses out of the mills."[37]

In order to build a solid working-class community, the English and Irish, together with the French Canadians, had to develop an informal social structure whereby they could share and understand their working-class condition and, from that tradition, create organizations which would effectively "emancipate" the "factory slave" from "capitalist tyranny."[38] That informal structure was built around the activities of the strikers during strikes and their social interactions before and after the struggles. Although it is difficult to piece together that activity during periods of relative labor peace, the strikes of 1884-1894 give a glimpse of that social interaction. Spinners and weavers, especially during the early years, worked together and shared their common understanding of their position in the industrial system. The English, Irish, and French Canadians paraded together, dancing and singing the songs of discontent. During these strikes, workers took over much of the activity of the strikes themselves with spontaneous parades, rallies, and demonstrations. These activities unified them, and they soon realized the power of labor solidarity.

THE STRIKE OF 1884

Most of the strikes during this period centered around wage cuts, but they quickly took on a larger meaning: whether the workers themselves would have any control over their lives and their work. In the beginning of this period, as before, the most skilled and best organized spinners led the strikes. It was they who, following the Fall River Board of Trade announcements in January 1884 of a 10 to 12 percent reduction in wages, sent out the call for a strike.[39]

The spinners' strike soon spread to a spontaneous walkout of hundreds of other operatives. Center city mills located near the strike center experienced walkouts, especially by nonspinners, even when they were non-strike-designated mills.[40] The spinners looked to these other operatives, particularly the weavers, for support.

The spinner's activity spread to the other workers, and the community to whom the spinners appealed soon took over much of the dynamics of the strike. On the third day of the strike, operatives at the Pocasset Mill (in the central city area) held an impromptu meeting in the mill, voted to go out, gathered up their lunch pails, and left the mill in a body. Soon the streets were massed with elated strikers who felt the power of collective action and could not bring themselves to leave the scene of victory. On February 8, 1884, weavers walked out of the Barnaby Gingham Mill (in Rodman Village), despite the fact that the mill had not reduced wages and was not listed to be struck. But the spirit of struggle was in the air, and the Barnaby Gingham Mill weavers gathered in a spontaneous yard meeting, voting to walk out and demanding the firing of an abusive overseer.[41]

On the same day, operatives of all crafts met in Globe Village to formulate a plan of action for village support of the strike.[42] Three days later, on February 11, weavers in the King Philip Mills (in Globe Village) spontaneously walked out and met in a nearby vacant lot to decide upon a plan of action and demands. A committee of three English and three French Canadians was chosen and sent to the mill owners to demand the rescinding of any wage reductions. The owners offered a compromise, but the weavers voted to stay out anyway. It was decided to hold another meeting the following day to map out further action.[43]

The striking Barnaby weavers met daily in Rodman Village and held dances, while the committee was sent to negotiate with the superintendent of the mill.[44]

The excitement in the air and the spontaneous walkout of several groups of weavers led many weavers to call for a mass meeting to form a permanent weavers union. On Saturday, February 9, 1884, the weavers crowded

Carrolton Hall "to suffocation," refused admittance to local newsmen, and listened enthusiastically as speaker after speaker called for class unity and unionism. They voted to form a union and hold an organization meeting on the following day. Both men and women crowded into the hall and both were encouraged to join.[45] The women weavers were even more determined than the males in forming a militant organization. Speakers at the rally asked for "sympathy with the oppressed of all nations." They saw the strike as the tool of the working class which put the arms of the workers "in the cogs of the wheels" and stopped them.[46] The issue of wages which began the walkout had spread to that of a class struggle between the "oppressed of all nations" and "the bosses"; that oppression gave militance and focus to the strike.[47]

Not only the weavers, but also the card room operatives—who spontaneously left their jobs under the banner of "united we stand, divided we fall"—decided to organize into a union.[48] By mid-March, the loom-fixers had organized and signed up over 150 members.[49] On March 18, the women spoolers, warper-tenders, and drawing-in girls formed the Young Ladies Union of Spoolers, Warper-tenders, and Drawing-in Girls, with over two hundred members.

The spontaneous organizing efforts of the various crafts reflected the feelings of class and community solidarity. A circular sent out by the spinners suggested as much: "Remember . . . the emancipation of the working class must be achieved by the working classes themselves, and labor can stand on equal terms with capital only if united."[50] Strikers of all crafts flooded the local paper with letters and poems calling for unity and depicting the plight of the "factory slave" under the present condition.[51]

Thus defining themselves as "factory slaves," strikers argued that, although politically free, they were tied to a system which denied them control over their lives and the fruits of their labor. Under such conditions, they saw the strike not merely as a struggle for higher wages, but as a struggle for the working class.

Manufacturers responded to this strike as they had to those that preceded it with all the pressure they could bring. They too saw it as a struggle for control, and not just for higher wages. They brought in strikebreakers and attempted to isolate the union from the rest of the community by penalizing union members in other sectors of Fall River. Strikers and strike sympathizers were evicted from their homes; they were denied credit in stores which depended upon the mill family-controlled banks and real estate companies; and their relatives were discharged from nonstrike-designated mills. Company spies reported on union meetings and union activities. Workers from other communities and newly arrived immigrants were brought in and housed in guarded company barracks. Back-to-work movements were encouraged by company supporters in the French Canadian community, under the leadership of the local priests and shopkeepers.[52]

The owners also used their control over the city police force to protect knobsticks and to discourage the strikers from rallying and renewing solidarity. The police harassed strikers by preventing street gathering or catcalling against scabs, and they also coordinated an assault against the informal community institutions. Police under Sergeant Ling intimidated the strikers who gathered in Coleman's Tavern in Bowenville. Timothy McDonald complained to the union and the city that Ling interpreted the law freely in his attempt to arrest and discredit strikers. McDonald claimed that Coleman's was under constant surveillance and that union men were continually interfered with.[53] In late March, the city marshall posted notices throughout the town "forbidding tumultuous assemblies," and he authorized the police authorities and magistrates to take measures to suppress them.[54]

The workers responded to the tactics of the manufacturers by mobilizing their numbers and utilizing the power of community pressure and violence to keep the scabs out of the mills. The strikers held daily rallies and meetings to keep the ranks solid and as a show of strength to other workers. Meetings were convened for different subgroups of the community as well as for the community at large. Strikers from each mill held local strike meetings, rallies, clambakes, and fund-raising balls.[55]

The workers also appealed to community organizations, which they dominated, for aid and endorsement. In late April, twelve weeks after the strike began, the workers won the endorsement of the Hibernians, the Robert Ernets Club, the Irish-American Club, the Clanin a Geals, the Foresters, the Celtic Library, the Young Men's Protestant Society, and the Odd Fellows.[56]

The Hibernians and St. John's Society voted to hold a social benefit for the strikers, and one week later the united societies of Fall River decided to sponsor a grand concert and ball to raise funds.[57] The strikers also demanded that the Hibernians take action against any scabbing members. Patrick Henrahan was accordingly expelled from the order for "knobsticking."[58] Feelings in the community ran so deep against scabbing that Henrahan's father's milk customers refused their patronage because of his son's actions.[59]

To discourage backsliding, a striker urged the union to publish a list of all "informers, spies, and other creatures of the land," so that pressure could be directed against them.[60] The union took up the proposal in late February and began publishing the names of knobsticks who should be shunned by the rest of the community.[61] The strikers made the life of the scab as difficult as possible. In the early days of the strike, this meant harassing, booing, hissing, and throwing mud on those who attempted to pass through the crowds and enter the mills. Peter Toomey required police protection to return home safely after he broke ranks and entered the mill. Children were encouraged by their parents to throw mud and stones at scabs at the Union Mill (in Mt. Pleasant Village) in order to make the scabs see the error of their ways.[62]

In the sixth week of the strike, tensions and hostility erupted into violence. On the night of March 9, John Lee, a strikebreaker in the Sagamore Mill (in Mechanicsville), was jumped and severely beaten on his way home from work. On the way home from a saloon, "a Knobstick and a female housekeeper of a knobstick boarding house" were also attacked. Five days later, Henry Devine, "the traitor to his trade," was severely beaten after an exchange of gunfire with strikers.[63]

On March 17, a group of armed strikers attacked Patrick Fallon's boarding house, which was used to house strikebreakers. After an exchange of gunfire and rocks, Fallon was able to drive off the strikers with his own gun. Later that night, a group of men and boys attacked and beat to death John Schofield, a strikebreaker who lived in a wretched tenement on Buffington Street in Rodman Village and had been driven back to work by starvation.[64]

On March 25, a group of six armed strikers entered a brothel run by Annie Brennan, in search of knobsticks. Brennan assured the strikers that there were no such "low types" in her place, and, after a careful search, the men left.[65]

On April 24, incendiaries set three separate fires inside the Sagamore

Mill, which had continued to run despite the strike (see Photograph 14). The fire completely destroyed the five-story, twelve-year-old brick building.[66]

Despite this violence and the community support, need and hunger began to drive the workers back to work. On May 12, the newly formed Weavers Union voted to abandon its longest strike against the Crescent Mills (in the southwestern section of the city). The spinners with greater resources voted to stay out, but by the end of the month, their ranks also began to break. On May 24, spinners in the Slade and Union Mills (in Globe Village and Mt. Pleasant Village, respectively) asked to hold separate shop meetings on whether to stay out. Two days later, they voted to go back to work. In the Border City Mills (in the extreme northern section of the city), union and nonunion workers began to return to work despite the strike.[67]

Throughout the late nineteenth century, the villages most remote from the central area of union activity were the first to break ranks and desert the strike. Conversely, much of the most militant and spontaneous action came from the villages close to the center of activity. This pattern demonstrates the extent to which urban dispersion weakened community and class solidarity.

A little over a week later, June 7, the rest of the spinners voted to quit the strike and go back on the agents' terms. After eighteen weeks, one death, some injuries, a mill burned to the ground, and several members of the community permanently isolated and shamed, the strike ended in defeat. The mills, victorious again, attempted to blacklist the organizers and crush the unions. At the very moment of defeat, the community began rebuilding the unions for the next battle, which would come five years later.[68]

In the 1884 strike, the operatives proved that they could pull together. Both workers and nonworkers noted that the French Canadians, previously accused of remaining "heretofore . . . aloof from the labor movement" and of being "unreliable," were as "uncompromising and unyielding as the others and [were] eager to join the organization."[69] Some organizers even considered them the "best contributors" to the struggle.[70]

Despite the loss of the strike and ethnic and craft differences, the community of workers had been able to unite and had tried to relate their common experience to an ideology of class conflict. Upon that common experience they built a strike struggle and a union organization. Although

14. Fire in the Old Print Works

Fire was not an unknown horror for Fall River textile workers. The large amount of oil and grease which soaked into the wood, coupled with the high speeds of the machines which could easily begin burning, made the mills constant fire hazards.

the owners had defeated the strike and weakened the unions, they had not destroyed the experience of unity, having failed to understand the commonality of the workers' condition.

STRUGGLE AGAINST EXHAUSTION: THE STRIKE OF 1889

The spinners began the union movement in Fall River and led many of the early strikes, but by the late 1880s, the leadership was shifting to the weavers. The first and probably the most important reason for this shift lay in the central role which the weavers played in the struggle against speedups and stretchouts. Although the spinners also experienced the deterioration of conditions, it was the weavers who most felt the manufacturers' pressures for increased production. Their struggle against this labor-intensive pressure pushed them to center stage in the struggle against capital in Fall River. As Karl Marx observed twenty-five years earlier, "by increasing the intensity of labour, a man may be made to expend as much vital force in one hour as he formally did in two." The weavers who found themselves tending twelve looms when they had previously tended six knew Marx's meaning without ever having to read "Value, Price, and Profit." Moreover, from their experience in the mills, they also understood that "in checking this tendency of capital, by struggling for a rise of wages corresponding to the rising intensity of labour, the working man [and woman] only resists the depreciation of his labour and the deterioration of his race."[71] The weavers were on the front line in the manufacturers' battle to increase the intensity of labor, and they were in turn the most militant in opposing the manufacturers. They also moved to the front line because the Spinners Union had been weakened and had turned conservative as a result of technological change. Although Fall River still depended heavily upon skilled mule spinners, the introduction of the ring spinner in many mills, which required only unskilled female labor, had introduced an element of caution, especially among the leadership.

The weavers had collapsed temporarily after the loss of the 1884 strike. By 1889, however, under the name of the Weavers Protective Union, their membership had risen to two thousand active workers, and they claimed the support of over 75 percent of the nine thousand weavers in the city.[72]

Many considered the weavers too heterogeneous to organize.[73] More than any other department, the weavers were mixed ethnically with

French Canadians, Irish, English, and native males and females working side by side. Despite this lack of homogeneity, they were driven together by the pressure of their work, the constant speedups, and their sense of exploitation.

The weavers were continually harassed by the stretchouts and low wages. The machines dictated the weaver's pace, his only choice being whether to operate or not; at the low wages his piece work commanded, not operating meant near starvation. When coupled with low wages and lack of speed control, piece work did not mean more control over the job, but more exploitation of the worker. Most of the textile workers suffered under these pressures, but for the weaver, the central figure in the production of cloth, they were even more severe. The following anonymous song reveals the severe pressure under which the Fall River weaver labored:

> A shuttle flew swiftly through
> A tunnel of warp with its woof
> As if it knew the best it could do
> Would still meet a tyrant's reproof.
> An old man stood over the loom
> With his head dejectedly hung
> For he thought the loom a voice did assume
> And this song it derisively sung.
>
> Clickity-click, clickity-clack,
> You've got to stick till I break your back.
> Clickity-click, clickity-clack,
> The longer you stick, the worse your back.
>
> Said the old man addressing the loom
> Forty years I've served you well,
> Forty years amid sorrow and gloom,
> Forty years of earthly hell.
> But now I am old and in want
> And the hours seem doubly long
> And the pay I get is more scant;
> Then why sing such a song.

Oh, why sing clickity-click,
And why sing clickity-clack?
When hunger compels me to stick,
Though you've already ruined my back.

Once you furnished good vitals to eat,
And I loved your clickity-clack
Till others began to compete
Was then you ruined my back.
Your speed they increased each day
Till they couldn't increase anymore,
But they never increased my pay,
And that's why my heart feels sore.

When you sing your clickity-click
Though hunger compels me to stick
And then with a clickity-clack,
You inform me you'll break my back.

Said the loom, "It is not my fault
If you don't get good vitals to eat.
I'll yet furnish both meat and salt
But your master takes all the meat.
You run me ten hours each day
Common sense would run me six,
While demand must all wages fix."

"So I'll sing my clickity-click
And I'll sing my clickity-clack.
As long as you're able to stick
I'll stop when I break your back."

Heartbroken the old man fell;
The last straw had just touched his back.
And the loom ran his funeral knell
With its clickity, clickity-clack.
In a pine box they bore him away
A worn-out forsaken old hack

And the loom for another next day
Sang gaily its clickity-clack.

And this song of the loom
T'is imprinted on each weaver's back
Many millions it has sung to the tomb
With its clickity-clack.[74]

The pressures on the weavers continued throughout the nineteenth and early twentieth centuries. In 1972, a retired garment worker explained that she quit the mills and entered the garment shops in the late 1920s, despite her parents' pressure to stay in the mills, because "every time I put the shuttle in the loom there was a tear." A 1904 worker complained that working twelve looms "makes you crazy watch' 'em."[75] The machines were so fast that even in 1889 Fall River weavers made more hourly than other New England weavers, even though the city's piece rates were significantly lower.

In the 1880s and 1890s, the weavers struggled to maintain their wage rates, hoping that once liberated from the yoke of below-subsistence wages, they could relax their speed, have greater control over the job, and take more breaks.[76] By the end of the century, however, the pressure of speedups was so great that they were striking to work less looms, despite the loss of pay.[77]

In March 1889, the weavers began to hold daily meetings to protest their low wages. On March 7, 1889, at separate meetings in Globe Village and Border City, they voted overwhelmingly to strike for higher wages. On March 8, they packed the union meeting screaming for strike, and they overwhelmingly voted to go out on March 11. In order to discourage knobsticking, the crowd voted to have the union print up and display the names of anyone going to work. The meeting broke up after calling for a 10:00 A.M. rally on March 11.[78]

The following night, the weavers held another rally and encouraged the French Canadians in particular to join the struggle. Many of the speeches were in French, and the French Canadians appeared to local observers to be "enthusaistic" about the strike. The Granite Mill (in Flint Village) weavers, who had a separate organization, met and voted to join the growing strike movement.[79]

When the whistles blew on Monday morning, March 11, the mills did not reverberate with the noise of the shuttles banging back and forth between the warp. All but a few of the city's mills were quiet. Only a handful of the city's nine thousand weavers attempted to pass through the angry crowds that gathered at the gates to witness their success in halting the machines. Almost half of the city's weavers gathered at the Fall River Park for a rally, despite the cold March winds blowing in from the harbor.[80] Following the rally, the weavers drifted about town talking to friends and dropping in at the union hall. Throughout the day, the hall was "thronged with people" talking about the strike, meeting friends, or signing up with the union.[81]

On Tuesday, even fewer weavers entered the mills. After picketing the gates, over five thousand weavers gathered on Pleasant Street in Mt. Pleasant Village and, led by a fife and drum, marched to the park in Little Canada where they heard union leaders urge them to remain solid.[82] After the rally the weavers broke up, with some going to the union hall and others drifting back to their separate districts to organize nightly meetings and rallies within the villages.

On the third day of the strike, a reporter from the local paper which had argued against the strike visited the union hall and reported that it had become a social club for the strikers. Workers made idle by the strike sat around playing cards, checkers, or dominoes, or simply read the papers and talked to friends. For many strikers who lived outside the center of town, the strike gave them an opportunity to visit the union hall and socialize with weavers from other areas. Although the women were members of the union, they did not participate in the social activity around the union hall; the union, therefore, decided to plan activities specifically to include female weavers.[83]

Thursday, March 14, produced an even larger rally and parade than Tuesday's and ended with a songfest of labor and protest songs.[84] On March 15, despite bad weather, hundreds of striking weavers held an impromptu rally in the rain and denounced the scabs and the company. Expressing the anger and frustrations of many, one weaver shouted that "a little dose such as the anarchists gave the police in Chicago would be a fit remedy to some of the agents of this city."[85] Considering the attitude of the rest of the country toward the violence in Chicago, this statement reflected the extreme feelings of some of the Fall River workers.[86]

The Granite Mill weavers organized their own social events and met daily for concerts and dances in Flint Village. After a rally and meeting, the weavers enjoyed a concert at Foresters' Hall where a local weaver "ground out music on his accordion for quadrilles, reels, jigs, and waltzes until the 12:00 bells."[87] French Canadians, English, Irish, and native Americans would all participate in these social exchanges which helped break down ethnic barriers and weld the community together.

On Saturday, one week after the strike began, the weavers were holding firm. Despite a heavy rain, they marched to Quinn Woodland and Company Hall singing an enthusiastic version of "Hold the Fort," and they listened to speeches calling for unity and solidarity. The Darvel weavers met earlier in the central city area so as to march to the rally in a body and thereby demonstrate that their ranks were solid and their spirit united in struggle.[88] Throughout the strike, local areas were the center for strike activity and integrated strikers into the struggle. Each mill and each district held its own daily rallies in the afternoon to keep everyone solid. This type of federalism and local competition to prove militancy and strength helped the union hold the widespread and diverse community together. It also gave rise to isolation and local back-to-work movements in the more isolated villages such as Border City where the union was not so strong.[89]

On March 20, the Bourne Mill weavers, from the southern edge of Globe Village bordering Rhode Island, who had previously not been on strike, left the mills en masse and marched to the union rally to join the walkout. At a rally of their own, French Canadian speakers urged the French Canadian weavers to join ranks with all the striking weavers of the city.[90]

The manufacturers admitted to a local reporter that they could afford the wage increase but that they did not want to capitulate to union demands: "We positively will not recognize the Weavers Union if the mills remain closed until the belts rot on the shafts."[91] To the manufacturers the struggle was not over wages but over job control. If they yielded to the strike demands, then the strikers would have a say over working conditions. The profits of greater labor intensity would be siphoned off in wage increases, thus directly affecting the manufacturers' control over the production process.

On Friday evening, March 22, when the Seaconnet Mill closed, a crowd of fifteen hundred angry strikers was on hand to greet the scabs as they came out. The strikebreakers were forced to run a "gauntlet of hoots, hisses and yells of 'knobsticks' and 'scabs'" until they reached Pleasant Street in Mt. Pleasant Village, when the frustration of the crowd reached a breaking point and the strikebreakers were stoned and beaten.[92] Although the violence brought condemnation from some quarters, it was effective. According to an overseer of the Seaconnet Mill, the violence prevented further strikebreaking: "The weavers will be afraid to return to work now."[93]

Over the weekend, the mill owners decided to attempt to open on Monday, March 25, and to break the strike. The union responded by staging a massive rally on Saturday and local rallies and meetings in the various sections of the city, especially in the more isolated areas of Border City (see Photograph 15) and Flint Village, where they expected a break in the ranks. On Monday, the weavers turned out in even greater numbers than before and urged the continuation of the struggle despite the lack of union funds.[94]

On March 26, the union leadership, worried about the fate of the union in a protracted losing battle, voted to present the weavers at the mass meeting scheduled for March 27 with a resolution to quit the strike. At that meeting, the reading of the resolution was greeted with "No! No!" from the crowd. The leadership, arguing that to continue the strike would very likely mean the death of the union, was able to convince the weavers to go back and build a better organization for a future strike. After the speeches, a slight majority of the crowd voted to return to work and to build and organize for the next strike.[95]

The weavers lost the strike, but they were able to keep their organization together. They had demonstrated that they could mount an effective strike and unify the disparate weavers. They brought French Canadian, Irish, English, and native men and women together not only in struggle, but also in social activities—dances, concerts, clambakes, and other social gatherings. The weavers had forged a community from among their ranks.[96]

Through these activities they both demonstrated and cemented their solidarity. The informality and spontaneity of the strike encouraged interaction and reinforced a sense of collective power and unity. Since no one was excluded from the rallies, demonstrations, and mass meetings of the strikers, all felt they had a full part in the struggle. Rank-and-file activity broke down divisions between the leadership and par-

15. Old Border City Mill (Now a Garment Factory)

The mill was typical of many of the mills built in Fall River in the late nineteenth century. It was located on the extreme northern edge of the city, removed from the central social area. The walk from Border City to the downtown or the parks just south of the downtown areas, which were used for rallies, demonstrations, and meetings, was almost prohibitive for the residents of the Border City area. Border City was usually the last to go out on strike and the first to break ranks and go back.

ticipants, as well as between the primarily English and Irish leadership and the heterogeneous community.

ORGANIZATION AND SPONTANEITY: THE STRIKE OF 1894

In 1890, the weavers reorganized into the Weavers Progressive Association, which by the end of the year was considered one of the most powerful unions in the city. The carders, encouraged by the weavers, reorganized in the early 1890s into the Card Room Protective Association, with almost 75 percent of the members women and children. Even the conservative loomfixers reorganized. Under the pressure of a 15 percent reduction in 1893 and with the aid of the weavers, the slasher-tenders and drawing-in girls reformed into a more permanent union.[97]

In the summer of 1894, the Fall River Board of Trade announced a 10 percent reduction in wages which would go into effect on August 20.[98] On August 10, Thomas Evens, a local labor leader and spokesman for the workers in Fall River, urged the operatives to unite and attack the capitalists on all fronts to "deem capitalist tyranny."[99] On August 13, the five unions of the Fall River textile workers formed an amalgamation in order to coordinate a joint attack on the manufacturers and the Board of Trade. However, the amalgamated, fearing a losing struggle and failing to bluff the manufacturers into rescinding the reduction, backed down and accepted the reduction under protest.[100] When the weavers were asked to uphold the decision of the amalgamation, they voted seven to one against accepting the reduction and decided instead to stay out of the mills on a four-week vacation.

On the first day of the reduction, a majority of the weavers stayed out of all but the Iron Works Mills, which had not reduced wages. Robert Howard of the Spinners Union, anxious that the weavers' action might lead the spinners in their weakened situation to stay out, urged his members to remain calm.[101] Even though several spinners urged their union to strike in support of their brother and sister weavers, the leadership was able to keep a tight rein on the members, and by a close vote it was decided to wait at least a week before voting on a strike.[102]

In the second week of the strike, the carders, under the leadership of thirty-year-old James Tansey who had recently arrived from Lancashire, voted to go out in support of the weavers.[103] The Amalgamated Council of all unions, hoping to end the strike before it dissipated union funds, sent a committee to the manufacturers asking that the reduction be rescinded. The manufacturers refused to talk to the operators.[104] The carders and weavers greeted this news with votes to remain out until the old rates were reinstated. The spinners and slasher-tenders voted to go out with the others.[105] On September 26 and 27, over a month after the weavers began their walkout, the mills attempted to reopen, hoping that four weeks of no wages would force enough workers back into the mills to begin operation. Although there was some break in the ranks, especially in the more isolated mills in Border City and Flint Village where the workers were less involved in the strike activity, the majority of workers remained out.[106]

On October 11, the manufacturers changed their tactics from resistance to manipulation. Hoping to break the ranks of the strikers, create distrust and discouragement, and thus start a general back-to-work movement, the manufacturers offered the spinners a 5 percent reduction, leaving the others at 10 percent, but promising to rescind it if the market improved.[107] After much arguing, Robert Howard was able to persuade a majority of the spinners to accept the 5 percent reduction and quit the strike. The weavers and carders were shocked by what they considered a "sellout" by the leadership of the Spinners Union.[108] The following day at a regular meeting, the weavers voted not to go back to work and to protest the spinners' sellout.[109]

When the mills opened on Monday, October 15, five thousand workers paraded the streets in protest, and fewer weavers entered the mills than had at the start of the strike. The march, swelling to six thousand as it passed by the mills, gathered in the park to protest the opening of the mills. The rally ended with another impromptu march through the city, with the crowds singing and chanting songs of victory.[110]

On October 17, the weavers began gathering in the center of the city for a march. One thousand marched en masse from Bowenville with chants proclaiming their solidarity and militancy. By 10:00 A.M., the march which paraded through the streets, passing many mills, had grown to seven thousand. Many weavers who had not supported the strike or had gone back after over two months of no wages left their looms to join the demonstration as it passed by the mills. Over two thousand of the marchers were women, some of them well over fifty years of age.[111] The tactic which began as a spontaneous response to the attempted reopening of the mills proved effective in holding the ranks solid and in drawing knobsticks out of the mills. As the days went by and the parades continued, more and more workers left the mills and joined the struggle. A local observer unsympathetic to the strike claimed that "the parades through Flint Village last week had a demoralizing effect in that vicinity. The mills in that section have been losing ever since and this morning there were less looms running than there were Saturday." The strikers kept up enthusaism by supplementing the parades with local shop meetings all over the city to prevent any area from losing contact with the strike movement.[112]

On Monday, October 22, the weavers organized one of the largest demonstrations and marches ever held in the city. Over ten thousand weavers, carders, and supporters gathered in the park, with many sections marching to the demonstration from their own villages in a body chanting and singing. Following the rally, the march weaved through the city, passing mills and urging scab workers to join them. Each mill still in operation emptied out workers into the parade.[113] On October 24, the weavers with their ranks still strong, asked for a conference with the manufacturers, hoping to win a compromise. The manufacturers refused to meet.[114]

The strikers were now feeling the pinch of debt and lack of credit.[115] On October 29, after two months of struggle and with their ranks still solid, the weavers and carders voted to quit the strike before hunger drove them back against the strike pledge.[116] The weavers had again proven that they could remain unified and keep their ranks tight, but they were not able to command the solidarity of the spinners who, although small, had one of the best organized unions in the city. Their failure to maintain the support of the spinners convinced them of the importance of building a powerful amalgamation of textile workers.

The late nineteenth-century strikes had involved the whole community. The union had successfully mobilized the community around the issues of job control and wages, and had involved it in daily demonstrations as well as more formal union activities. They had been able to mobilize the community because the community felt it was part of the struggle. They had been able to hold community support and maintain their struggle against the manufacturers because their members saw the commonality of their condition and shared that understanding with the community. It lost these strikes not because of the failure of the union or the community, but because the manufacturers were able to hold out beyond the resources of the community.

10

The Twentieth Century: Unity and Fragmentation

The difficult but successful process of developing working-class cooperation among the French Canadian, English, and Irish immigrants in Fall River is in marked contrast to the response of the working-class community to the arrival of the Portuguese and Polish immigrants around 1900. Although the Poles and Portuguese stood by the unions during the strikes, they were not accepted into the social activity of the unions.

The 1904 strike marked the beginning of community fragmentation into separate ethnic units of social activity and the failure of the unions to act as socializing and integrating institutions. Although Fall River workers demonstrated unprecedented unity during the strike itself, there were signs of growing divisions between the English-speaking and non-English-speaking workers which hardened as time wore on. Despite tremendous hardships, wage-earners joined together during the strike, but their leadership and their formal institutions failed to support that unity or build upon it. In response to the increased number of Portuguese and Polish workers, the unions abandoned their social role and their position of speaking for the community as a whole. Beginning to lose sight of their class identification, they increasingly functioned as "business unions." They began to represent only their own members and craft. This happened at the same time that structural changes occurred: they were acting more as industrial unions, in response to the industry and to the tactics of the manufacturers. The unions began to coordinate the collective action of all workers as the only tactical response to employers; yet, socially they were moving in the opposite direction.

By the 1920s, the divisions which first emerged at the end of the 1904 strike had become widespread; by then, too, the working class had abandoned the informal interactions by which the whole community could be integrated into the struggle. In 1899, the Fall River textile unions formed the Textile Council, elected James Tansey president, and began coordinating and negotiating for all of the city's textile workers. By 1900, it appeared that labor was moving into the camp of the industrial unionists. Yet, conditions in the industry and in the community would radically change that direction in the coming years. Between 1890 and 1900, Fall River added almost a million more spindles to its factories. Profits were high in 1900 and the city's future as an industrial center seemed secure; that prosperity brought its workers jobs and a limited amount of security. Conditions were not *that* stable for wage-earners, however. Severe competition from the growing southern textile centers where wages were lower and machinery more modern was on the horizon. By the turn of the century, Fall River manufacturers were forced to increase the labor intensity of their work force in order to compete, and the workers saw the cracks in their limited security. As in the 1894 strike, union leadership began to retrench into craft unionism, especially after the 1904-1905 downturn.[1]

The economic depression in the textile industry was not the only cause of the shift toward conservative unionism. The move toward industrial unions was also halted by the immigration of the Portuguese and Eastern European workers who flooded Fall River around 1900. Following the strike of 1904, in which both skilled and unskilled and immigrant and native-born demonstrated unity and solidarity, Fall River unions retreated from an ideology which emphasized the unity of the whole class into craft-oriented business unionism. The new immigrant workers were not encouraged to join the established unions, nor did the established unions act in unity with nonskilled workers. James Tansey withdrew from the presidency of the United Textile Workers in 1903, and in 1908, weavers and slasher-tenders unions also left— with the support of the Fall River Central Labor Union which refused to expel them, despite AF of L pressure. Seven years later, the other locals deserted the United Textile Workers, and in 1916, they formed the conservative National Association of Textile Operators. These unions accused the United Textile Workers of failing to protect the skilled positions which were dominated by the English, Irish, and French Canadian workers.[2]

This craft ideology resulted from the skilled operatives' fear of the immigrant worker and did not reflect the functioning or success of the Fall River unions. The restrictive craft approach was not a tactical decision, for since the late 1890s the unions, through the Textile Council, had been functioning as an industrial union. The Textile Council, in the words of the National Labor Relations Board, "although . . . represent [ing] only craft locals . . . nevertheless customarily bargained for all employees in the plants."[3] The National Labor Relations Board found that in Fall River the "crafts were merely arbitrarily defined segments of an integrated operation, and where bargaining by crafts had always been on an industrial basis."[4]

The craft unions had depended upon the unskilled and semiskilled workers to follow their direction and carry out "industrial strikes," but the unions became more and more indifferent to the unorganized unskilled or semiskilled workers.[5] The labor community had divided along ethnic lines, even though functionally it depended upon a united community.

Following the strike of 1904, the English, Irish, and French Canadian workers and their unions continued to withdraw from the community. The new workers who entered the work force did not participate in union activity and were not part of a labor community tied together by union activity. They were isolated in their own ethnic communities and were only able to break out in the second quarter of the twentieth century.

Fall River workers in the nineteenth century took pride in their tradition of militancy; they were particularly proud that their unions had made the city famous as a radical union center.[6] By the early twentieth century, workers were losing touch with that tradition. Younger members of the work force were not part of the strong union movement. The unions had withdrawn so extensively into the upper reaches of the skilled crafts that the workers below had little consciousness of their existence. When asked in 1973 if Fall River was a union town or had a union tradition, retired Polish, Portuguese, and even French Canadian workers responded negatively: "There was no talk about unions."[7] "There was no such thing as unions in 1925 in Fall River." "It was after 1930 that the unions got active in Fall River."[8] The workers had lost continuity with their union past because the community institutions which would have passed on the tradition had fragmented under excessive on-the-job pressure and alienation, and continual immigration of new members of the work force. As the work became more exhausting and alienating under the stretchout system, the workers had less energy or inclination to keep the informal class institutions viable. In turn, these institutions became more formalized and removed from the direct participation of the workers. The city itself became more spread out, breaking up central areas where the working class gathered. When the new immigrants began to flood the city, the class institutions, especially the trade unions, were unable to integrate them into the informal structure which itself was becoming less important.

THE STRIKE OF 1904

Between 1894 and 1904, the time of the great strike, Fall River's working-class community organized under the Textile Council to prevent the division between the trades which had occurred during the 1894 strike. The council was given authority to negotiate with the manufacturers and to direct strikes, acting for all the operatives and speaking for no single craft. With support and pressure from the Textile Council, the AF of L chartered the United Textile Workers of America in 1901, with James Tansey as the first president from 1901 until 1903. The new union was located in Fall River, which was its strongest center.[9] By 1904, Fall River workers belonged to a craft union which was part of the city-wide Textile Council, which itself was part of the city-wide Textile Council, which itself was part of the National United Textile Workers of America, AF of L.

Structurally, the operatives were united. Through the strikes of 1884, 1889, and 1894, they had proved that they could unite the community behind them and even integrate the French Canadian workers into their movement. They had built a united trade union movement which gave them an organized community-wide structure with which to take on the manufacturers.

Between 1894 and 1904, however, the working-class community had undergone a change which the workers did not control. On one level, the already excessive "drive" increased. Weavers could barely keep up with the eight looms the manufacturers required them to work. Between 1900 and 1904, the manufacturers increased the work load to ten to twelve looms, without, in many cases, improving the looms: "They gave us twelve looms, I didn't see that we could make it out alive at all. They talk about the electric stop makin' it easy. The girls say it's harder anyway with twelve looms and you don't make as much. We never seen no electric stop in our mill—just got four more straight looms."[10]

The workload had increased so greatly that the textile worker felt the pressure of the job from the time of the rising bell to the exhausting tramp home at the end of the day. After a hasty breakfast, the workers found their machines before the break of day. No longer could they spend a few minutes before operating talking to friends at the mill gates. The early hours were spent "prepar[ing] their work for the moment when the wheels begin to roar at 6:30." The noon meal "was eaten from the floor of the mill" and had to be rushed even more than usual, for the time was "encroached upon by more cleaning and preparing the machines."[11] One weaver claimed that he had to quit work every so often to "recuperate because the work was so hard."[12] The stretchouts which affected almost all of the textile operatives tired them so much that they had less time and energy to socialize after work; they also had less time and possibility for socializing on the job. Workers were now expected to tend several more machines, were further separated from each other, and had little opportunity for contact with fellow operatives while on the job. They were quickly becoming isolated workers lost amongst a sea of machines.[13]

The workload was not the only change faced by the workers in 1904. The *Massachusetts Labor Bulletin* observed that

the nationality of the operatives is changing. . . . Some time since the textile foreign population in Massachusetts was largely English, but we find them supplemented by French Canadians, who in turn gave way largely to the Portuguese. Now the Poles, Jews, and Greeks in large numbers are being employed in textile work.[14]

A worker in one plant expressed her consciousness of a change in the ethnicity of the work force when she complained of the workload: "But that don't make no matter—there's plenty waiting at the gates for our jobs, I guess. The Polaks learn weaving quick, and they just as soon live on nothing as work like that," and there was also the "Portagee," waiting to be let into the community of workers.[15]

As noted earlier, the "Portagees" first began to move into Fall River at the end of the nineteenth and early twentieth centuries. When they arrived, they were initially used in the most unskilled positions as bobbin boys, doffers, combers, drawers, twisters, spoolers, beamers, and eventually carders, and even weavers. The Portuguese communities, one located in the south end of the city and the other between the river and Little Canada, grew at a tremendous rate, so that by 1922, they outnumbered all other foreign-born groups.[16]

With their darker skin and even stranger languages, the Portuguese and Poles were even more alien to the extisting working-class community than the French Canadians were. Their customs, too, were even more different than those of the French Canadians. The poverty they were forced to live in shocked the other workers and came to be identified as a character trait rather than as a symptom of their exploitation. The Portuguese and Poles were actually believed to desire poverty and unbearable working conditions: "Poles and Portuguese, who live in crowded tenements . . . will sleep and live and eat according to the needs of the employers."[17]

Between 1895 and 1905, over eight thousand Portuguese immigrated into Fall River. This was but the first wave of the tide, but it was sufficiently large to affect the community structure and change the pattern of class and union behavior. In the very heat of the 1904 strike, the president of the United Textile Workers qualified his praise of the newly arrived immigrant groups "for the splendid way in which they have stood by their English-speaking brothers and sisters" by stating that he hoped "all questions of nationality will be buried *for the time being.*"[18]

The social activities which had been so important in the nineteenth century in integrating new workers into the union ended with the 1904 strike. After 1905, union members withdrew from the working-class community and saw themselves purely as skilled craft workers. They encouraged the division between skilled and unskilled workers, and between the older ethnic groups and the newly arrived Portuguese and Polish workers. This division was even greater in Fall River, the center of trade unionism, than it was in Lawrence, Lowell, or New Bedford.[19] A 1956 study of textile workers maintained that in the early twentieth century "members of the [Fall River] unions differed from the rest of the workers by skill and national background."[20]

Traditionally, the work place and the community were central to the integration process of new members of the work force. It was in the work place that newcomers learned their jobs and their larger role as members of the industrial labor force. There they met members of different nationalities and shared their common experience as workers. The commonality of that experience was analyzed in the community. Community institutions gave meaning and definition to their position in the industrial world, and provided the base for a common working-class culture. From the 1880s to World War I, a combination of factors both on the job and in the community began to hinder their functioning as integrative forces. The increased speedups and stretchouts isolated the workers on the job. The increased dispersal of the city and the greater isolation of ethnic neighborhoods worked to weaken class-wide community institutions. When, after 1900, job competition and recession in the textile industry added to occupational insecurity, the established unions and their membership, isolated on and off the job, retreated into the apparent safety of craft identity and business unionism which hopefully would protect them.

Although engaged in Fall River's largest and most prolonged struggle, the unions deliberately excluded strikers from union halls unless they came for business and called off public demonstrations. No longer were the dances, parades, and clambakes held. The strike was conducted in the most organized and businesslike fashion possible. Its very orderliness drew praise from several sides.[21]

The strike of 1904, like the strikes of 1889 and 1894, was prompted by a combination of wage reductions and increased "drive" on the weavers and, as in the earlier strikes, the weavers were the leading force behind the walkout. The Northrop loom, introduced in 1898, enabled a weaver to handle more than eight looms and was widely used in the newly developing textile areas of the South and rural New England. In order to meet this competition, Fall River manufacturers increased the number of looms per weaver to ten, twelve, or even fourteen. They added to the looms the "long bobbin" which held more thread and required less changing. On the looms themselves, an electric warp thread-breaker, or electric stop-motion, was added which would stop the loom if a thread broke.[22] In some mills, additional looms were added without any change.[23]

The weavers claimed that the additional looms were too much to work, even with the electric stop-motion, and that the larger bobbins caused more breaks in the yarn, requiring more stops and harder work. Although the weavers admitted they could make more money on the twelve-loom system, they argued that the increase would not compensate for the extra "drive."[24]

During the early part of the century, weavers in several mills successfully struck against the ten- and twelve-loom system, returning to work on eight looms at a loss of 10 to 20 percent in pay.[25] Where the Northrop or Draper looms were introduced, the weavers accepted the increase. It was the increase with the modified and ordinary looms that the weavers opposed.[26]

In November 1903, the manufacturers, in an attempt to combat the rising costs of cotton and the decreased demand for cotton cloth, decided to reduce wages 10 percent through the Cotton Manufacturers Association, an outgrowth of the old Board of Trade. The Textile Council voted, without dissent, to accept the reduction resulting from the depressed condition of trade.

From November 1903 until July 1904, however, few of the city's mills ran continuously, and the speedups and stretchouts caused considerable bitterness among the operatives. Complaining of working conditions, weavers refused to go back to work in several mills after shutdowns.[27] On April 8, 1904, the weavers in the Bourne Mills (in southern Globe Village), who were particularly hard hit by stretchouts as they were expected to work twenty modified looms, voted to strike. The strikers attempted to keep the spirit of the strike alive through meetings and rallies as had been done in 1889 and 1894.[28] The mills remained open by using scabs willing to risk humiliation and violence. The striking weavers gathered at Tierney's Saloon and hissed, booed, and threatened strikebreakers as they entered the mill. One loomfixer, Joseph Provost, was attacked and beaten on his way home from work.[29]

At the general weavers' meeting of May 3, complaints about the stretchout dominated the discussion. On May 12, the weavers' meeting was filled to capacity with members demanding that the union act to stop the increase in looms. They voted to have the executive committee immediately formulate plans of action.[30] On May 23, one hundred weavers from the Seaconnet Mills (in Rodman Village) walked off the job in protest of the additional looms. Only a minority of those leaving were union members. The sentiment against overwork was unanimous and militant. The striking workers formed their own committee to negotiate with the manufacturers and bring about a change in job conditions.[31] On June 8, three hundred Chace Mill (also in Rodman Village) weavers walked off, protesting the electric-stop motion. Many weavers claimed that the strike was the beginning of a general strike over job conditions in Fall River.[32] At the June 9 union meeting, the members voted to endorse the Chace Mill strike and denounce the speedups. Despite this continual agitation by the membership, the secretary of the union remained cautious, maintaining that the strikes and grievances were really an issue of wages, and discouraging the membership from taking any rash action.[33] Nonetheless, the weavers called for a special union meeting to protest the stretchouts and the manufacturers' attempts to "disrupt the union." The members held shop meetings in every mill in the city to protest the stretchouts. Women particularly complained of having to work too many looms and signed up for the union in ever-increasing numbers.[34]

The slasher-tenders also went out on isolated strikes over job conditions during the tense period in late 1903 and early 1904. Their actions, like those of the weavers, were usually spontaneous walkouts by the rank and file.[35]

On July 14, 1904, the mill agents posted notices of a 12.5 percent reduction of wages to begin July 25. The reduction followed a signed agreement by the mill agents "of a common stand . . . regarding wages even in the future in order to keep wages permanently lower."[36] The response of the workers was hostile and immediate. The reduction ignited the fires of resistance, inasmuch as it was announced at a time when the atmosphere was already tense, when "slasher-tenders have to run extra machines, drawing-in girls have been reduced due to machinery changes, loomfixers have had their number of looms increased, and weavers were asked to run ten looms on an eight loom basis or . . . twelve to fourteen."[37] As one spinner stated, "four or five first-class funerals among those who have charge of the corporations in the city [would be a] blessing."[38]

The *Fall River Globe,* realizing that a vote of the membership "in their present temper would result in a strike," hoped that the "leaders" would be able to control "the violent feelings of the operatives."[39] The paper did recognize, however, that if there was a strike, "it would be brought by the weavers."

On July 18, the Textile Council voted against a strike and recommended that the union members vote against striking. The council also voted to allow each member union to take separate strike votes.[40] On July 20, the unions voted on what action to take. The leadership of the spinners and carders was able to keep the pro-strike forces in their unions just short of the needed two-thirds majority, but the loomfixers, slasher-tenders, and weavers all voted overwhelmingly for a strike. The leadership of the weavers and loomfixers urged their members to vote against the strike, but the mood of the workers was so bitter that those opposed to the strike did not even come to the meeting. After the vote, thousands of weavers marched through the streets cheering for strike.[41] Following the vote of the weavers, slasher-tenders, and loomfixers, the carders and spinners voted to join the strike and thus make the strike unanimous.

At 5:50 A.M. on July 25, the waking whistles blew. Again at 6:00 and at 6:30 they blew, but the mills remained quiet. Twenty-three thousand operatives stayed home on the first day of the biggest strike in Fall River's history. Except for the Fall River Iron Works and a few small mills which did not belong to the Cotton Manufacturers Association and which did not reduce wages, the mills shut their gates for the day and sent the overseers home.[42]

The unions discouraged their members from congregating either at the union halls or in the streets or near the mills, but the workers still gathered at the plant gates to prevent scabbing. There were too few scabs to make waiting worthwhile, so after a few minutes the crowds broke up and the strikers drifted home.

Both the union and nonunion operatives remained solid in their opposition to the mill owners and in their support of the strike. Leaders of the various unions complimented all "for their stand both union and non-union."[43] Jackson, secretary of the slasher-tenders, praised the non-unionists for rallying to the cause: "Although we have not got all the operatives of the city into our organizations, when our cause is just we can depend upon them as well as upon the union men and women to help us out."[44] The Textile Council, organized after the strike of 1894 to represent all the operatives of the city, reaffirmed that position at the outset of the strike: "In this strike all operatives are brothers and sisters fighting for one common cause and there will be no discrimination made on the part of these committees between union and non-union operatives."[45]

The unskilled immigrant workers supported the struggle and remained out with their union "brothers and sisters," despite the skepticism of many union workers.[46] Staying out caused great suffering for the immigrant. The unskilled nonunion workers had the greatest burden to bear during the strike. They were less likely to belong to a benefit organization and did not have the advantage of union strike benefits. In most cases, the immigrants could not apply to the city for aid because they had not lived there long enough to establish residence.[47] By August, many of them were forced to live in tents set up on the beaches.[48] In order to remain out, they had to depend on the support and solidarity of the skilled workers for their survival.

The union leaders simply expected the support of the nonunion workers and had little appreciation of either their solidarity or their consequent suffering. Their solidarity was expected on the basis of past experience and it was no longer cultivated. The secretary of the spinners expressed his expectation when reporting on the progress of the strike:

> The non-union operatives are with us and will stand with us until the last ditch. It is only extreme cases of suffering that will cause them to enter the mill gates. . . . They stood by us in 1894 until the last minute. There are any number of non-union help in the city who have saved up sufficient money to struggle alone.[49]

James Tansey echoed this acceptance of nonunion help: "There never was a strike in this city where the non-union people were not with the union and stayed out until the strike was declared off. That has been the experience of all strikes in this city."[50]

John Golden, president of the United Textile Union, emphasized the division between the unionists and nonunionists in his description of the situation: "Eight thousand textile workers, or all of the skilled were organized in Fall River; the remainder, consisting largely of women, are not organized."[51] Golden's statement is revealing in its inaccuracy. Union membership in Fall River was closer to forty-five hundred than to eight thousand, and even if it were eight thousand, to relegate twenty thousand textile workers to the category of "the remainder" at the very least misrepresents the proportion of union workers to nonunion workers.[52] If only males were union members, and this was not the case, half the remaining workers would also be males; thus, the remainder did not "consist largely of women" but was fairly evenly divided between males and females. The remainder, however, did consist largely of foreigners, a growing number of whom were Portuguese and Polish. Golden's flippant dismissal of almost twenty thousand operatives, both male and female, reflects the failure of the union leadership and the skilled union members to see the newly arrived immigrant workers as equal members of the community, or even as co-members of a community of operatives. The leaders of the skilled workers saw themselves as one community "followed" by others.[53]

Golden's conception of the nonunionists following the unionists out "as in the past" distorts the past experience of Fall River workers as well. In many cases, the unionists followed the nonunionists, or, more often, the unionists and nonunionists were indistinguishable in their struggles to stop the mills. Golden also failed to understand the active role women played in the struggles of the operative class in Fall River, not only in the past but in the 1904 strike as well. Much of the push to go out in the 1904 strike came from women who were opposed to the increased workload:

> Those who have looked into the matter closely believe that the bottom line of the intense anger which is found among the operatives is in large part drawn by the feelings of . . . women. Union leaders and overseers all felt that it was the class of women employed in the mills who are thoroughly steeped in anger and who are heard from at times in a way that leaves the settlement of the strike a very questionable matter for weeks to come.[54]

It would appear that on many levels the men were following the women. By denying the community among the union and nonunion workers in past struggles and by not recognizing the active participation by women and immigrants in the present struggle, Golden reflected the feelings of many of the skilled English-speaking workers. They did not see the immigrants as part of their community and denied that community in the past.

By the first week of August, nonunion workers were coming to the union offices "clamouring for aid."[55] The unions reported that "the greatest proportion of calls for relief have come from the Portuguese," despite the fact that contingents of nonunion French Canadians from Globe Village had also marched on the office demanding food.[56]

By the middle of the fourth week of the strike, the ethnic and craft divisions within the community began to emerge, with the skilled English,

Irish, and French Canadian unionists taking the lead in creating the division. On August 17, the unions and the Textile Council, set up to represent all operatives, decided to divide the union and nonunion members and relegate nonunionists to secondary importance. Aid and attention would be devoted to union members. The labor leaders set up two separate funds, one for union members and one for nonunionists. The state Board of Charity was expected to pick up much of the nonunion relief, and when enough donations came in, funds would be diverted for nonunion relief.[57]

When asked whether ignoring nonunionists would hurt the strike, Thomas O'Donnell of the spinners expressed indifference to the unskilled and semiskilled workers. He argued that it would make no difference if the nonunionists returned to work, for the unionized skilled workers could win the strike themselves.[58]

On September 1, a relief committee formed by the union refused aid to the Portuguese community until the committee could thoroughly investigate the "colony." When committee representatives did try to investigate, they were treated with hostility and abused as spies. The Portuguese colony, while in the midst of great deprivation and struggle, resented the patronizing attitudes of the committee and treated its representatives as symbols of that degradation even at the risk of losing the aid. The committee responded to the colony's protests by cutting off aid until the Portuguese accepted the investigation.[59]

That year, the unions voted against holding a Labor Day demonstration. The leaders believed that, although Labor Day demonstrations had been a traditional symbol of unity, they might arouse too much excitement and bitterness among the workers. They voted instead to save their funds for the struggle which lay before them.[60] They also discouraged socializing or gathering at the union halls. Even members were encouraged to come to the union only for business and then to leave.[61]

On October 3, after thirty-nine days of strike, the Weavers Union, which in 1889 and 1894 had held daily parades, rallies, and dances, convened its very first mass meeting. The crowd that jammed the Bijou Theater, most of them women, enthusiastically shouted for solidarity and unity.[62] The following day, the unions held their first event of the strike, a rally for Samuel Gompers who came to encourage the unionists "to stand up against the degradation of slavery."[63]

On November 14, after sixteen weeks of strike, the mills decided to open their gates. On the first day of the attempted opening, the workers remained home. With the exception of five hundred operatives who gathered around the Chace Mills to harass the scabs, most of the workers obeyed the unions' request not to leave home.[64]

By late November, most of the mills had given up attempting to operate. In the eastern sector of the city, the Seaconnet, Davis, and King Philip Mills were able to run at partial capacity through a small number of rotating workers who were willing to work a few days to prevent starvation, eviction, and harassment by mill agents and police.[65] The mills had hoped for a break in the nonunion ranks, but by December it had not occurred.[66]

In January, the new governor, William Douglas, took office. He had polled 7,357 to 4,351 for John L. Bates. Labor, often politically divided, viewed him as a pro-labor candidate and worked against Bates who had vetoed a woman and child labor law. Upon taking office, the new governor attempted to settle the conflict.

On January 16, 1905, Douglas met with both labor and management.[67] Two days later, the union agreed to return to work at the 12.5 reduction, with the understanding that there would be no discrimination against the strikers, and upon the condition that, as the governor worded it:

> after resumption of work I [Governor Douglas] will take up and investigate the matter of margin [between the cost of cotton and the price of cloth] and submit to you my conclusion as to what average margin shall prevail on which the manufacturers shall pay a dividend of five percent on wages earned from the present time to April, 1905. It is agreed by both parties present that the margin fixed by me shall in no way prejudice future wage schedules.[68]

Stated another way, the governor negotiated a sliding wage scale for Fall River, whereby, if the difference between the cost of cotton and the price of cloth was such as to guarantee a certain profit, wages would be raised.

Both sides claimed victory. The mills got their reduction, but the workers got a promise of better wages in the future. The workers' biggest and most important victory was the mills' agreement to reduce the number of looms per weaver to eight for non-rebuilt looms and ten or less for rebuilt looms.[69] This agreement eliminated one of the weavers' major grievances and represented a major concession by the manufacturers: the right of labor to have a say over conditions as well as wages.

During the strike, the manufacturers had employed two tactics to defeat the strikers. First, they completely shut down all the mills and by agreement would not open them until all opened, hoping to starve the workers when the price of cloth was low and they had little to gain by continual operation. Once the mills opened in the middle of November, the mill owners expected that hunger would break down the ranks of the unskilled and semiskilled workers, weaken the influence of the union, and divide the ranks of the skilled workers by attrition. Second, they gained the support of the textile manufacturers throughout New England in order to overcome local difficulties. Through the Association of Textile Interests, an organization which represented textile companies in New England, the Fall River companies were able to insure themselves against the strike. The organization guaranteed the companies' income even when they were shut down because of labor difficulties. The Fall River mill agents admitted their affiliation with the association and claimed that their membership was in the best interests of the Fall River stockholders.[70] Like the National Association of Leather Manufacturers, the Association of Textile Interests gave the companies a larger arena from which to combat local union efforts. The local unions, in turn, had the aid of the American Federation of Labor to augment their local efforts.

The workers themselves looked not only to the union, but also to the community and to the national labor movement for aid. The American Federation of Labor, after hearing a Fall River delegate describe the suffering of the strikers (which brought tears to the eyes of the husky labor delegates), voted in November to assess members $75,000 to support the strike. Over a thousand dollars a day came into the city from trade unions around the country, especially in New England. Samuel Gompers promised the strikers that the strike "was the only one to engage the attention of organized labor."[71]

Local grocers gave heavily to the strike fund, bakers offered bread, many boarding houses free meals, farmers from surrounding farms food, and the Salvation Army its traditional soup.[72] These grocers and retail tradesmen were closely aligned with the working-class community either by family ties or by the local nature of their enterprise; hence, they tended to contribute to the strike fund. The wealthier merchants, organized into the Merchants Association, attempted to steer a middle course between the mill owners and the operatives. Economically, they were tied to both groups. Many of their customers were operatives, but on the other hand, the families of the mill owners controlled most of the capital in the city, and so the merchants could not afford to alienate them. The merchants formed a committee to bring about an "adjustment of the difficulty between the manufacturers and the operatives."[73] They emphasized that they were interested in what was best for the city, and not just in the concerns of the operatives or the manufacturers. They therefore refused to take a position on the strike itself, hoping not to antagonize either group. They noted that both the reduction and the strike brought hardship to the city.[74]

The merchants' middle course was supported by most of the churches of the city, which urged a peaceful resolution of the strike through conciliation. Reverend W. Dixen, pastor of St. Luke's Church, expressed the position of most of the clergy when he argued for the neutrality of the church: "It is not the part of a clergyman to decide questions of that kind."[75] A Baptist minister, after hoping that a more "optimistic spirit [would] spread in the city," exclaimed, "of the merits of the strike, I do not care to say anything!"[76]

The churches and the merchants were not the only elements in the city hoping to avoid taking sides. For example, in the elections of 1904, neither candidate for mayor mentioned the strike, except briefly. The incumbent argued that the strike should not be brought "into politics," and his opponent, after stating that more should be done to end it, agreed.[77] At the inaugural address of the challenger, Democrat John Coughlin, the only mention of the strike was a passing reference to "an unfortunate circumstance."[78]

Statistically, the strike of 1904 was one of the nation's largest up to that time. It affected thirty-three corporations, closing down seventy-two mills and idling 2.3 million spindles, at a weekly loss of over $150,000 in wages. It cost the Fall River unions over $200,000 and gained more trade union support than any strike to that date.[79] It involved twenty-six thousand striking operatives, many of whom left the city permanently. It shut down the nation's largest cotton textile center and demonstrated nationally the power of collective class-wide action. The strike looked in both directions: forward to the rank-and-file unionism of the 1930s and backward to the craft ideology of the conservative AF of L. It was an industrial strike, as much a product of rank-and-file discontent over job conditions as of trade union bread and butter unionism. It demonstrated a high degree of class unity and cohesion, especially among the unskilled and semiskilled workers who remained out despite deprivation, and among the weavers whose militance during the struggle helped win the important concession over the workload.

On another level, the strike of 1904-1905 demonstrated a growing loss of unity and withdrawal between the skilled union members (especially their officers) and the unskilled immigrant workers who were cut out of union activities. Statements of unity and solidarity between skilled and unskilled at the beginning of the strike were replaced by statements of indifference by its end, even though the unskilled and semiskilled, and the rank and file generally, had shown increased class unity and cohesion. The newly arrived Portuguese did not prove to be knobsticks, but rather class comrades to the point of martyrdom, for it was they who endured the greatest hardships during the strike. The walkout reflected the loss of contact between the union leadership and the community of operatives, which in the past had provided the support and an integrating structure for the union movement, and which was now swelled by Portuguese and Polish workers. In turn, the widening gap left both the union movement and the community open to fragmentation. Metaphorically, the 1904 strike was the forceps for the stillbirth of industrial unionism.

POSTSCRIPT

Between 1904 and 1934, Fall River's skilled workers continued to withdraw from the community of workers around them. Between the strike of 1904 and the boom years of World War I, the Portuguese population grew markedly and found its way into the mills, especially in the unskilled positions. As the more skilled English and Irish workers began to move into the outer perimeter of the city, the newcomers came to dominate the southern districts. This heightened the ethnic and skill-level segregation which had already become evident in the late nineteenth century. Such patterns of segregation began to reverse themselves in the 1920s when the industry's depression tended to force many skilled textile operatives to return to the city and double up with relatives, and when the Portuguese slowly acquired skills. However, such trends simply increased the isolation of the unskilled.

Four years after the 1904 strike, Fall River's skilled weavers in effect protested against the United Textile Workers' growing recognition of unskilled and semiskilled workers. For they voted "that the members of the weavers union think that the best interests of the textile workers can be best served by being organized in national craft unions."[80] On April 1, 1908, they decided to leave the United Textile Workers, and, a week later, the slasher-tenders followed them out.[81] In 1915, the rest of the local unions left the United Textile Workers, and in 1916, they formed the National Association of Textile Operatives, renamed the American Federation of Textile Operatives (AFTO) in 1920.[82]

AFTO represented Fall River's skilled operatives. While not excluding Portuguese or Polish workers, it did not encourage their membership. Thus, the skilled workers withdrew from association with the unskilled or semiskilled.[83] In 1919, when the Portuguese organized the Doffers Union and struck the mills, union spinners went into the doffing room and did the doffers' work to break the walkout. The skilled, then, were so removed from the Portuguese workers that they were willing to scab against the strike. Their unionism did not extend to semiskilled or unskilled immigrant labor.[84]

The unions of Fall River's skilled workers had so withdrawn from the community that most workers lost touch with unionism before 1934.[85] After the defeat of the doffers' strike, one operative stated, "they didn't talk union for a long time."[86] A female worker who eventually went to work in the garment shops observed that while she was in the mills, "never, never did anyone approach us for unions in the mills."[87]

Below the AFTO and the isolated community of skilled workers, a new community was stirring—one that was forged in adversity. Fall River textiles, although prosperous for a short period around and shortly after World War I, began to falter and then collapse during the 1920s. The South began capturing a growing share of the nation's textile industry, and much of that was drawn from Fall River. Low wages and adverse work conditions in the southern textile industry generated massive strikes during the late 1920s. Overproduction and shrinking textile markets plagued both North and South and led to a nationwide depression in the industry by 1924. Initially, neither northern nor southern workers were strong enough to fight declining wages, short-time, and layoffs, but as the depression deepened and spread into other industries and other sectors of the economy, a general wave of discontent began to sweep the nation's work force.

By the 1930s, the revolt had become general, especially among industrial workers. The initiative which Franklin Delano Roosevelt's first programs and their rhetoric inspired, especially Section Seven A of the National Recovery Act (NRA), led to a dramatic increase in union and working-class activity. Fall River labor was no exception. Semiskilled Portuguese workers who now dominated the work force were building a new union movement, as well as new institutions that would bind the community. In the midst of the Depression which forced thousands of workers to return to the community, double up in homes, or move in with older relatives, ethnic divisions began to break down and the ghettos lost some of their previous isolation. Less skilled labor, such as Portuguese weavers and doffers, now worked with other immigrants and were developing interethnic contact.[88]

Ethnic clubs began to lose their homogeneous character and became neighborhood clubs which crossed ethnic lines. The evolving new community also built a new union movement under the auspices of the United Textile Workers. In this way, the operatives solidified their community and began building institutions which would serve as integrating agents in it.[89]

The strike of 1934 reflected the dichotomy between the isolation of the skilled workers in AFTO and the community of workers evolving below them. Not a local struggle as past Fall River walkouts had been, it was a national general strike against the entire textile industry. In Fall River, the semiskilled and unskilled went out in support. Thus, they became part of a national struggle, while at the same time confronting local problems which had plagued the Fall River working-class community since 1900— the segmentation of the work force.

The textile industry, like many of the nation's large industries, was a central part of Roosevelt's NRA. As was the case in many industries, however, management soon came to dominate the board set up to administer the industry. Management was eager for government intervention in textiles. Despite the reduction of the number of spindles during the late 1920s, production continued at above market-demand and wages dropped to below-subsistence, with even whole families working. In 1933, the Cotton-Textile Institute under the leadership of George Sloan pushed through the Code of Fair Competition for textiles. It provided labor with a minimum wage of $13 in the North and included Section Seven A. The act also set up the Cotton Textile National Industrial Relations Board; yet, labor had but one voice there and that a nontextile worker. The board was dominated by the textile manufacturers through B. E. Greer and George Sloan. Management ignored the labor provisions of the act, while the board ignored the labor complaints which flooded them. When the board reduced hours and cut production, labor's initial wage gains were lost. The bitterness over the board's treatment of the union and workers' complaints finally produced the nationwide strike of textile workers in 1934 mentioned above.

Fall River workers, like textile workers throughout the nation, were ripe for a strike. The city had struggled through ten long years of depression. By early 1933, conditions had improved somewhat, but part-time work and unemployment still haunted most families. The depression and fear which first accompanied the downturn of the 1920s had been replaced by anger and hostility. Companies were being blamed not only for low wages and bad conditions, but also for purposely failing and keeping out alternative industries. Membership in the United Textile Workers was high, especially among semiskilled and unskilled workers, and continued to increase.

In July 1934, the United Textile Workers' officers called a special convention to consider how to deal with flagrant company violations of the NRA and the failure of the board to enforce the code it had been established to administer. The delegates of the United Textile Workers met in August 1934 and, in a militant mood, demanded a national strike against the industry. They instructed the officers of the union to strike in early September 1934.

After the strike was announced, the Fall River United Textile Workers issued a statement calling for class solidarity and struggle "against the challenge of the reactionary employers. . . . We urge all textile workers to join us in our fight."[90]

The skilled members of the AFTO, under the leadership of James Tansey, president of the carders and leader of the 1904 strike, voted against supporting the strike.[91] AFTO claimed 100 percent membership of the skilled loomfixers, slasher-tenders, and knot-tiers and warp-twisters, as well as most of the more experienced Irish, English, and French Canadian weavers.

On the first day of the strike, September 4, the AFTO members went to work. The United Textile Workers, which was particularly strong among the Portuguese doffers, the carders (also strongly Portuguese), and the female spinners, was able to pull out over 50 percent of the work force on the first day, despite the AFTO strikebreaking.[92]

Two workers were arrested on the first day of the strike, one of whom was a Portuguese United Textile worker. It was not until the second day, however, that members of the United Textile Workers turned out in force, despite an appeal by the union "not to gather in groups, side-walks, or street corners."[93] Police used tear gas to disperse over six thousand workers gathered at the Pepperroll Mill to prevent strikebreakers from entering. Pickets and the crowds that joined them threw stones and bricks at both scabs and mill windows. By noon, the pickets had effectively closed all the mills in Fall River.[94] After the successful use of pickets and violence to close down the mills, the local United Textile Workers organized "flying squadrons" to go to the other textile areas and help close down their mills. The flying squadrons proved their mettle not only in Lawrence and Lowell, where several Fall River workers were arrested, but especially across the state line in Rhode Island where the governor called out the National Guard and the company hired New York "goons" to prevent the squadrons from setting up pickets.[95]

On Friday, September 7, the United Textile Workers held a huge march of over fifteen thousand strikers. The march ended with a rally during which the strikers were told to "hit back if hit, shoot back if shot at."[96] Over 350 new members, many of whom were former AFTO members who left in protest over their union's conservative position, joined the United Textile Workers by the third day of the strike.[97] At the end of the first week of strike, the semiskilled and unskilled United Textile Workers had idled over twenty-one thousand Fall River workers.[98]

AFTO publicly protested the methods used by the United Textile Workers pickets against the AFTO members.[99] AFTO officials met with Mayor Joseph L. Hurley and asked for the opening of the mills and city police protection for nonstrikers.[100] The leaders of the unions, which fifty years earlier had fought against strikebreakers and had attacked the city for supplying police protection for scabs, now asked for that same protection themselves.

On September 22, the leaders of the United Textile Workers accepted an agreement worked out with the NRA and the representatives of the textile industry, and called off the strike. For the national union the strike had been lost, but in Fall River the strikers held their ranks. The following Monday, twenty-one thousand Fall River workers returned to work.

The issue which divided the AFTO from the United Textile Workers was not one of craft versus industrial unionism. The structure of the United Textile Workers was not significantly different from that of the AFTO. Rather, it was the commitment of the local United Textile Workers members to organizing the community of operatives, not just the skilled workers.

The local members of the United Textile workers did not distrust the unskilled and semiskilled immigrant workers from Portugal, Poland, Russia, or Italy.[101]

In March 1937, the United Textile Workers and the CIO leadership agreed to form the Textile Workers Organizing Committee (TWOC) in order to organize the unskilled textile workers around the country. In Fall River, the United Textile Workers leadership under Mike Doolan, Manuel Bishop, Mike Botelho, and Manuel Mellow quickly moved over to TWOC and began pushing their locals into the new organization.[102] The Fall River union leaders in the United Textile Workers and activists in the strike of 1934 became the leaders in the TWOC drive.[103] Locally, there was little conflict between the United Textile Workers and the TWOC.

Manuel Bishop was typical of the leadership of the new community of workers. An immigrant from the Azores, he entered the Fall River mills as a doffer at ten years of age. He lived in the Portuguese South End and socialized at the Liberal Athletic Club. In the 1920s, he became president of the dyers unit of the United Textile Workers, and through his position he became friends with Mike Doolan, a United Textile Worker, weaver, and Irishman. Bishop and Doolan tried to organize the immigrant workers to unite the different ethnic groups. In 1934, they were leaders in the local strike, and in 1937, they switched over to TWOC and began organizing workers into the new movement.[104]

In 1941, the Textile Workers Union of America (TWUA), which was formed from the TWOC, appealed to the National Labor Relations Board for elections in Fall River to determine which union, TWUA or AFTO, would represent the declining number of textile workers in Fall River. AFTO claimed that the elections should be divided up according to the different crafts inside the plants, with separate bargaining units for loom-fixers, loom-changers, slasher-tenders, knot-tiers, drawing-in machine operators, and warp-twisters. It was hoped that they would be able to maintain bargaining rights for a few of the skilled crafts. The National Labor Relations Board ruled against them on two counts. First, the board determined that structurally the craft divisions were arbitrary. Second, it argued that traditionally the AFTO craft unions had in fact acted as an industrial union: "bargaining of the craft had always been on an industrial basis."[105]

By the end of World War II, the newer Portuguese immigrants dominated the labor force and the labor movement in Fall River. The older English, Irish, and French Canadian workers who were still active in the labor struggle united with the more recent recruits in a common struggle against the manufacturers. Portuguese leader Manuel Bishop headed TWUA along with Irish Mike Doolan and Portuguese Manuel Mellow. The older Anglo-Irish workers either joined with the Portuguese or left the movement.

The success of the United Textile Workers in 1934 and the TWOC in the late 1930s was based upon the ability of the organizers and the unions to build upon an integrated community and to maintain that community. The strike of 1934 in Fall River utilized the tactics of the city's earlier strikes—massive rallies, parades, demonstrations, and activities which called for the unity of the community, including all skill levels and all ethnic groups; that is, it achieved a unity based upon class allegiance. Once that community was strong enough, it was easy to move from the United Textile Workers to TWOC because the community behind the formal union had already developed class ties which held them together and facilitated their integration into an industrial union.

The movement that the textile workers struggled to create in the second quarter of the twentieth century had to battle not only against the racial and craft bias of the older workers, but also against the slow process of re-location of the textile industry in the South. It was this second battle that the textile workers lost. By the end of the 1950s, textiles were a relatively unimportant industry in Fall River. In the huge old mills, the hum of "power machines" replaced the clanging of looms. The once-powerful textile workers' unions were replaced by the International Ladies Garment Workers Union and the American Clothing Workers Union.

The Fall River textile operatives worked in mills that covered several hundred acres of floor space and dominated the landscape of the city. The mills woke the workers with their rising bells and whistles, and held them inside the walls until the late night whistle sent them home exhausted. They employed the whole family and indirectly dictated the careers of the children, and for many, they even supplied housing. By the end of the first half of the twentieth century, however, the mills dominated Fall River only in the depressed shadow they spread over the city. They had been transformed to house the garment shops which employed a fraction of the number of workers the mills had.

Textile workers, whose halls and buildings were once the center of social life, were now barely able to keep up a small building in the south-ern part of town. Workers who once gathered at the Weavers Hall for social activity now came to the union center only to pay into the death fund or to register a change of address.

11

Conclusion

The question of whether class or community solidarity ever existed in the United States has been a major problem for social historians. Many historians have maintained that no coherent class solidarity developed and have traditionally cited ethnic conflict and the possibility of upward mobility as reasons.[1] In fact, however, American history contains several evidences of class and community solidarity.

This study has examined three strategic factors in the development of that solidarity: first, the demands of the work place; second, the relative geographic dispersion or centrality of social centers, residences, and work places; and third, the dilemma of integrating new members into the work force and community. These factors relate to the existence of a substructural community larger than the factory or trade union itself. The concept of community we have examined entails a sense of the wholeness of the life experience encompassed by the role of the worker as a worker. The institutions of the community contributed to its cohesion and continuity and helped define the members' sense of being. The viability of the institutions enabled the community to hold itself together over time and to maintain class solidarity among its members.

Reverend Cook's lectures in 1871 on factory reform emphasized that the Lynn of the pre-Civil War and pre-factory years was a coherent community with common interests, concerns, and moral character. With the new factories, Cook saw Lynn gaining power and wealth, but losing its old community and instead developing into a new city with two opposing classes: "an operative class and an employing class." Yet, the new Lynn was not without community and coherence. What disturbed Cook was that the new community had become a community of workers which totally excluded the middle and upper classes. When the factory system was finally adopted in Lynn, the workers maintained their solidarity with in-shop discussions and after-hours socializing in neighboring lunchrooms and union halls.

The workers who joined Lynn's expanding shoe industry in the 1880s were mostly native Americans who had connections with pre-industrial shoemaking. These natives were augmented by the Irish between 1865 and 1895, many of whom originally settled in the shantytown Brickyard area. English and French Canadians followed the Irish in the 1870s and 1880s. In the mid-1880s, Lynn's working-class population saw the addition of a number of Germans and Scandinavians. By 1905, Polish, Russian, Italian, Greek, and Austrian immigrant groups grew rapidly, and the names on the dues list of the local unions began to reflect this new immigration from Eastern and Southern Europe.

A series of formal and informal institutions within the working-class community helped the Lynn workers cope with the problems of industrial workers in a changing and often alienating environment. They supplied job information, fellowship, and, in times of pecuniary needs, especially during layoffs, financial aid. These institutions also provided the workers with a center for entertainment, socializing, and group and class interactions. They reinforced class alliances and established class identity.

Layoffs, seasonal unemployment, and accompanying job rotation, as well as continual in-shop discussions and out-of-work socializing, helped to break down worker isolation and to integrate the newly arrived immigrant into the urban working-class world. Shoe workers were in constant contact with other shoe workers despite ethnic and craft differences.

Most of the shoe workers' social activity was conducted in central Lynn. The downtown area, with its lunchrooms, pool halls, theatres, and union halls, created a central gathering place for the workers. Emptying out of the various shops into the lunchrooms and cafes, they socialized with workers from other shops and crafts within the trade. These centers bound the workers together and helped integrate the world of work and the world of leisure. ("Years ago it seemed that everybody came from the brickyard or something, you knew everybody who worked next to you, you knew him from somewhere, you either met him for coffee, or you met him for lunch."[2]) When hard times came or when there was a cut in wages, these social institutions became the focal point for class discussions and actions.

The central location of the shops in the Central Square area also contributed to the concentration of the working-class residential area within easy walking distance of both the work place and the central entertainment area. Lynn's working class lived close together near the central work place.[3]

The very structure of his work gave the shoe worker a sense of common identity with his fellow workers. Work in the shoe shops approximates Robert Blauner's model for relatively nonalienating work.[4] The shoe workers had control over the pace of their work. They worked together in small shops employing between fifty and two hundred workers. Although by the second half of the nineteenth century the industry had specialized to a degree which shocked contemporaries, that division of labor did not isolate the shoe workers.[5] Their awareness of their relationship to each other and their identification with the group were heightened by the continual in-shop discussion which went on above the hum of the machines.[6]

During periods of conflict between labor and capital, these institutions were vital in supporting class solidarity and maintaining a common front. Workers looked to their community institutions for communication and programs for action concerning wages, labor conditions, and the possibility of the success or failure of a strike. These institutions linked together workers of different skills and crafts and even different industries, reinforcing a common class consciousness and action, as well as supportive links between workers for both financial and boycotting purposes.[7] The institutions permitted the interchange of common experiences and values which allowed them to develop an analysis of society based on class antagonism and which encouraged ethnic and craft cooperation.

In a broader sense, these institutions were the schools of class consciousness, where the workers learned who their enemies and friends were. They defined the relationship between labor and capital; this definition was preeminent for the working-class community during the late nineteenth and early twentieth centuries.

While Lynn's institutions centered in the community, they had their origin within the history of shoemaking. Shoe workers brought to these institutions values and a culture which was deeply rooted in their experience in Lynn's shops, their conflict with the manufacturers, and their understanding of their role in the production process. In turn, the institutions carried that understanding to new workers entering the shops and provided a forum for analyzing that experience.

Fall River workers, like Lynn workers, looked to their institutions and community. Yet, the nature of their work and the structure of their community also affected the makeup of their institutions. Textile workers were part of a highly mechanized industry; they worked in large mills, tending several machines. Fall River's textile industry during the late nineteenth century fits Blauner's description of alienation and machine-tending work.[8] The on-the-job "gaps and pores" which Marx saw eroding in the middle of the century, and which were so important for the Lynn shoe workers, were almost completely eliminated for the late nineteenth-century textile worker. With speedups and stretchouts, the worker's few remaining freedoms were whittled away.

Following the Civil War, Fall River began building the huge granite mills which came to dominate the city's landscape. The number of spindles increased more than tenfold and the population almost fourfold. With the development of steam power in the factories, the mills began to spread from their central location along the fall of the Quequechan River to other watersite locations. The expansion of the textile mills brought increasing numbers of workers into the city, especially workers escaping the depressed conditions in Lancashire County, England. These English and Irish workers became the heart of Fall River's trade union and working-class movement. Their taverns, lodges, and unions helped transform the city from a quiet community during the pre-Civil War period into a mill town with two distinct communities: that of the mill owners and their supporters, and that of the workers.[9] And the community of workers earned for the city a reputation as the most militant trade union town in New England.

Despite their extensive structure of community institutions, the Fall River workers endured long hours of exhausting and intensive labor with low pay throughout the nineteenth and twentieth centuries. The low wages forced the children of mill families into the textile factories. In order to survive, the workers depended upon the labor of the family, and as they worked in the mills, they became trapped in a cycle of low wages, long hours, and exhausting work. The textile worker of the 1880s and 1890s relied upon the social institutions outside the mill—friendship ties and kin, coops, clubs, and unions—to compensate for the alienation and oppressive conditions inside and to protect their interests in labor relations.[10]

With the extensive building of newer and ever larger mills in the late nineteenth century, Fall River spread out from its central river location.

The newer mills moved out to the periphery of the city; some of them were located several miles from the downtown area, and around the scattered mills separate villages emerged. With the relocation of the mills and the creation of separate villages, those who lived outside downtown Fall River no longer had easy access to the working-class institutions. The very distance to the downtown, coupled with the long hours and exhausting working conditions, discouraged participation in these institutions. Instead, these workers tended to remain in their villages, socializing in a local tavern or on the doorsteps of their tenements. Only workers within the older mills continued to socialize at the union hall or other social centers.

This process of decentralization was paralleled by the stretchouts and speedups within the mills, which broke down the informal socializing within them. The stretchouts affected all workers in the production process, from carders and spinners to weavers and loomfixers. All were subjected to the strains of excessively long and tiring labor with low wages. There was little communication or socializing in the mills, and little energy or time to do so afterwards. The community institutions, which were brought over from England and had been used to integrate new members into the community and working class during the 1870s and 1880s, began to feel the pressure of a tired and residentially fragmented community.

Although the workers had important social centers in their scattered villages, these centers reinforced residential isolation. As the residential areas became identified with ethnic minorities, the local institutions produced further ethnic isolation and class fragmentation.

Such forces were not solely responsible for a segmented work force, but urban dispersion and excessive on-the-job demands weakened these community institutions. They left the working-class community ready to fragment under the pressure of mounting immigrant entry into the work force after 1900.

Between 1895 and 1905, when urban dispersion and job competition reached their peak, Fall River experienced a new flood of immigration. This time the community was not able to absorb the immigrants, and so it became fragmented into isolated craft and ethnic subgroups which eroded collective action and community cohesion. By 1900, the southern edge of Little Canada had become identified with the Portuguese. The English, Irish, and French Canadian workers were unable to socialize in the mill, owing to excessive on-the-job pressures (low wages, piece time, and stretchouts), and they were also dispersed residentially into separate villages and ethnic ghettos. It follows, then, that they looked upon the newcomers not so much as fellow workers but as threats in an increasingly unstable job market and as depressors of wages. Their response was to close off their community institutions and to transform them from class-oriented to ethnic- and craft-oriented institutions.[11] They eliminated the informal socializing of the trade unions and discouraged gathering at the union halls.

The Portuguese and Poles who poured into Fall River brought with them customs and values which they used as support systems within the alien and hostile industrial environment. Their language and cultural traditions, alien to the established working class, provided them with a common bond within their ethnic communities. Yet, without strong class institutions to facilitate the assimilative process, that bond also acted as a barrier to integration within the working class.

In the twentieth century, the kind of work available in Lynn changed radically. This change affected the city much as urban dispersion and excessive job demands affected Fall River's working-class community.

With the decline of Lynn's shoe industry, the General Electric plant, located on the southwestern edge of the city, replaced the old shoe shops as the city's major employer. The plant transformed the work pattern, and ultimately the very community, of the workers. General Electric workers eventually built a militant trade union movement, but that movement differed from the strong community-oriented labor movement and class solidarity of the shoe workers.

General Electric workers did not work together in small cooperating groups. The structure of the plant and the demands of the jobs isolated them from the informal socializing of the shoe workers in the cafes and lunchrooms. With the exception of the Depression layoffs, General Electric provided its employees with year-round work. Even during the Depression the company recalled employees through its own formal channels rather than relying on those informal contacts which had dominated both the shoe industry and General Electric before the 1930s. The new worker at General Electric no longer owed his job to the community, his friends, his kin, or the union, but rather to the personnel office. The older institutions which the shoe workers used for job placement and security had no function in the modern General Electric plant.

The nature of the work at General Electric also discouraged the informality and comradeship which spilled over into after-hours social activity. Taylorism brought time-motion studies to the plant, and the workers, faced with speedups and intense job pressures, saw their freedom to socialize and control the work process scientifically removed.

During the early twentieth century, electrical workers had joined in the activities of the shoe workers, but as the shoe industry died out, so did the shoe workers' institutions. The electrical workers became increasingly isolated and alienated from the community and their work. The process was accelerated by the structure of VA and FHA loans which encouraged the workers to buy homes in the city's growing lower- and middle-class suburbs. As the workers were required to commute greater distances between home and work, the institutions which were dependent upon the integration of work, leisure, and home became less meaningful.[12]

Without strong supporting institutions, Lynn's working-class community began to atomize. The job pressures and suburbanization of the work force slowly took their toll on the community. Workers participated less in the social institutions of the community and more and more began to look outside the community to fulfill their needs. By the 1970s, both retired shoe and electrical workers felt a lack of class identity among the workers. The city was not the strong supportive community they had known.

In both Lynn and Fall River, the structure of work and of the city affected working-class cohesion and class solidarity. In both cities, centralized institutions furthered class solidarity and facilitated the integration of new members into the work force. Class solidarity suffered in both cities as the work force lost its informal social contacts. The excessive numbers of unskilled nonindustrial workers who flooded Fall River during the turn of the century, competing with local workers for a dwindling number of jobs, overwhelmed the city's working-class institutions. The new immigrants themselves did not reject class solidarity, as is evident from their strong support of the strike of 1904-1905. Rather, they were rejected by the skilled workers. The established working class closed off their institutions to the uninitiated and transformed these

institutions into self-serving exclusive institutions to protect the already
initiated members of the working class.

The Lynn shoe workers maintained strong integrative institutions
despite extensive job competition during the late nineteenth and early
twentieth centuries, when the city's shoe industry was declining. The city's
electrical workers had much greater difficulty holding on to strong class
institutions. Even with the effects of work demands and urban dispersal,
however, in both Fall River and Lynn, the workers were drawn together
by the work itself, and in time collective action developed.

Workers in both cities experienced work-related insecurity and community support. That support rested upon a wide variety of institutions
which not only integrated new members into the community, but also
became schools of class consciousness. They interpreted events in class
terms and, in the case of trade unions, provided the vehicle for class
actions. Yet, these same institutions proved vulnerable to rapid and far-
reaching urban change. As the work force became spatially dispersed
and isolated, both residentially and on the job, the class-based institutions were weakened and failed to act as either integrative agents or as
schools of class consciousness. This process did not prove to be irreversible.
In Fall River, continual economic insecurity, the rise in the 1930s of the
class-based institutions of the United Textile Workers and the TWOC, and
the emergence of the Portuguese institutions to a position of dominance
increased class awareness and solidarity. In Lynn, the decline of class
institutions which took place during the 1950s may have been halted
with the workers' struggles over health and safety measures and job
security.

Appendix A

Oral History

By providing an anthropological tool, oral history allows the student of working-class culture to go beyond an outline of events in the lives of those interviewed. It permits the urban or labor historian to look into the very experiences and consciousness of the groups who are studied and gives him or her the means to bridge the behavior and consciousness of the "inarticulate."

Before oral history can be effectively used, however, the historian must know how to use it. To employ anthropological or sociological techniques does not make the historian an anthropologist or sociologist, or equip him or her to use the techniques of other disciplines correctly. What follows are some problems which I have confronted in my work and some tentative solutions.

Many pitfalls await the oral historian. Historians do not as yet have a sophisticated method for or approach to oral history. Until sampling problems and methods have been worked out, the historian must grope along in the dark as best as possible, fully aware of the difficulties which lie before him. Oral history is a unique historical tool. Unlike quantitative or traditional historical data, oral history data are not manipulated by existing information but rather are created by the historian. The oral historian must be particularly careful not to create answers he or she wants by posing leading questions or presenting an authoritative bearing.

The interviewee must control the interview as much as possible, with the interviewer only adding direction. The more control by the interviewee, the less likely the interviewer will force answers which please him but do not reflect the real feelings or attitudes of the person being interviewed.

In the interviews conducted for this work, I attempted to stay out of the interview as much as possible, allowing it to take its own course no matter how much it deviated from the interests of this study. Group interviews were used as much as possible to broaden the sample and to relax the interviewees. The group provided a check on each other's recollections, broadening them at times, correcting them at others. The group technique also reduced the need for participation by the interviewer.

The shoe workers selected for interview were chosen because of their formal contact with the union. The local union's secretary introduced me to the interviewees, and the interview sessions were held at the union hall. I spent several hours at the Lynn Union Hall between December 13 and 14 1972. When the taped interviews were made on December 14, I had established greater ease with the nine interviewees. The electrical workers, who were volunteers as were the shoe workers, were members of the IUE local 201 retiree club. A group of six was interviewed on December 19, 1972, after a brief preliminary discussion of the aims of this study. The garment workers were interviewed in September 1973 and, like the retired electrical workers, were members of the local union retiree club. The interview with these workers was followed up with an interview with the local business agent who was born and raised in Fall River. Because no formal organization existed for retired workers in Fall River, I used contacts through the union for interviews with a local retired textile worker and his wife, both of whom had been textile workers in the 1910s and had been active in the organizing drives of the 1930s. This interview was conducted in the fall of 1973.

Oral history obviously suffers from the same problem as autobiographies—selective memory. Whenever possible, the oral historian must attempt to correlate oral history with testable behavior; I have done so in this study as much as possible.

Appendix **B**

Immigration Patterns in Lynn and Fall River, 1885-1920

Place of Birth	Lynn					Fall River				
	1885	1895	1905	1910	1920	1885	1895	1905	1910	1920
Native Born	36,009	46,060	55,070	61,992	71,290	28,912	44,683	59,371	68,421	78,154
England	643	1,479	1,662	1,920	1,850	8,751	12,959	11,394	10,995	7,968
Ireland	4,609	5,374	5,322	5,153	4,527	8,720	8,434	6,107	5,194	3,201
Canada, French	423	1,035	1,607	2,369	2,164	8,219	11,079	15,780	15,277	10,734
Canada, British	393	3,074	1,872	7,511	7,382	208	846	591	965	826
Portugal	4	6	17	29	21	313	1,707	7,020	9,365	5,663
Scandinavia	96	606	1,756	1,399	1,119					
Germany	138	260	328	305	219				234	135
Russia		87	1,164	3,880	3,074		762	1,366	2,143	1,661
Italy	45	102	814	1,354	1,943				1,025	945
Poland	23	22	659	958	1,391		109	418		2,525
Greece			409		1,685				103	149
Total Population	45,867	62,358	77,042	89,336	99,148	56,870	89,203	105,762	119,295	120,485

Appendix C

Average Yearly Wages of Shoe, Leather, and Cotton Textile Workers in Massachusetts, 1886, 1890

Year	Shoe Workers	Leather Workers	Cotton Textile Workers
1886	$510.68	$521.99	$308.72
1890	518.96	541.07	339.73

SOURCE: *Annual Report, Massachusetts Statistics of Manufacturers, 1890* (Boston, 1890).

Appendix **D**

Nativity of the Labor Force in Massachusetts, 1903
(percentage distribution)

Country of Descent	Boot and Shoe Industry	Leather Industry	Cotton Textile Industry
Native Descent	46.23	21.19	8.42
Foreign Descent	53.77	78.81	91.58
Ireland	28.51	52.55	29.57
Canada, French	9.45	6.57	30.25
Canada, British	2.43	1.71	1.57
England	3.29	3.25	16.06
Germany	1.14	2.72	2.80
Nova Scotia	2.28	1.95	. . .
Sweden	1.76	1.84	. . .
Italy	0.53	. . .	. . .
Scotland	1.18	1.48	. . .
Russia	0.69	. . .	. . .
Portugal	. . .	. . .	2.38
Poland	. . .	. . .	2.26

*All others under 1 percent.

SOURCE: *Thirty-fifth Annual Report MBLS, 1904* (Boston, 1905).

Notes

CHAPTER 1

1. Joseph Cook, *Outlines of Music Hall Lectures, Embracing Five Addresses on Factory Reform* (Boston: W. H. Halliday, 1871), p. 52.

2. Ibid.

3. John R. Commons, et al., *History of Labor in the United States* (New York: Macmillan Co., 1918-1935); Selig Perlman, *Theory of the Labor Movement* (New York: Macmillan Co., 1928).

4. This traditional school assumes that the working class of America differs from the working class of Europe in having no class consciousness. This assumption boils down to the following circular argument: The American worker is not socialist because he has no class consciousness. We know he has no class consciousness because he is not socialist. See Daniel Bell, "Marxian Socialism in the U.S.," in Conrad Egbert and Stow Person, eds., *Socialism and American Life* (Princeton, N.J.: Princeton University Press, 1952), pp. 216-217; Daniel Bell, *The End of Ideology* (New York: Free Press, 1960).

5. See Herbert Gutman, "Work, Culture, and Society in Industrializing America, 1815-1919," *American Historical Review* 78 (June 1973): 531-588; Paul Faler, "Cultural Aspects of the Industrial Revolution: Lynn, Massachusetts, Shoemakers and Industrial Morality, 1826-1860," *Labor History* 13 (Summer 1974): 367-394.

6. In many cases, the Irish immigrants did not come directly from the Irish countryside but moved first to the mills and mines of England, where they had a strong working-class apprenticeship before emigrating to America. Many individuals who received funds from trade unions in Lancashire, England, to come to America were Irish. Many of the trade union leaders in Fall River were Lancashire Irish. See the *Annual Reports of the Bolton and Oldham Mule Spinners Union*, Webb Collection, London School of Economics, 1870-1900. The leather and shoe workers who came to Lynn, Massachusetts, were often experienced shoemakers from urban areas before they came to America. See U. S. Congress, Senate, Immigration Commission, *Immigrants in Industry*, 61st Cong., 2d Sess., S. Doc. No. 633 (Washington, D.C.: 1909-1910), Vols. 72, 74.

7. Clark Kerr and Abraham Siegel, "The International Propensity to Strike—An International Comparison," in Arthur Kornhauser, Robert Dublin, and Arthur

Ross, eds., *International Conflict* (New York: McGraw-Hill Book Co., 1954), pp. 195-196.

8. William L. Warner and J. O. Low, *The Social System of the Modern Factory* (New Haven, Conn.: Yale University Press, 1947). Charles Tilly and Edward Shorter, *Strikes in France, 1830-1968* (London: Cambridge University Press, 1974) contains a critique of the Kerr and Siegel argument.

9. In this study, the formal unions which occupied the attention of the earlier labor historians constitute but one of a series of class institutions which may or may not contribute to community cohesion and collective action.

10. David Ward, *Cities and Immigrants: A Geography of Change in Nineteenth Century America* (New York: Oxford University Press, 1971), p. 91, discusses the impact of the historical structure and development of industry and its relationship to centralization or dispersal of the manufacturing district.

11. Fall River cotton manufacturers in 1890 had a total of $24,860,081 invested in plant expenditures and only $6,724,452 in wages. Fall River manufacturers also expended only $9,500 in rents. This compared to Lynn's shoe industry with its external economies where $1,750,930 was expended in plant costs (of this, $1,379,849 was in machines), $6,832,938 in wages, and $2,815,000 in rents (U.S. Census Bulletins, 1890).

12. See Herbert Gans, *The Urban Villagers* (New York: Free Press, 1962) and Edward Thompson, *The Making of the English Working Class* (New York: Random House, 1963), pp. 9-11.

13. *Nineteenth Annual Report of Massachusetts Bureau of Statistics of Labor, 1888* (hereafter cited as An. Rpt. MBLS) (Boston: 1889), p. 195.

14. Ibid., p. 211.

15. Ibid., p. 223.

16. See David Montgomery, *Beyond Equality: Labor and the Radical Republicans, 1862-1872* (New York: Random House, 1967) for a discussion of politics and working-class consciousness. Alan Dawley, *Class and Community: The Industrial Revolution in Lynn* (Cambridge, Mass.: Harvard Univeristy Press, 1976) and Philip Silvia, "The Spindle City: Labor, Politics, and Religion in Fall River, Massachusetts, 1870-1905," Ph.D. dissertation, Fordham University, 1973, discusses the role of electoral politics in the two respective cities.

CHAPTER 2

1. Joseph Cook, *Outlines of Music Hall Lectures, Embracing Five Addresses on Factory Reform* (Boston: W. H. Halliday, 1871), p. 9.

2. "Lasters Union Minutes," Vol. 1, June 23, 1896, Lynn Lasters Union Papers, Baker Library, Harvard University.

3. Robert Billups and Phillip Jones, *Labor and Conditions in the Shoe Industry in Massachusetts, 1920-1924* (Washington, D.C.: U. S. Government Printing Office, 1925), p. 24.

4. Statement of December 13 and 14, 1972, in tape sessions with retired shoe workers at the Lynn Union Hall. Since the sessions were made in groups, and indi-

vidual workers were often unidentified, in many cases statements made in the interviews can only be referred to as "tape sessions." The tapes are available at the Lynn Historical Society; statement at the entrance of the General Electric plant in Lynn.

5. William Betts, "Lynn, A City by the Sea," *Outlook* 68 (May 1901): 207.

6. Paul Faler, "Workingmen, Mechanics and Social Change: Lynn, Massachusetts, 1800-1860," Ph.D. dissertation, University of Wisconsin, 1970, Chap. 2.

7. Cook, *Music Hall Lectures*, p. 4.

8. "Shoe Manufacturing in Lynn," *Boot and Shoe Recorder* (Lynn: 1892): 11.

9. *Sixteenth An. Rpt. MBLS, 1885* (Boston: 1885), p. 175; E. A. Start, "Lynn, Massachusetts," *New England Magazine* 4 (June 1891): 502.

10. *Lynn Scrapbooks*, Vol. 48, p. 15; Vol. 41, p. 72.

11. Betts, "Lynn, A City," p. 208.

12. See Alan Dawley, "Artisan Response to the Factory System," Ph.D. dissertation, Harvard University, 1971, for a discussion of the putting-out system; see also Paul Faler, "Workingmen," for his discussion of the developing division of labor within the shoemaking craft, and David Johnson, *Sketches of Lynn* (Lynn: Thomas Nichols, 1880), pp. 332-335, for a description of the division of labor developing in Lynn during the nineteenth century.

13. *Sixteenth An. Rpt. MBLS, 1885*, p. 175.

14. Johnson, *Sketches*, pp. 338-389.

15. Ibid., pp. 336-356.

16. Ibid., pp. 340-341. For a discussion of this process, see also Betts, "Lynn, A City," and Dawley, "Artisan Response."

17. Faler, "Workingmen," Chap. 9.

18. "Testimony of Horace Eaton," U.S. Congress, House, *Report of the Industrial Commission*, 56th Cong., 2d Sess., House Doc. No. 495 (Washington, D.C.: 1901), Vol. 7, p. 363.

19. Johnson, *Sketches*, p. 341.

20. "Shoe Manufacturing in Lynn," *Boot and Shoe Recorder*, p. 14.

21. Ellen Wetherall, *After the Battle* (Lynn: n.p., 1903), p. 1.

22. Betts, "Lynn, A City," p. 209.

23. Johnson, *Sketches*, p. 209.

24. Letter to *Lynn Item*, 1884, located in unfiled ms., Lynn Historical Society.

25. Cook, *Music Hall Lectures*, p. 4.

26. Ibid., p. 3.

27. Ibid., pp. 8-9.

28. Ibid., p. 9.

29. Ibid., p. 14.

30. Ibid., p. 29; for a discussion of middle-class moral reform in Lynn as exemplified in the Music Hall Lectures, see also Dawley, "Artisan Response."

31. Interview with Harold Walker, son of a shoe manufacturer and officer of the Lynn Historical Society, December 4, 1972; Bessie Van Vorst and Marie Van Vorst, *The Woman Who Toils* (New York: Doubleday, Page, 1903), p. 294.

32. Ira Haskel, "Union Street Now and Then," ms., Lynn Historical Society.

33. Betts, "Lynn, A City," p. 209. See also the Papers of the Gregg House

(nineteenth-century settlement house), Swedenberg School of Religion, Newton, Massachusetts; Papers of the Lynn Associated Charities, located at Lynn's Family Service of Greater Lynn; tape sessions made with a group of retired shoe workers who grew up in the Brickyard.

34. Dawley, "Artisan Response," p. 123.

35. "Railroads," Vol. 1, ms., Lynn Historical Society.

36. *Boston Evening Transcript,* November 13, 1886.

37. *Massachusetts State Census, 1895* (Boston: 1896), Vol. 4, p. 392; U.S. Congress, Senate, Immigration Commission, *Immigrants in Industry,* 61st Cong., 2d Sess., S. Doc. No. 633 (Washington, D.C.: 1909-1910), Vol. 4, p. 225. The Lynn Lasters Union rolls show that there were more foreigners in Lynn than the state figures indicate.

38. George Strayer, *Report of the Survey of the School of Lynn* (Lynn: 1927), p. 9.

39. See Appendix B for the city's immigration patterns at the turn of the century.

40. *Twentieth An. Rpt. MBLS, 1889* (Boston: 1889), p. 538.

41. *Lynn City Directories,* 1908, 1914.

42. *Immigrants in Industry,* Vol. 74, p. 391.

43. *Thirty-second An. Rpt. MBLS, 1901* (Boston: 1901), p. 27.

44. *Scrapbook 2,* Gregg House Papers.

45. *Report of Lynn Park Commission, 1911* (Lynn: 1911), p. 22.

46. Vincent Ferrini, *No Smoke* (Portland, Me.: Falmouth Publishers, 1941), pp. 58-59; *Report of Lynn Park Commission, 1910;* "Lynn, One Hundred Years a City," ms., Lynn Historical Society, 1950. For a discussion of subsistence among Lynn's shoe workers, see Alan Dawley, *Class and Community: The Industrial Revolution in Lynn* (Cambridge, Mass.: Harvard University Press, 1976).

47. *Sixth An. Rpt. MBLS, 1875* (Boston: 1875), pp. 240-241.

48. *Scrapbook 1,* Gregg House Papers; *Thirty-second An. Rpt. MBLS, 1901* (Boston: 1901), pp. 13, 14, 22, 23, 36-41; Peter Kenen, "A Statistical Survey of Basic Trends," in Seymour Harris, ed., *American Economic History* (New York: McGraw-Hill Book Co., 1961), p. 80.

49. Cook, *Music Hall Lectures,* p. 67.

50. For a discussion of the difficulty of moving from workingman to manufacturer in nineteenth-century Lynn, see Faler, "Workingmen" and Dawley, "Artisan Response."

51. In 1921, twenty-seven new shoe manufacturing concerns opened in the city. Billups and Jones, *Labor,* p. 2.

52. Ibid., pp. 1, 23.

53. Ibid., p. 24; *Immigrants in Industry,* Vol. 74, p. 361.

54. Billups and Jones, *Labor,* p. 24.

55. Ibid.

56. Ibid., p. 25.

57. Tape sessions with shoe workers.

58. Mike Carrucho, one of the retired workers who participated in the tape sessions, was typical of this pattern. His parents were shoe workers, and he worked in

the shoe shops until the Depression. When the shoe shops began to close down, he went to work for the Works Progress Administration; later, he entered the General Electric plant, from which he finally retired in the late 1950s.

59. *Lynn Scrapbook,* Vol. 41, p. 93; *The Union Worker* (Lynn), January 31, March 13, 1922.

60. See Table 3.

61. Interview with Thomas Coleman, an eighty-year-old shoe worker, December 13, 1972, at the United Shoeworkers Union Hall, Lynn.

62. *Lynn Scrapbooks,* Vol. 48, p. 30.

63. Tape sessions with shoe workers and electrical workers.

64. Papers of the Associated Charities of Lynn; the names have been changed to insure confidentiality.

65. Ferrini, *No Smoke,* p. 96.

66. Billups and Jones, *Labor,* p. 24. It was estimated that in 1923 between one thousand and two thousand Lynn workers were commuting to Boston to work in shops there (*The Union Worker* [Lynn], February 7, 1924).

67. "Sweatshops," ms., Consumer League of Massachusetts (1938), Folder 482, Woman's Archives, Schlesinger Library, Radcliffe College, p. 17.

68. Unfiled ms., Gregg House Papers.

69. General Electric was not new to Lynn. It had its origin in the old Thomson-Huston Company which Charles Coffin brought to the city in 1883. In 1892, when Coffin merged with Edison Electric, the main offices and control of the Lynn plant were centralized in Schnectady. Lynn workers were now part of a national corporation; even their huge plant was secondary to the one in Schnectady. Charles Coffin, G. E. Second An. Rpt., quoted in General Electric, *Professional Management in General Electric* (1953), p. 4. U.S. Department of Labor, *Bulletin of the U.S. Bureau of Labor Statistics,* No. 180 (Washington, D.C.: 1915), p. 15.

CHAPTER 3

1. Tape sessions with retired shoe workers and electrical workers.

2. U. S. Bureau of the Census, *Twelfth Census of the United States, 1900,* Vol. 1, p. 621; *Massachusetts State Census, 1885* (Boston: 1886), Vol. 1, pp. 4, 162, 507.

3. William Betts, "Lynn, A City by the Sea," *Outlook* 68 (May 1901). The Brickyard was originally an area of boarding houses and shanties set up on the edge of a marsh west of the city. It was occupied by poor native and Irish workers, many of whom worked in the brickyard which gave the area its name. For descriptions of the mixed ethnic community in the Brickyard, see the Papers of the Lynn Associated Charities and The Papers of the Gregg House.

4. *The Union Leader* (Lynn), May 29, 1920.

5. "Lynn Lasters Union, Receipt Book," Vol. 10, Lynn Lasters Union Papers.

6. Ira Haskell, "Union Street Now and Then," ms., Lynn Historical Society.

7. Bessie Van Vorst and Marie Van Vorst, *The Woman Who Toils* (New York: Doubleday, Page, 1903), p. 203.

8. Tape sessions with shoe workers; advertisements in *Boot and Shoe Cutters*

Assembly 3662, Knights of Labor Official Report (Lynn: 1904-1905); *Calander,*
7 (November 1902), official publication of the Lynn Catholic Church; *Law and
Order,* Temperance Journal (Boston: October 4, 1884), p. 8.

9. Tape sessions with retired shoe workers; "Receipt Book," Vol. 10, 1894-
1896, Lynn Lasters Union, Lynn Lasters Union Papers.

10. "Minutes of Lynn Lasters Union Benefit Association," Vol. 24; *Record
Book,* Lasters Aid Association, Vol. 26, June 1890-November 1890, Lynn Lasters
Union Papers; U.S. Department of Labor, *Bulletin of the U.S. Bureau of Labor
Statistics,* No. 180 (Washington, D.C.: 1915), p. 101.

11. Betts, "Lynn, A City," p. 209.

12. These figures were drawn from the City Directory of 1905 from a random
sample of just under 1 percent of the shoe workers of Lynn. Their residency was
plotted according to street location on a 1905 city map *(Lynn City Directory,*
1905). See also U.S. Bureau of Census, *Twelfth Census of the U.S., 1900, Population,*
Vol. 1, p. 621.

13. *Lynn Daily Item,* February 24, 1891.

14. Tape sessions with shoe workers, Frank Cacicio.

15. Tape sessions with shoe and electrical workers.

16. Vincent Ferrini, *No Smoke* (Portland, Me.: Falmouth Publishers, 1941),
p. 62.

17. Advertisement in *Boot and Shoe Cutters Official Report, 1903* (Lynn: 1903);
The Union Leader, May 1929. Advertisements in *The Union Worker,* January 3,
1924, for Wymen's and Mt. Vernon Lunch both stressed they were prounion and
were open from 4:30 A.M. to 1:30 A.M.

18. Tape sessions with Lynn shoe workers.

19. Ibid.

20. *Boston Evening Transcript,* November 13, 1886.

21. Joseph Cook, *Outlines of Music Hall Lectures, Embracing Five Addresses
on Factory Reform* (Boston: W. H. Halliday, 1871), p. 53.

22. Tape sessions with shoe workers; Mike Carrucho, one of the participants
in the tape sessions, took jobs in Boston during lean times in Lynn; *The Union
Leader,* July 9, 1920.

23. Van Vorst and Van Vorst, *Woman Who Toils,* p. 207.

24. Cook, *Music Hall Lectures,* p. 53.

25. Tape sessions; Mike Carrucho and Frank Cacicio were typical of this pattern, for both left the city during their young adulthood to look for work and adventure elsewhere. Carrucho took a job in Boston for a few years, while Cacicio
went to California. They both returned to Lynn and its shoe factories after a few
years. An electrical worker who participated in the tape session of electrical workers
noted that he tried to get work in the Maine shoe factories before returning to Lynn
to work in the General Electric plant. For similar findings, see Tamara Hareven,
"The Laborers of Manchester, New Hampshire, 1912-1922," *Labor History* (Spring
1975): 225. See also Stephen Thernstrom and Peter Knights, "Men in Motion," in
Tamara Hareven, ed., *Anonymous Americans* (Englewood Cliffs, N.J.: Prentice-Hall,
1971); and Peter Knights, *The Plain People of Boston, 1830-1860* (New York:
Oxford University Press, 1971).

26. Tape sessions with shoe workers.

27. Betts, "Lynn, A City," p. 210.

28. Ibid.

29. Papers of the Associated Charities of Lynn.

30. Betts, "Lynn, A City," p. 210.

31. *Scrapbook 1,* Gregg House Papers.

32. Gregg House Papers.

33. Ibid.

34. *Lynn Daily Bee,* September 19, 1890.

35. Betts, "Lynn, A City," p. 210.

36. Nathan Hawkes, "An Historical Address Delivered before Bay State Lodge, #40, I.O.O.F." (Lynn: 1894), ms., Lynn Historical Society.

37. "Constitution and By-Laws of Lynn Lodges of I.O.O.F." (Lynn: 1900), ms., Lynn Public Library.

38. *Lynn Scrapbooks,* Vol. 48, p. 16.

39. See Table 5 for the occupational makeup of the Odd Fellows membership.

40. Interview with Harold Walker, son of a shoe manufacturer, who worked in the Lynn General Electric plant just after World War I and was an officer in the Lynn Historical Society, December 1972; tape sessions with electrical workers.

41. To determine the class membership of these benefit or social organizations, the occupations of the officers and trustees listed in the city directories (usually about six or more in number) were checked in the directories. If the total membership was available in the various repositories, such as the Odd Fellows and Masons, the occupations of all members were checked. It has been assumed that by choosing the officers in these organizations, the sample is biased against working-class members. That is, it is more likely that members with white collar occupations could more easily handle officer duties. Thus, if an organization had working-class officers, it was assumed that the general membership was working class. This method is also biased in favor of the more skilled working-class members. Keeping this in mind, the Lynn Mutual Benefit Association, whose officers were skilled shoe workers and clerks, may have had a membership that was much more representative of the Lynn working class than its officers' occupations imply.

42. John Cumbler, "Three Generations of Poverty," *Labor History* 15 (Winter 1974): 78-85.

43. *Calander,* the official organ of the Lynn Catholic Church, 10 (August 1903): 317-318.

44. Ibid.

45. Ibid., 10 (September 1903): 339.

46. Ibid.

47. *The Union Worker,* March 20, 1924.

48. Following Oscar Handlin's model in *Boston's Immigrants* (New York: Atheneum, 1969), the Irish Catholic church became a central counter-institution for Boston's Catholic community, partly in response to the nativist hostility directed against the newcomers. It is interesting that in Fall River the church was used by the city's Irish population and further solidified the Irish workers. When the French Canadians came to Fall River, they brought with them a strong church system which

had been developed in Canada as a counter-institution to the English rule there, much as the Irish had used the church in Ireland. In contrast, the Portuguese came to Fall River without the tradition of a strong counter-institution. Thus, Catholicism was a weak force in their community, and the Portuguese looked to ethnic clubs rather than to the church for support in the hostile environment.

49. *Lynn City Directories*, 1880-1885; pamphlet of Lynn's Workingmen's Aid Association, Boston Public Library.

50. Tape sessions with General Electric workers.

51. *Lynn City Directories*, 1880-1895.

52. Charter of Lynn Damascus Lodge of the Masons, ms., Lynn Public Library; *Lynn City Directories*, 1898-1914.

53. Membership list, Lynn Damascus Lodge. Only 17 percent of the lodge's members were working class.

54. *Lynn City Directory, 1905*. For a description of the learning process, see U.S. Department of Labor, *Bulletin of the U.S. Bureau of Labor Statistics*, No. 180 (Washington, D.C.: 1915), p. 49.

55. Ibid.

56. Richard Kelly, *Nine Lives for Labor* (New York: Frederick A. Praeger, 1946), pp. 42-44. In Fall River, the ethnic organizations cushioned the immigrants from each other. Here, the ethnic club served as a neighborhood tavern and community center for the first- and second-generation immigrants. It integrated them into the ethnic subcommunity. Officers in these ethnic clubs were the oldest and most respected members of the ethnic community. See also Donald B. Cole, *Immigrant City* (Chapel Hill, N.C.: University of North Carolina Press, 1963); Tamara Hareven, "The Laborers of Manchester, New Hampshire," in Humbert Nelli, ed., *The Italians of Chicago* (New York: Oxford University Press, 1970); Gerald D. Suttles, *The Social Order of the Slum: Ethnicity and Territory in the Inner City* (Chicago: University of Chicago Press, 1968), all of which discuss ethnicity and ethnic clubs and social groupings.

57. The occupational makeup of these organizations was determined by cross-checking the officers listed in the city directories with their occupations. It has been assumed that if the officers were unskilled workers, a sign of recent arrival, the membership also consisted of recent immigrants since members with longer periods of residence and more skilled positions would most likely be elected officers. Thus, a club with unskilled officers most likely had recent arrivals for members. The life histories of the participants in the tape sessions bear out this assumption.

58. Tape sessions with shoe workers.

59. *Lynn City Directories*, 1900, 1905.

60. Interview with Morac Roam, secretary of the Lynn Workingmen's Circle, Branch 937, December 1972. After World War II, the Circle lost much of its earlier socialist orientation in Lynn.

61. *Lynn City Directories*, 1900, 1905, 1910. See note 57 above.

62. Tape sessions with Mike Carrucho.

63. Tape sessions with Nick Pappas.

64. Ibid.

65. Ibid.

66. Ibid.

67. *Lynn Scrapbooks,* Vol. 34, p. 74.

68. Ibid.

69. Tape sessions with shoe workers.

70. Ibid.; *Lynn Daily Bee,* September 4, 1890.

71. Tape sessions with retired shoe and electrical workers.

72. Interview with Thomas Coleman, a retired Lynn shoe worker, at the Lynn Union Hall, United Shoe Workers, AF of L-CIO, December 13, 1972.

CHAPTER 4

1. *The Union Worker,* August 31, 1922.

2. In his work on the industrial worker in the Gilded Age (*Work, Culture, and Society in Industrializing America* [New York: Alfred A. Knopf, 1976]), which emphasizes the conflict between the local workers and their community and the developing capitalist system, Herbert Gutman has pioneered much of the work which has been done on the industrial worker in his local setting. Gutman points to the importance of the workers' pre-industrial culture and social tradition in their resistance to capital. For other innovative studies, see David Brody, *Steelworkers in America; Non-Union Era* ((Cambridge, Mass.: Harvard University Press, 1960); Stephen Thernstrom, *Poverty and Progress: Social Mobility in a Nineteenth Century City* (Cambridge, Mass.: Harvard University Press, 1964); and David Montgomery, *Beyond Equality: Labor and the Radical Republicans, 1862-1872* (New York: Random House, 1967). Several young historians, such as Paul Faler in his work on early shoe workers, Alan Dawley in his study of early shoe workers' unions, Daniel Walkowitz in his work on Troy, New York, Tamara Hareven in her examination of Manchester textile workers, and Thomas Dublin in his study of Lowell's textile workers, have also broken new ground.

3. From the late nineteenth century until the middle of the twentieth, Lynn shoe workers were continually seceding from national unions which in many cases they themselves set up. From the late nineteenth century, the Lynn lasters went in and out of the Knights of Saint Crispin; the Socialist Trade and Labor Alliance; the Lasters Protective Union, AF of L; The Boot and Shoe Workers Union, AF of L; the Lasters Protective Union, independent; the Independent Lasters Union; the United Shoe Workers Union; and the Amalgamated Shoe Workers Union. They generally bolted from the national organizations because of conflict between national directives and local concerns.

4. Class solidarity on the local level often involved a parochial view of the working class. Workers in Lynn felt solidarity and unity with other workers, but that solidarity and unity was strongest with local Lynn workers around local issues.

5. See Paul Faler, "Workingmen, Mechanics and Social Change: Lynn, Massachusetts, 1800-1860," Ph.D. dissertation, University of Wisconsin, 1970, and David Johnson, *Sketches of Lynn* (Lynn: Thomas Nichols, 1880), for a discussion of the older system and of the social institution which the Lynn craftsmen built to support themselves.

6. See Faler, "Workingmen," pp. 457-460.

7. Ibid., pp. 461, 467.

8. For an extended discussion of the Knights of Saint Crispin in Lynn and the level of skill among their membership, see Alan Dawley, *Class and Community: The Industrial Revolution in Lynn* (Cambridge, Mass.: Harvard University Press, 1976).

9. "Lynn Lasters Union, Receipt Book," Vol. 10; "Minutes of Lynn Lasters Union," Vol. 1, November 9, 1898; "Minutes of Benefit Association," Vol. 24, September 10, 1894; *Record Book,* Lasters Aid Association, Vol. 26, June 1890-November 1890, Lynn Lasters Union Papers. The pool or billiards room operated by the Lasters Union was so successful that it brought $10 to $20 weekly into the treasury. "Dues Book," Vol. 10, 1894-1896, Lynn Lasters Union Papers.

10. *Boston Evening Transcript,* November 13, 1886.

11. *Lynn Daily Bee,* September 2, 1890; *Lynn Transcript,* September 5, 1890.

12. "Testimony of Horace Eaton, Sec. of Lynn Lasters," *Industrial Commission,* Vol. 7, p. 364.

13. *Annual Report,* Knights of Labor, Cutters Assembly, No. 3662, 1905.

14. "Minutes of Benefit Association," Vol. 24; *Record Book,* Lasters Aid Association, Vol. 26, June 1890-November 1890, Lynn Lasters Union Papers.

15. "Testimony of Horace Eaton," *Industrial Commission,* Vol. 8, p. 351. Lasters Union officials were not allowed to act unless given instructions by the "crew" involved in the particular dispute. "Minutes of Lynn Lasters Union," Vol. 1, 1897, 1898.

16. *Thirty-eighth An. Rpt. MBLS, 1907* (Boston: 1908), p. 142. See "Lest We Forget," pamphlet of the United Shoe Workers of America, 1913, for a discussion of why the shoe workers in Lynn became disillusioned with the leadership of the Book and Shoe Workers (especially on the issue of compulsory arbitration which the local rank and file felt was a sellout to management of shop floor militance) and how the local militants broke off to form independent unions which ultimately became the United Shoe Workers.

17. Massachusetts Bureau of Statistics of Labor, "Directory of Labor Organizations," *Labor Bulletins,* 1909-1913.

18. A. E. Galster, *The Labor Movement in the Shoe Industry, With Special Reference to Philadelphia* (New York: Ronald Press Co., 1924), pp. 145-155.

19. Ibid., p. 156.

20. Ibid., pp. 162-163; Edward Burt, *The Shoe Craft* (Boston: Everett Press, 1917), p. 69.

21. "Minutes of Lynn Lasters Union," Vol. 1, December 1897, January 1898, Lynn Lasters Union Papers.

22. Robert Billups and Phillip Jones, *Labor and Conditions in the Shoe Industry in Massachusetts, 1920-1924* (Washington, D.C.: U. S. Government Printing Office, 1925), pp. 26-27.

23. *Immigrants in Industry,* Vol. 74, p. 399. Based on a sample of 641, the Immigration Commission estimated that over 41 percent of the workers were union members.

24. "Directory of Labor Organizations," *Labor Bulletins,* 1903-1915.

25. *The Union Worker,* March 20, 1924.

26. Ibid., May 29, 1924.

27. Ibid., June 26, 1924.

28. Ibid., February 14, 1924.

29. Ibid.

30. Ibid., January 31, 1924.

31. Ibid.

32. Ibid.

33. Ibid., June 26, 1924.

34. Ibid.

35. *Thirtieth An. Rpt. MBLS, 1889* (Boston: 1889), p. 19.

36. Ibid.

37. In the late nineteenth and early twentieth centuries, Lynn had the third largest number of trade unions of any city in the state (*Massachusetts Labor Bulletin,* Nos. 1-38, 1897-1905).

38. Tape sessions with shoe workers.

39. In the shoe shops, the workers would help each other so that all would finish their batches together and could leave the shop together. "Minutes of Lynn Lasters Union," Vol. 1, June 23, 1897, Lynn Lasters Union Papers. Also in a taped interview with Nick Pappas, a business agent for the shoe workers, Pappas claimed that when he worked in the shops, the faster cutters would help the slower ones so that they could all leave together.

40. *Thirty-fourth An. Rpt. MBLS, 1903* (Boston: 1903), p. 381.

41. Ibid., pp. 378, 380-381.

42. *The Union Leader* (Lynn), May 29, 1920. In his work on machinists and the workers' control struggles in America, David Montgomery has found that the struggle for job control in Lynn dated back to 1904 when the Lynn machinists successfully blocked the introduction of premium pay.

43. Finn Malm, "Local 201, U.E.-C.I.O.," Ph.D. dissertation, Massachusetts Institute of Technology, 1946, discusses General Electric's attempts to keep out the union with such tactics.

44. Quoted in *The Union Leader,* May 29, 1920.

45. Ibid., June 19, 1920.

46. "Fifteen Years with 201, U.E.-C.I.O.," ms. of the Lynn Local (Lynn: 1948).

47. Ibid.; and James J. Matles and James Higgins, *Them and Us: Struggles of a Rank-and-File Union* (Englewood Cliffs, N.J.: Prentice-Hall, 1974), p. 34.

48. "Fifteen Years with 201, U.E.-C.I.O."

49. Ibid.

50. Ibid.

51. *Electrical Union News,* 1938, 1939, 1940.

52. Ibid., 1938.

53. For a discussion of the process of conservatism in organized labor's interaction with large-scale corporations, see Lorin Lee Cary, "Institutionalized Conservatism in the Early C.I.O.: Adolph Germer, A Case Study," *Labor History* 13 (Fall 1972): 375-478.

CHAPTER 5

1. For the best and most complete statement of this process, see E. P. Thompson, *The Making of the English Working Class* (New York: Random House, 1963). For an

American version of Thompson's work, see Herbert Gutman, "Work, Culture, and Society in Industrializing America, 1815-1919," *American Historical Review* 78 (June 1973): 531-588. For two studies on the process of transition from pre-industrial to industrial environments in Lynn, see Alan Dawley and Paul Faler, "Working-Class Culture and Politics in the Industrial Revolution, 1820-1890," *Journal of Social History* 9 (July 1976) and Alan Dawley, *Class and Community: The Industrial Revolution in Lynn* (Cambridge, Mass.: Harvard University Press, 1976).

2. For a discussion of anthropological methodology for analyzing community structure and institutions during conflict, see W. Lloyd Warner and J. O. Low, "The Factory in the Community," in E. Digby Baltzell, ed., *The Search for Community in Modern America* (New York: Harper and Row, 1968), pp. 22-39.

3. David Johnson, *Sketches of Lynn* (Lynn: Thomas Nichols, 1880), pp. 31-32.

4. "Shoe Manufacturing in Lynn," *Boot and Shoe Recorder* (Lynn: 1892), p. 14.

5. U.S. Department of Labor, *Description of Occupations, Boot and Shoe and Tanning* (Washington, D.C.: U.S. Government Printing Office, 1918), pp. 63-70; Leo Brown, "Collective Bargaining in the Leather Industry," Ph.D. dissertation, Harvard University, 1940, p. 14.

6. Calculated from statistics of *Massachusetts State Census, 1895,* Vol. 4, pp. 392-393, using shoe workers, both male and female, and leather workers, only male. See Table 6 for data on changing ethnicity in the Lynn labor force.

7. *Lynn Transcript,* August 1, 1890; *Massachusetts State Annual Report of Manufacturers, 1891* (Boston: 1892), p. 255.

8. *Lynn Transcript,* August 1, 1890.

9. *Lynn Daily Item,* October 2, 1890.

10. *Annual Report, Shoe and Leather Reporter, 1886* (Boston: 1886).

11. *Lynn Transcript,* September 5, 1890.

12. On September 5, 1890, John T. Moulton returned from New York where, after a conference with the executive committee of the NALM, he obtained a pledge of support from the national association. *Lynn Daily Item,* September 5, 1890; Leo Brown, *Union Policies in the Leather Industry* (Cambridge, Mass.: Harvard University Press, 1947), pp. 24-25, 31; *Lynn Transcript,* September 5, 1890; *Lynn Daily Item,* October 4, 1890.

13. *Lynn Transcript,* September 5, 1890.

14. *Lynn Daily Bee,* September 4, 1890.

15. *Lynn Daily Item,* September 11, 1890.

16. Ibid., September 16, 1890.

17. Ibid., September 14, 1890.

18. Herbert Gutman has called attention to the support merchants and small businessmen gave to the strikers. For example, see "Workers Struggle for Power," in H. Wayne Morgan, ed., *The Gilded Age, A Reappraisal . . .* (Syracuse, N.Y.: Syracuse University Press, 1970), p. 20. According to Gutman, the difference between the support given in the small industrial towns and by Lynn merchants was one of motivation. Gutman attributes the merchants' support to personal ties between workers and small businessmen which went back to earlier stages of development. Although personal ties were clearly a factor in Lynn, many of the

merchants acted because of the organized workers' economic "clout." The Lynn workers were accustomed to using their buying power to punish local merchants and tradesmen for not supporting strikes. In 1894, the Lynn Lasters Union refused to buy coal from the local dealers because they were "not progressive" and had failed to support the city's workers. "Minutes Book, Lynn Lasters Benefit Association," Vol. 24, September 10, 1894, Lynn Lasters Union Papers.

19. *Lynn Daily Item,* September 16, 1890.

20. *Lynn Daily Bee,* September 24, 1890.

21. For a more complete discussion of this concept, see Dawley, *Class and Community.*

22. *Lynn Daily Item,* October 6, 1890.

23. Ibid.

24. Local hotels, fearing a boycott, refused to board strikebreakers. H. Hitcock, proprietor of the Ideal Dining Room, stated to the local newspapers that he refused to have anything to do with the strikebreakers. He "did not want such boarders." *Lynn Daily Bee,* September 20, 1890.

25. Ibid.

26. Ibid., October 9, 1890.

27. Ibid.

28. Ibid., October 4, 1890.

29. Ibid.

30. From an early age, working-class children from the Brickyard identified with local working-class peer groups who were centers for the activity and in constant conflict with the police. Much of their activity was directed against the symbols of the controlling elite of the city, such factories and abandoned tenement buildings. Papers of the Gregg House, *Scrapbook 1,* 1907.

31. *Lynn Daily Bee,* September 19, 1890.

32. *Lynn Daily Item,* September 19, 1890.

33. Ibid.

34. *Lynn Daily Bee,* September 19, 1890.

35. *Lynn Daily Item,* September 20, 1890.

36. Ibid.

37. Ibid., September 23, 1890.

38. *Lynn Daily Bee,* September 24, 1890.

39. *Lynn Transcript,* September 19, October 3, 1890; *Lynn Daily Item,* October 2, 1890; *Lynn Daily Bee,* September 27, 1890. By late September, the national association began sending unemployed leather workers to Lynn for the purpose of breaking the strike there (*Lynn Daily Item,* September 27, 1890).

40. *Lynn Daily Item,* September 26, 1890.

41. Ibid., October 2, 1890.

42. *Lynn Daily Bee,* September 27, 1890.

43. One old shoe worker who reportedly followed the course of labor in Lynn from 1860 to 1890 stated that Lynn was on "the eve of the greatest struggle of organized labor and capital that this country has ever known." *Lynn Daily Item,* October 20, 1890.

44. Ibid.

45. Ibid., November 15, 1890.

46. "Lynn Lasters Union Treasurer's Cash Book," Vols. 3, 4, September 5, 29, October 13, 28, November 25, December 23, 1890, January 20, Feburary 21, June 1, 1891, Lasters Union Papers.

47. *Lynn Daily Item*, January 1, 1891.

48. Ibid., October 6, 1890.

49. Ibid., December 24, 1890.

50. Fogg ran on the Republican ticket against the Workingmen's party. Fogg was a member of the Knights of Labor and came out of the strong working-class third ward. Although the city-wide Republican party was making much of law and order, their candidate for mayor was running on his connections with the working class and was calling for the "impartial enforcement of the laws." In the confusion of the strike and with two working-class union members running against one another, one for the Republican and one for the Workingmen's party, the election was a close one. Fogg polled 3,736 votes and Newhall, the Workingmen's candidate, 3,118. The leaders of the strike told their members to "vote strike" and support Newhall, but many shoe workers, along with the majority of the city's middle class, voted for fellow heeler E. Knowlton Fogg. *Lynn Daily Item*, November 18, November 26, December 9, December 10, 1890; *Lynn City Directories*, 1885.

51. During the strike in Lynn, the leather manufacturers began locking out Knights of Labor workers in New York City.

52. In an interview on December 13, 1972, with Thomas Coleman at the Lynn Union Hall, United Shoe Workers, I asked Mr. Coleman what non-shoe workers such as salesmen and real estate agents did in their spare time. He responded that "in the old days there were only shoe workers in Lynn."

53. Although the men were part of the Knights of Labor with its national organization, the Knights were unable to coordinate an effective national boycott against scab leather. The power of the Knights in Lynn was in the local support they enjoyed. The manufacturers dealt mostly with nonlocal markets. Shoe towns like Brockton and Haverhill were not as organized as Lynn in the 1880s, and coordination and communication were not sufficiently developed to organize an effective state-wide boycott.

54. *Thirtieth An. Rpt. MBLC, 1889* (Boston: 1899), p. 197; *Twenty-ninth An. Rpt. MBLS, 1898* (Boston: 1898), p. 613; "Minutes of Lynn Lasters Union," Vol. 1, August 23, 1899, January 21, 31, 1900, Lynn Lasters Union Papers, Baker Library.

55. *Shoe Workers Journal* (January 1903): 10-12, as quoted in A. E. Galster, *The Labor Movement in the Shoe Industry, With Special Reference to Philadelphia* (New York: Ronald Press Co., 1924), p. 82.

56. *Thirty-fourth An. Rpt. MBLS, 1903* (Boston: 1903), pp. 374-375, 377-379; *Official Report, Boot and Shoe Cutters Assembly, Knights of Labor* (Lynn: 1905).

57. *Official Report, Boot and Shoe Cutters Assembly, Knights of Labor* (Lynn: 1905).

58. "Strike of 1903," ms., Lynn Historical Society.

59. *Lynn Daily Item*, January 21, 1903.

60. *Thirty-fourth An. Rpt. MBLS*, 1903, pp. 377-381.

61. Ibid.

62. *Shoe Workers Journal* (September 1910): 8, as quoted in Galster, *Labor Movement,* p. 8.

63. *Lynn Daily Item,* September 1, 2, 1917.

64. Ibid., September 6, 7, 8, 1917.

65. Ibid., September 14, 1917.

66. Ibid., September 20, 1917.

67. See John Laslett, *Labor and the Left: A Study of Socialist and Radical Influence in the American Labor Movement* (New York: Basic Books, 1970), pp. 55-91.

68. *Lynn Daily Item,* September 9, 1925.

69. Tape sessions with shoe workers.

70. *Lynn Daily Item,* January 20, 1938.

71. Sumner Slichter, *Union Policies and Industrial Management* (Washington, D.C.: Brookings Institute, 1941), pp. 363-364.

72. Tape sessions with shoe and electrical workers.

CHAPTER 6

1. Tape sessions with retired shoe workers.

2. Ibid.

3. Ibid.

4. Ibid.

5. Ibid.

6. Taped interviews with retired workers of any community usually reflect this nostalgia and a sense of lost community. Much of this nostalgia has to do with the vagueness of the concept of community. Ultimately, community is a feeling of social cohesion tied together by ritualized and institutionalized interactions. These interactions are greatest in youth, for it is at this time that friends are most likely local and that the closest ties are formed to institutions such as schools, churches, and clubs. What is significant about the reflections of the Lynn workers is that their "good old days" were times when class and class cohesion were strong. These workers are not reminiscing about a time in which everyone was equal or when there was a cohesive society of all classes. The "good old days" were times in which there was a strong sense of class solidarity and class consciousness, when *workers* stuck together.

7. Taped interview with Mike Carrucho.

8. Tape sessions with shoe and electrical workers.

9. Tape sessions with retired shoe workers.

10. Tape sessions with retired electrical workers; also life history of Mike Carrucho and tape sessions with retired shoe workers.

11. Tape sessions with retired electrical workers.

12. Ibid.; also interview with Harold Walker, officer of the Lynn Historical Society, who testified to the importance of the Odd Fellows when he worked for General Electric as his first job.

13. Tape sessions with retired electrical workers; also interview with Thomas Coleman at the Lynn Shoe Workers Union Hall, December 1972.

14. For a discussion of the impact of Taylorism on the worker, see George Friedmann, *The Anatomy of Work* (New York: Free Press, 1964 ed.), pp. 4, 64-76.

15. Tape sessions with retired electrical workers.

16. Herbert Northrup, "The Case of Bowlwareism," *Harvard Business Review* 41 (September-October 1963): 86-97; James J. Matles and James Higgins, *Them and Us: Struggles of a Rank-and-File Union* (Englewood Cliffs, N.J.: Prentice-Hall, 1974), pp. 245-253.

17. Matles and Higgins, *Them and Us,* pp. 250-253.

18. For a discussion of consumerism and the working class, see Stuart Ewen, *Captains of Consciousness* (New York: McGraw-Hill, 1976).

19. For a discussion of working-class culture in suburbia, see Bennett Berger, *Working-Class Suburb: A Study of Auto Workers in Suburbia* (Berkeley, Calif.: University of California Press, 1960) and Herbert Gans, *The Levittowners* (New York: Alfred Knopf, 1967).

20. Informal interviews with individual workers at local 201, International Union of Electrical (IUE) Workers Union Hall, both the old guard and the younger disgruntled challengers. Not represented here are the supporters of the Progressive Labor party which had a small but noticeable following in Lynn's General Electrical plants. Also missing are the opinions of the sizable but older supporters of the United Electrical Workers which, until recently, accounted for almost 50 percent of the General Electric workers in Lynn.

CHAPTER 7

1. William Robinson, "Fall River; A Dying Industry," *The New Republic* 39 (June 4, 1924): 38.

2. Lizzie Borden, who came from one of the city's leading families, was found innocent of the murder of her father and stepmother.

3. Memorandum by J. T. Lincoln, Fall River Iron Works Papers, Baker Library, Harvard University.

4. Henry Fenner, *History of Fall River* (New York: F. T. Smiley Publishing Co., 1906), p. 72; Robert Lamb, "Development of Entrepreneurship: Fall River, 1813-1850," Ph.D. dissertation, Harvard University, 1935, Chap. 5, pp. 12-13; Chap. 15, p. 22; Chap. 3, p. 10; Chap. 9, pp. 1-2.

5. Lamb, "Development," Chap. 9, p. 11.

6. See Lamb, "Development," which describes the marriage patterns of Fall River's elites; see also Thomas Smith, *The Cotton Textile Industry of Fall River* (New York: King's Crown, 1944), pp. 77-78, and Sylvia Lintner, "A Social History of Fall River, 1859-1879," Ph.D. dissertation, Radcliffe College, 1945, p. 16.

7. Harriet Robinson, *Loom and Spindle* (Boston: Thomas Y. Crowell and Co., 1898), p. 31.

8. For a discussion of early strikes and activity in the New England textile towns of the 1830s and 1840s, see Thomas Dublin, "Women, Work, and Protest in the Early Lowell Mills," *Labor History* 16 (Winter 1975): 99-116.

9. Quoted in Lamb, "Development," Chap. 15, p. 18.

10. Ibid., p. 19.

11. Lintner, "Social History," pp. 86-88.

12. Smith, *Cotton Textile Industry*, p. 69.

13. Jonathan P. Harrison, *Certain Dangerous Tendencies in American Life* (Boston: Houghton, Osgood, and Co., 1880), p. 160.

14. Quoted in Lamb, "Development," Chap. 14, p. 5.

15. Testimony of Clare De Graffenried before the *United States Industrial Commission*, Vol. 7, 56th Cong., 2d Sess., House Doc. No. 495 (Washington, D.C.: 1900), p. 219.

16. Unlike Lynn, where the workers were essentially located near the central city, in Fall River the working-class residential areas were scattered throughout the city. Since the Fall River mills depended upon internal economies, they did not require close location to the central business or warehouse sectors of the city. Once liberated from the waterfalls by steam power, they sought the more spacious peripheral water sites. A comparison of the population density of Fall River and Lynn wards indicates the process of this working-class dispersal by the mid-1880s. Lynn's central wards were ever increasing in density, with the population of the fourth, fifth, and sixth center wards totaling 31,607, while that of the first, second, and seventh was only 4,716 (by 1910, this disparity had grown even greater). Fall River's wards, although much higher in overall population, did not vary in density between the various wards. Most of its wards included very high density working-class areas as well as some middle-class and upper-class areas. The high density working-class areas were distributed widely about the city with the dispersion of the various mills.

17. Testimony taken by the Senate Committee, "Relations Between Labor and Capital," 1883, Vol. 1, pp. 60-65; quoted in Herbert Lahne, *The Cotton Mill Worker* (New York: Farrar and Rinehart, 1944), p. 27.

18. Payroll records, Metacomet Mills, October 26, 1886, Fall River Iron Works Papers, Baker Library, Harvard University.

19. Lamb, "Development," Chap. 15, p. 10.

20. George Gunton, *Wealth and Progress* (New York: D. Appleton, 1887), p. 370.

21. *Annual Reports, Bolton and District Operative Cotton Spinners, 1882-1913; Annual Reports, Oldham Cotton Spinners, 1882; Annual Reports, Amalgamated Society of Operative Lacemakers, 1886*, located in the Webb Collection, London School of Economics.

22. See Donald Cole, *Immigrant City* (Chapel Hill, N.C.: University of North Carolina Press, 1963); Vira Slakman, *Economic History of a Factory Town* (Smith College Studies in History, Vol. 20, Northamptom, 1936); John Coolidge, *Mill and Mansion* (New York: Russell and Russell, 1942); and Philip Silvia, "The Spindle City: Labor, Politics, and Religion in Fall River, Massachusetts, 1870-1905," Ph.D. dissertation, Fordham University, 1973. Silvia argues that Fall River Irish followed patterns similar to Handlin's Boston Irish. However, his data reflect mostly the earlier migration and do not deal with Fall River Irish who came from Lancashire. A comparison of the ethnic makeup of a sample of skilled spinners from Bolton, Lancashire, who received funds to migrate to this country, with skilled Fall River textile workers for the same years (1880-1905) shows similar percentages of Irish

workers in both groups. Of the Lancashire workers receiving emigration funds, 32 percent were of Irish origin. This corresponds roughly to the percentage of Irish in the skilled trades in Fall River. Moreover, the number of Irish coming over with lesser skills was much higher than the 32 percent of the spinners—hence, the large number of Irish textile workers in Fall River, many of whom had industrial and trade union experience.

23. The annual reports of various textile unions in Lancashire, England, list the amounts given for emigration funds and show that the grants were given to loyal trade unionists who had become "victims" of the union struggle because of blacklisting or striking. The funds were given to strikers according to union seniority. Many unions listed not only the total amounts given in emigration grants, but also the names and destinations of the recipients of the grants. By tracing these names, a pattern of migration from England to Fall River as well as from Ireland to Lancashire to Fall River emerges (*Annual Reports*, Oldham and Bolton Cotton Spinners, and Operative Lacemakers, Webb Collection). Fall River's expansion, combined with the great cotton famine in Lancashire in the 1860s and the gradual reduction of wages in Lancashire from 1835 to 1876, created both a pull to Fall River and a push from Lancashire which began the great migration of English and Irish Lancashire workers to Fall River. This migration reached its height in the late 1870s (*Report of the Industrial Renumeration Conference* [London: January 1886], p. 50).

24. Fenner, *History*, p. 146.

25. Address to International Textile Conference, England, 1894, quoted in *Fall River Daily Herald*, August 7, 1894.

26. Arthur Phillips, *Phillips History of Fall River* (Fall River: Dover Press, 1945), p. 145.

27. Quoted in Rowland Berthoff, *British Immigrants in Industrial America* (Cambridge, Mass.: Harvard University Press, 1953), pp. 32-33.

28. *Thirteenth An. Rpt. MBLS, 1882* (Boston: 1882), p. 199.

29. Thomas Young, *The American Cotton Industry* (New York: Charles Schribner's and Son, 1903), pp. 1-2.

30. Harrison, *Certain Dangerous Tendencies*, p. 201.

31. J. Gilmore Speed, *A Fall River Incident* (New York: J. J. Little and Co., 1895), p. 18.

32. Ibid.; Gertrude Springer, "Up from Bankruptcy," *Survey* 66 (July 1931): 341.

33. Smith, *Cotton Textile Industry*, p. 76; Lintner, "Social History," pp. 86-88.

34. *Fall River Daily Herald*, March 2, 1889.

35. Ibid., March 22, 1889.

36. William Hale, "The Importance of Churches in a Manufacturing Town," *Forum* 18 (September 1884-February 1895): 295.

37. Ibid.

38. Ibid.

39. Fall River earned the infamous distinction of having the highest death rate of any northern city, far surpassing New York and even the mill cities of Lancashire, England. Charles Verrill, "Infant Mortality and Its Relation to the Employment of Mothers in Fall River Massachusetts," *Transactions of the 15th International Congress*

on Hygiene and Demography, Washington, D.C., 1912 (Washington, D.C.: 1913), Vol. 3, pp. 319-320.

40. *Sixth An. Rpt. MBLS, 1875* (Boston: 1875), p. 287.

41. Ibid., p. 291; sample of textile operatives from payroll records, Fall River Iron Works, 1886, 1887, 1895, 1896, 1897, 1902, 1907. See below.

42. Harrison, *Certain Dangerous Tendencies,* p. 190.

43. Quoted in Lintner, "Social History," p. 49.

44. *Fall River Daily Herald,* March 22, 1889.

45. Ibid.

46. Monthly wages actually fell from $18.50 in 1884 to $17.32 in 1904. *1907 MBLS,* Bulletin No. 51 (July-August), p. 33. Wages for the sampled operatives from the payroll records of the Fall River Iron Works, although fluctuating greatly among the various occupational groups, generally remained consistent throughout the decades mentioned above.

47. Testimony by Clare De Graffenried, *United States Industrial Commission,* Vol. 7, p. 219.

48. *Massachusetts State Census, 1898,* Vol. 1, pp. 389-390; *Massachusetts State Census,* 1905, Vol. 1, pp. 67, 110. Thirty-eight percent of the families in Fall River, compared to only 27 percent in Lynn, had larger than five-person families.

49. *Fall River Daily Herald News,* September 19, 1953.

50. *Massachusetts State Census, 1905,* Vol. 1, p. 69; Ira Podea, "Quebec to Little Canada," *New England Quarterly* (September 1950): 373-374.

51. *Massachusetts State Census, 1885,* Vol. 1, p. 501.

52. Hale, "Importance of Churches," p. 295; *Fall River Daily Herald News,* September 19, 1953; Lintner, "Social History," pp. 86-88.

53. One percent of the French Canadians worked in the Iron Works Mills in 1886. It was not until 1890 that substantial numbers worked in the mills outside of the American Linen Mills. Sample of operatives from the payroll records of the mills of the Fall River Iron Works, Baker Library, Harvard University. Ethnicity based upon surname (see Table 11).

54. At first, the French Canadians were called "annual Canadians" because they worked only during the winter months. Testimony of Rufus Wade before the U.S. Industrial Commission, *U.S. Industrial Commission Reports,* Vol. 7, p. 72.

55. U. S. Congress, Senate, Immigration Commission, *Immigrants in Industry,* 61st Cong., 2d Sess., S. Doc. No. 633 (Washington, D.C.: 1909-1910), Vol. 71, p. 39.

56. For a more complete discussion of the French Canadian culture and migration to the United States, see Leon Truesdell, *The Canadian Born in the United States: An Analysis of the Canadian Element in the Population of the United States, 1850 to 1930* (New Haven, Conn.: Yale University Press, 1943), p. 45; Marcus Lee Hansen, *The Mingling of the Canadian and American Peoples* (New Haven, Conn.: Yale University Press, 1940); and Ralph Vicero, "The Immigration of French-Canadians to New England, 1840-1900," Ph.D. dissertation, University of Wisconsin, 1968.

57. For a more complete discussion of stem-migration, see Conrad Arenberg

and Solon Kimball, *Family and Community in Ireland* (Cambridge, Mass.: Harvard University Press, 1940), and Harry Schwarzweller, James Brown, and J. J. Mangalam, *Mountain Families in Transition* (University Park, Penn.: Pennsylvania State University Press, 1971).

58. Truesdell, *The Canadian Born*, p. 44; Arenberg and Kimball, *Family*.

59. Family employment is reflected in the high percentage of related workers found in the payroll records of the mills. Frequently, 20 percent of the operatives in a single room would have close relatives in the same room. Payroll records of the Fall River Iron Works, 1896, Mill Number 4 operatives in spinning and weaving rooms, 1897, Mill Number 2, spinning and weaving rooms, Fall River Iron Works Papers, Baker Library, Harvard University.

60. U. S. Congress, Senate, Immigration Commission, *Immigrants in Industry*, Vol. 71, p. 395; this is also reflected in the size of the Fall River families.

61. Even as late as the mid-twentieth century, the French Canadians maintained their reputation for a close-knit community. Interview with Manuel Mellow, Fall River operative and organizer for the Textile Workers Organizing Committee (TWOC), November 1973, Fall River, Massachusetts; taped interviews with retired garment workers, available at the Fall River Local, International Ladies Garment Workers Union.

62. *Forty-first An. Rpt. MBLS, 1910* (Boston: 1911); "Living Conditions in Massachusetts" (Boston: 1911), p. 278; Podea, "Quebec to Little Canada," p. 380.

63. Podea, "Quebec to Little Canada," p. 380.

64. Gunton, *Wealth*, p. 362.

65. U. S. Congress, Senate, Immigration Commission, *Immigrants in Industry*, Vol. 72, p. 73.

66. These figures were calculated from samples drawn from the payroll records of the Fall River Iron Works Mills, Baker Library, Harvard University.

67. Donald Taft, *Two Portuguese Communities in New England* (New York: Longmans, Green, and Co., 1923), p. 98.

68. Massachusetts Bureau of Statistics of Labor, *Massachusetts Labor Bulletin*, No. 37 (September 1905): 136.

69. *Massachusetts State Census, 1905*, Vol. 1, p. 67.

70. Taft, *Two Portuguese Communities*, p. 30.

71. *Forty-first An. Rpt. MBLS, 1910*, p. 279.

72. U. S. Congress, Senate, Immigration Commission, *Immigrants in Industry*, Vol. 72, p. 39; *Massachusetts State Census, 1885*, Vol. 1, p. 501; *1895*, Vol. 2, p. 597; *1905*, Vol. 1, p. 67.

73. Sample of operatives from the payroll records of the Fall River Iron Works. It is interesting to note that in 1902, the Portuguese, as the French Canadians in the 1890s, were employed in occupations that had the greatest standard deviation from the mean wage, and thus the least security.

74. *Massachusetts State Census, 1895*, Vol. 2, p. 597; *1905*, Vol. 1, p. 67.

75. *Fall River Daily Herald News*, September 19, 1953.

76. Ibid.

77. Report No. 2, National Industrial Conference Board, "The Cost of Living

Among Wage Earners in Fall River, Massachusetts, October, 1919" (Boston: November 1919), p. 2.

78. *Massachusetts State Census, 1885,* Vol. 1, pp. 160, 162.

79. Smith, *Cotton Textile Industry,* p. 76; *Thirteenth An. Rpt. MBLS, 1882* (Boston: 1882), p. 206; Rhetta Dorr, "The Woman's Invasion," *Everybody's Magazine* (November 1908): 580-591.

80. Lintner, "Social History," pp. 117-118.

81. Payroll records, Fall River Iron Works, Mill Number 4, Papers of the Fall River Iron Works, Baker Library, Harvard University.

82. Payroll records, Fall River Iron Works, Metacomet Mill, Mills number 4, 2, and 5, Papers of the Fall River Iron Works, Baker Library, Harvard University.

83. Ibid.; and Thomas Uttley, *Cotton Spinning and Manufacturing in the United States* (Manchester, U.K.: University of Manchester, 1905), p. 31.

84. *Fall River Daily Herald,* March 22, 1884, February 28, 1884; *Thirteenth An. Rpt. MBLS, 1882,* p. 225; Smith, *Cotton Textile Industry,* p. 76.

85. *Forty-first An. Rpt. MBLS, 1910,* p. 278.

86. In 1902, the weekly mean wages of the most numerous occupations ranged from $10.43 for weavers, $4.37 for spinners, $5.17 for doffers, $7.78 for flay-frame enders, and $7.11 for spoolers. These figures are somewhat high since 1902 was one of the best years for wages from before 1880 until the upswing in 1907. The figures quoted here may be somewhat high since state-wide the mean weekly wages paid weavers were a little under $8 for women and under $9 for men. Stanley Howard, *The Movement of Wages in the Cotton Manufacturing Industry of New England Since 1860* (Boston: National Council of American Cotton Manufacturers, 1920), pp. 17, 67; payroll records, Fall River Iron Works Mill Number 4, Papers of the Fall River Iron Works, Baker Library, Harvard University.

87. U.S. Department of Labor, *Women and Children Wage Earners,* 61st Cong., 2d Sess., Senate Doc. No. 645, Vol. 16, Part 3 (Washington, D.C.: 1909-1910), p. 976; Lahne, *Cotton Mill Worker,* p. 280. Rhetta Dorr claims that the individual wage became meaningless. "The family wage is everything" ("Woman's Invasion," pp. 588-589).

88. Taped interview with Manuel Mellow, retired textile worker, organizer for the local TWOC; "Testimony of Thomas O'Donnell" before the Senate Committee upon the Relations Between Labor and Capital, 1883, quoted in John Garraty, ed., *Labor and Capital in the Gilded Age* (Boston: Little, Brown, 1968), p. 33.

89. *Report of Massachusetts Commission on Minimum Wage,* Massachusetts House Doc. No. 1697 (Boston: 1912), p. 17.

90. U. S. Department of Labor, *Women and Children Wage Earners,* pp. 745-776.

91. Ibid.; U. S. Congress, Senate, Immigration Commission, *Immigrants in Industry,* Vol. 72, p. 114.

92. Louis Dublin, "Infant Mortality in Fall River," *American Statistical Association Quarterly Publication* 14 (June 1915); Verrill, "Infant Mortality," Vol. 3, p. 319.

93. U. S. Department of Labor, *Women and Children Wage Earners,* p. 754.

Both the U. S. Congress, Senate, Immigration Commission of 1909 and Donald Taft, in 1923, placed the figure higher.

94. Woman's Trade Union League, ms., 1922-1928, Folder 33, Woman's Archives, Schlesinger Library, Radcliffe College; *Child Labor Bulletin* (Boston: 1917), p. 214.

95. F. K. Brown, *Through the Mill* (Boston: Pilgrim Press, 1911), pp. 96, 103.

96. Gunton, *Wealth,* p. 362; taped interview with Manuel Mellow and his wife.

97. *Massachusetts State Census, 1895,* pp. 276-278; *Massachusetts Child Labor Bulletin, 1917* (Boston: 1917).

98. Ibid.

99. Verrill, "Infant Mortality," p. 318.

100. Ibid., pp. 319-320. Rhetta Dorr claimed the figure to be as high as 350 deaths per 1,000 births ("Woman's Invasion," p. 590).

101. Verrill, "Infant Mortality," pp. 319-320; Dublin, "Infant Mortality," pp. 505-520. Although one study in 1908 and another in 1913 emphasized that working mothers should stay home after birth, to care for and breastfeed their children, it is clear that impure water and surroundings, more than the actual working of the mothers, caused the high death rates, especially since the highest death rates were in the poorest working-class areas (Dublin, "Infant Mortality," p. 518). In almost 42 percent of the traceable stillborn deaths in Fall River, the mothers worked during pregnancy (Verrill, "Infant Mortality," pp. 319-320).

102. *Fall River Daily Herald,* July 2, 1902.

103. Carol Aronovici, *Housing Conditions in Fall River* (Fall River: Associated Charities, Housing Committee, 1912), p. 3; for a critique of Aronovici's study, see Taft, *Two Portuguese Communities.*

104. Ethel Johnson, "Fifteen Years of Minimum Wage in Massachusetts," ms., Ethel Johnson Papers, Folder 96, Woman's Archives, Schlesinger Library, Radcliffe College, p. 4; *Massachusetts Statistical Census, 1905,* Vol. 1, p. 67.

105. Aronovici, *Housing Conditions,* p. 9.

106. Ibid., p. 18.

107. *Forty-first An. Rpt. MBLS, 1910,* p. 279.

108. Ibid.

109. Ibid., pp. 16-17.

110. Ibid.

111. Fenner, *History,* p. 75.

112. See Lamb, "Development," for a discussion of the functioning of the interlocking directorships; and Lintner, "Social History," for their nineteenth-century problems.

113. Smith, *Cotton Textile Industry,* pp. 118-119.

114. Ibid., p. 117. It has been argued that Fall River's failure to install high-speed ring spinners to replace the slower mules also indicated the city's failure to meet competition as early as the 1870s. It is more likely that the mules were retained because the nineteenth-century ring spinners could not produce as fine a thread, and thus could not be used in the production of more finished cloth (ibid., p. 99).

115. Ibid., p. 115.

116. *Forty-first An. Rpt. MBLS, 1910,* p. 282.

117. Springer, "Bankruptcy," p. 342.

118. Smith, *Cotton Textile Industry*, pp. 82-92, 122; see also J. Herbert Burgy, *The New England Cotton Textile Industry* (Baltimore: Waverly Press, 1932), pp. 33-34.

119. William Miernyk, *Inter-Industry Labor Mobility: The Case of the Displaced Textile Worker* (Boston: Northeastern University, 1955), p. 91.

120. Testimony of Representative Thomas Smith of Fall River at "Public Hearings of the Massachusetts Industrial Commission in Fall River, 1930."

121. Robinson, "A Dying Industry," pp. 38-40.

122. Ibid., p. 38.

123. Ibid., p. 40.

124. Springer, "Bankruptcy," p. 341.

125. "Confidential Report," ms., Consumer League Papers, Folder 482, B-24, Woman's Archives, Schlesinger Library, Radcliffe College.

126. "Sweatshops in Fall River and New Bedford, 1938," ms., Consumer League Papers, Folder 482, B-24; Seymour Wolfbein, *The Decline of a Cotton Textile City* (New York: Columbia University Press, 1944), p. 115; Harry Crone, *Thirty-five Years of the Northeast Department* (New York: International Ladies Garment Workers Union, 1970), pp. 3, 20, 22.

127. "Confidential Report"; and Springer, "Bankruptcy," p. 345.

128. "The New Menace in Industry," *Scribner's* (March 1933): 141.

129. "Confidential Report."

130. "Sweatshops, 1938," pp. 4-8; Crone, *Thirty-five Years*, pp. 32-33.

131. Taped interview with Manuel Mellow, textile worker and local organizer.

132. Testimony of Martin Welsh at "Public Hearing of the Massachusetts Industrial Commission in Fall River, 1930."

133. Miernyk, *Inter-Industry Mobility*, p. 64. See also Robinson, "A Dying Industry," p. 40.

134. Carrie Glasser and Bernard Freedman, "Work and Wage Experience of Skilled Cotton Textile Workers," *Monthly Labor Review* 63 (July 1946): 8, 14-24. By 1945, the average age of the Fall River textile worker, based upon a sample of two hundred, was already over forty-five (p. 8).

135. Ibid., p. 21.

136. Ibid., p. 22.

137. Ibid., pp. 13-14; Burgy, *New England Cotton*, p. 150; Paul Whitehead, "The Assimilation of the Portuguese in Fall River," Master's thesis, University of Massachusetts at Amherst, 1966.

138. Robinson, "A Dying Industry," p. 39. In 1924, mills in Reading, Pennsylvania, were refused advertising for workers in the two local Fall River papers.

139. Glasser and Freedman, "Work and Wage Experience," pp. 27-28, 99-100.

CHAPTER 8

1. In the textile industry, machine tending means that the craft skills are incorporated into the machine, and the worker's job is to mind several machines doing the same operation from spinning to weaving.

2. Gertrude Barnum, "The Story of a Fall River Mill Girl," *The Independent* 58 (February 21, 1905): 243.

3. "Testimony of Thomas O'Donnell" before the Senate Committee, Relations Between Labor and Capital, 1883, quoted in John Garraty, ed., *Labor and Capital in the Gilded Age* (Boston: Little, Brown, 1968), p. 36.

4. "Testimony of Dr. Timothy Stow" before the Senate Committee, Relations Between Labor and Capital, 1883, quoted in Garraty, ed., *Labor and Capital*, p. 31.

5. "Testimony of Robert Howard," before the Senate Committee, Relations Between Labor and Capital, 1883, quoted in Garraty, ed., *Labor and Capital*, p. 25. In the textile mill, the cotton begins in the breaking room where it is loosened from the ball and cleaned. It is then moved to the carding room where the fibers are straightened and combed by the carding machine. Next it is doffed off the carder machine and taken to the spinning machine where in the early days the skilled mule spinners spun the fibers into threads and where, later in the century, rows of ring spinners accomplished this task. When the bobbins which accumulate the finished thread are full, the doffer removes them and replaces them with empty bobbins. The bobbins are then moved to the weaving room where the cloth is woven. The weaving room is the noisiest room in the mill (if not actually deafening). Like the spinner, spooler, carder, and doffer, the weaver was responsible for a number of machines—six to eight in the nineteenth century and as many as sixteen to twenty by the first quarter of the twentieth. (With the multiple-loom system, weavers were responsible for as many as seventy-five looms, but by the time this change occurred there were few mills still operating in Fall River.) The work performed by most textile operatives requires more speed and alertness than skill, and by the twentieth century strong feet were also necessary. For a discussion of the impact of a machine-tending technology on the worker's community and job interaction, see Robert Blauner, *Alienation and Freedom* (Chicago: University of Chicago Press, 1964). For a discussion of further labor-saving developments in the textile industry and the effect of the stretchouts on labor, see Eliot Dunlap Smith, *Technology and Labor* (New Haven, Conn.: Yale University Press, 1939).

6. This applied to spinners and carders as well as weavers. *Thirteenth An. Rpt. MBLS, 1882* (Boston: 1882), pp. 307, 351; Sylvia Lintner, "A Social History of Fall River, 1859-1879," Ph.D. dissertation, Radcliffe College, 1945, pp. 117-118; *Charities* 14 (February 4, 1905): 415.

7. *Sixth An. Rpt. MBLS, 1875* (Boston: 1875), p. 287.

8. *Thirteenth An. Rpt. MBLS, 1882*, p. 351.

9. William Hale, "The Importance of Churches in a Manufacturing Town," *Forum* 18 (September 1894-February 1895): 294.

10. Jonathan B. Harrison, *Certain Dangerous Tendencies in American Life* (Boston: Houghton, Osgood, and Co., 1880), pp. 163-164.

11. Sidney Chapman, *Lancashire Cotton Industry* (Manchester, U.K.: University of Manchester, 1904), p. 194. As early as 1801, Sir Frederick Eden observed that Lancashire with its 120 friendly societies had many more such clubs than any other county. He also noted that these clubs, centered in "ale houses," had an obvious tendency to facilitate combinations for improper purposes in trade,

religion, and politics. Sir Frederick M. Eden, *Observations on Friendly Societies*
(London: n.p., 1801), pp. 7, 23.

12. Quoted in Chapman, *Lancashire Cotton Industry,* p. 181.

13. Webb Collection, "Textiles, 4," Folder 4, London School of Economics.

14. Chapman, *Lancashire Cotton Industry,* p. 233.

15. *Report of the Industrial Renumeration Conference* (London: 1885), p. 433.

16. Herbert Lahne, *The Cotton Mill Worker* (New York: Farrar and Rinehart,
1944), claimed that the early Fall River unions were actually locals of the Manchester
union. I have not been able to substantiate this direct link. The Odd Fellows lodges,
besides the Manchester Unity, were also primarily working class, with working-class
officers. The Manchester Unity Lodge was chartered directly from Manchester and
was established in 1881. The Unity Lodge was charter No. 6434 of the Manchester
organization. Lancashire textile workers could then utilize their English membership
to integrate themselves into Fall River through the Odd Fellows. The Ancient Order
of Foresters like the Odd Fellows acted as a transitional institution for Lancashire
textile workers. All the Foresters charters numbered in the thousands, indicating
their English origins and ties (*Fall River City Directory, 1887*).

17. *Thirteenth An. Rpt. MBLS, 1882,* p. 254.

18. Ibid., p. 255.

19. Ibid.

20. Jonathan Lincoln, *The City of the Dinner Pail* (Boston: Houghton-Mifflin,
Co., 1909), p. 53.

21. For a discussion of British workingmen's clubs, see John Taylor, *From Self
Help to Glamour: The Workingmen's Club 1860-1872,* History Workshop Pamphlet,
No. 7 (Oxford: Ruskin College, 1971).

22. *Fall River Daily Herald,* August 9, 1894.

23. J. M. Baernreiter, *English Association of Workingmen,* English ed., A. Taylor,
trans. (London: Swan, Sonnon, Schein, 1889), p. 142.

24. *Cotton Factory Times,* 1885-1904, located in Colundale Library, London.

25. Ibid., January 16, 1885.

26. For a description of this process of self-definition, see E. P. Thompson,
The Making of the English Working Class (New York: Random House, 1963).

27. *The Textile Manufacturer,* November 15, 1883, quoted in Charlotte Erik-
son, "Encouragement of Emigration," *Population Studies* 3 (London: 1949): 266.

28. Thomas Young, *The American Cotton Industry* (New York: Charles Scribner's and Son, 1903), p. 18.

29. *Fall River Daily Herald,* March 1, 1884.

30. Charles Verrill, "Infant Mortality and Its Relation to the Employment of
Mothers in Fall River, Massachusetts," *Transactions of the 15th International Congress on Hygiene and Demography,* Washington, D.C., 1912 (Washington, D.C.:
1913), Vol. 3, p. 330.

31. *Massachusetts Child Labor Bulletin, 1917* (Boston: 1917), p. 214; F. K.
Brown, *Through the Mill* (Boston: Pilgrim Press, 1911).

32. Lintner, "Social History," pp. 107, 109.

33. Brown, *Through the Mill,* p. 85; interview with the curator of the Fall River

Historical Society, both of whose parents were textile workers, February 1, 1973.

34. Brown, *Through the Mill*, p. 85.

35. Ibid., p. 117.

36. *Report of the Fall River School Committee, 1919,* quoted in Donald Taft, *Two Portuguese Communities in New England* (New York: Longmans, Green, and Co., 1923), p. 231.

37. "Testimony of Fanny Ames," *Report of the Industrial Commission,* November 1900, Vol. 7, 56th Cong., 2d Sess., House Doc. No. 495 (Washington, D.C.: 1900), p. 56.

38. *Massachusetts Child Labor Bulletin,* 1914, pp. 7, 11-12.

39. Brown, *Through the Mill*, p. 117; Maurice Hexter, *Juvenile Employment and Labor Mobility in the Business Cycle* (Boston: Massachusetts Child Labor Committee, 1927), p. 13; interview with President Burns, local president of the Textile Workers Union of America in Fall River.

40. Gladys Palmer, "Mobility of Weavers in Three Textile Centers," *Quarterly Journal of Economics* 4 (May 1941): 465-485; *Thirteenth An. Rpt. MBLS, 1882,* p. 202; Brown, *Through the Mill*, p. 117. One French Canadian father went so far as to tell an investigator for the Massachusetts Bureau of Statistics of Labor, "I will not permit my girls to work in any other mill than the one I am in and where I can keep my eye on them" (*Thirteenth An. Rpt. MBLS, 1882,* p. 202).

41. Payroll records, Fall River Iron Works, Mill Number 4, 1896. Papers of the Fall River Iron Works, Baker Library, Harvard University. Twenty percent of the thirty-six weavers in Mill Number 4 also had close relatives working in the weaving room.

42. Brown, *Through the Mill*, p. 46.

43. *Massachusetts Child Labor Bulletin, 1913,* p. 8.

44. Tape sessions with retired garment workers, available at University of Louisville Oral History collection. Quote from Mary Felix whose parents were textile workers and who herself began work as a weaver.

45. Hale, "Importance of Churches," p. 295.

46. Interview with Manuel Mellow and his wife (April 1973 in their apartment in Fall River), both retired textile workers and organizers in Fall River since the early twentieth century; see also F. K. Brown's description of this mother's drinking in *Through the Mill.*

47. Harrison, *Certain Dangerous Tendencies,* p. 184.

48. Ibid., pp. 182-183.

49. *Fall River Daily Herald,* February 28, 1884.

50. Ibid., March 22, 1884.

51. Harrison, *Certain Dangerous Tendencies,* pp. 171-172.

52. Ibid., p. 167.

53. Ibid., pp. 169-170.

54. Ibid., p. 170.

55. "Testimony of J. G. Jackson," before the *United States Industrial Commission,* Vol. 17, 56th Cong., 2d Sess., House Doc. No. 183 (Washington, D.C.: 1901), p. 588, emphasis mine.

56. *Fall River Daily Herald,* March 13, 15, 1889.

57. Quoted in Rowland Berthoff, *British Immigrants in Industrial America* (Cambridge, Mass.: Harvard University Press, 1953), p. 103.

58. *Fall River Daily Herald,* August 7, 1884.

59. Henry Earl, *Fall River and Its Manufacturers* (Fall River: George Bamford, 1910); see also *Fall River City Directories,* 1880-1900.

60. Baernreiter, *English Association of Workingmen,* pp. 219-223.

61. *Fall River Daily Herald News,* March 17, 1963.

62. Conflict within the French Canadian and Irish Catholic communities erupted several times during the late nineteenth century, especially over which priest would head the various ethnic churches in Fall River. In 1870, a Catholic church was built specifically for the French Canadians, under Father Montaubricq, a conservative, anti-union, but pro-French Canadian priest. St. Anne's remained the major French Canadian church until the construction of Notre Dame de Lourdes under the leadership of another antilabor priest, the French Canadian born J. B. Bedard. With the appointment of an Irish priest to St. Anne's, Bedard became the leader of the French Canadian religious community. In 1884, French Canadian Catholics expressed their deep religious distrust of the Irish Catholics' hierarchy in a conflict with the bishop of the area over whether they would accept an Irish Catholic priest to replace Bedard. The heated controversy was finally settled in favor of the French Canadians a year later. Although this struggle reflected ethnic division within Fall River, it must be viewed with caution. The leaders of the conflict with the bishop were also the business elite of the French Canadian population. Moreover, their hostility to the Irish did not necessarily mean class division since the French Canadian religious community and the working-class community had different leaders. Hence, conflicts within the church may not have transferred to conflicts within the class or trade union movement. For a more detailed account of the collision between the Irish hierarchy and the French Canadian religious community, see Philip Silvia, "The Spindle City: Labor, Politics, and Religion in Fall River, Massachusetts," Ph.D. dissertation, Fordham University, 1973, pp. 381-425.

63. Hugo A. Dubuque, *Guide to Canadian-Francais de Fall River* (Fall River: 1889); *Fall River City Directories,* 1887, 1895.

64. Lincoln, *City of the Dinner Pail,* p. 59; Lintner, "Social History," pp. 72-81.

65. In "The Spindle City," pp. 351-306, Philip Silvia gives a vivid account of the conflict between English and Irish trade unionists and of the influx of French Canadians. The trade unionists, fearing the influence of the antiunion French Canadian priests and middle-class leaders, at first looked upon the French Canadians as strikebreakers, depressors of wages, and uninterested in trade unionism. The initial distrust seems to have abated by the late 1880s when the French Canadians were accepted into the working-class community.

66. Donald Taft, *Two Portuguese Communities,* p. 336; Paul Whitehead, "The Assimilation of the Portuguese in Fall River," Master's thesis, University of Massachusetts at Amherst, 1966, pp. 118-169.

67. Whitehead, "Assimilation of the Portuguese," pp. 119-128, and Taft, *Two Portuguese Communities,* p. 337. Typical of this pattern is the life story of Mariano

Biship who was born on St. Michale's Island in the Azores and later became a leader of the textile workers in Fall River. Soon after coming to Fall River with his parents at age ten, Biship entered the Stevens Cotton Mill. When he was old enough, he joined the Liberal Athletic Club where the old men sat and talked of work and the young of athletics and work. Biship met the woman he would later marry, Mary Sousa, in the doffing room where they both worked. Mary had begun working as a doffer at age fourteen. At the time of their marriage, she had never been outside of Fall River, and Biship had only been to New York to meet his father who had gone back to the Azores for a visit (Richard Kelly, *Nine Lives for Labor* [New York: Frederick A. Praeger, 1956], pp. 42-45).

68. Report No. Two, National Industrial Conference Board, "The Cost of Living Among Wage Earners in Fall River, Massachusetts, October, 1919" (Boston: November 1919), p. 3; Whitehead, "Assimilation of the Portuguese," p. 128.

69. See William Thomas and Florian Znaniecki, *The Polish Peasant in Europe and America* (New York: Alfred Knopf, 1927), Vol. 1.

70. See John Bodnar, "Immigration and Modernization: The Case of Slavic Peasants in Industrial America," *Journal of Social History* 10 (Fall 1976): 44-71.

71. *Fall River Herald News*, September 19, 1953.

72. Report No. Two, National Industrial Conference Board, "The Cost of Living," p. 9; taped interviews with retired garment workers.

73. Taft, *Two Portuguese Communities*, p. 223.

74. Whitehead, "Assimilation of the Portuguese," p. 143.

75. *First Annual Report, Associated Charities* (Fall River: April 1889), pp. 8, 15; pamphlet, Family Welfare Association of Fall River, 1938, located in Fall River Library, p. 1.

76. Taft, *Two Portuguese Communities*, pp. 238-246.

77. As is clear from other parts of this work, trade unions were not the exclusive institution of the working class, and their use here in the analysis is not to imply that labor history is only the study of unions and strikes. Unions were in the forefront of the battle between labor and capital, however, and as such they received visual notice by the press and provide the historian with another view of the world of the worker.

CHAPTER 9

1. *Thirteenth An. Rpt. MBLS, 1882* (Boston: 1882), p. 95; Charles Mullen, "Textile Labor Movement," ms., Fall River Historical Society Papers, p. 7. This strike and early conditions in Fall River are discussed in Norman Ware, *The Industrial Worker 1840-1860* (Chicago: Quadrangle Press, 1969), pp. 76-78, 116-118, 202-204.

2. *Fall River Daily Herald*, August 7, 1894.

3. Quoted in *Fall River Daily Herald*, March 15, 1885.

4. See Sylvia Lintner, "A Social History of Fall River, 1859-1879," Ph.D. dissertation, Radcliffe College, 1945, which deals with the functioning of the working-class cooperatives and benefit organizations to protect the workers from the wage squeeze.

5. David Montgomery, *Beyond Equality: Labor and the Radical Republicans, 1862-1872* (New York: Random House, 1967), pp. 271-295, discusses the context of the state- and nation-wide labor movement within which this stike took place.

6. Henry Fenner, *History of Fall River* (New York: F. T. Smiley Publishing Co., 1906), p. 138; Mullen, "Textile Labor Movement," p. 9; Herbert Lahne, *The Cotton Mill Worker* (New York: Farrar and Rinehart, 1944), p. 176; Lintner, "Social History," p. 140.

7. *History of the Fall River Strike,* written by an unknown worker, John Smith, ed., secretary of the Weavers Union (Fall River: n.p., 1875), pp. 10-11.

8. Although these three tradesmen did support the strike, most of Fall River's merchants refused support and sided with the owners because the elite families controlled all of the city's enterprises from banking to real estate. For a discussion of the merchants' reaction to strikes in the 1870s, see Lintner, "Social History," p. 148.

9. *History of the Fall River Strike,* pp. 10-15.

10. Ibid., pp. 25, 29-30. For a general description of the strike, see E. Abbott, "Employment of Women in Cotton Mills," *Journal of Political Economy* 17 (January-December 1909): 33.

11. During the 1875 strike, even the small French Canadian population held its own meeting and sent a message to the Irish and English workers: "The French Canadian operatives send greetings to their brother operatives of other nationalities, and that their motto like that of the Weavers Committee is 'Stand to the Last.'" During the strike, the spinners, weavers, carders, slashers, union members and non-union members, male and female, participated equally in the strike, rallies, demonstrations, and other actions. Women were the backbone of the strike. See Ronny Joseph, "The Great Vacation: A Study of Class Conflict in Fall River," unpublished paper, University of Massachusetts at Amherst, 1974.

12. The song was written by James Rooney, a local weaver who was a popular singer at union rallies. The tune is that of "Be Kind to Your Parents." *Fall River Daily Herald,* March 13, 1889.

13. For a history of the strike, see Fenner, *History,* p. 139; Mullen, "Textile Labor Movement," p. 10; and Lahne, *Cotton Mill Worker,* p. 179.

14. Lintner, "Social History," p. 164; Lahne, *Cotton Mill Worker,* p. 177.

15. Robert Lamb, "Development of Entrepreneurship: Fall River, 1813-1850," Ph.D. dissertation, Harvard University, 1935, Chap. 15, p. 49.

16. Fenner, *History,* p. 141; and Lamb, "Development," Chap. 15, p. 51. For a biographical sketch of Robert Howard, see *Fall River Daily Herald,* August 7, 1894.

17. Lamb, "Development," Chap. 15, p. 31.

18. "Testimony of Rufus Wade" before the *United States Industrial Commission,* Vol. 7, 56th Cong., 2d Sess., House Doc. No. 495 (Washington, D.C.: 1900), p. 69.

19. Lamb, "Development," Chap. 15, p. 56; Lintner, "Social History," p. 172.

20. Mullen, "Textile Labor Movement," pp. 11-12; Fenner, *History,* p. 139; "Testimony of Rufus Wade," *Industrial Commission,* p. 69; and Lintner, "Social History," pp. 169-175. See also Lamb, "Development," Chap. 15, for a discussion of the strike. Following the loss of the strike, the leadership of the spinners took a much more conservative position. Philip Silvia argues that this conservative leaning of Fall River's union leadership was indeed the central thread in Fall River's labor

history ("The Spindle City: Labor, Politics, and Religion in Fall River, Massachusetts," Ph.D. dissertation, Fordham University, 1973). Silvia fails to deal with two factors, however: the continuity of conservative attitudes of the leadership, including the fiery George Gunton in the strike of 1875, and the changing rank-and-file response to the other forces acting on the operatives.

21. Lintner, "Social History," p. 175.

22. *Fall River Daily Herald*, February 5, 1885.

23. Ibid.

24. Ibid.

25. Ibid., February 13, 1884.

26. "Testimony of Thomas O'Donnell" before the *United States Industrial Commission*, Vol. 17, 56th Cong., 2d Sess., House Doc. No. 183 (Washington, D.C.: 1901), p. 567.

27. "Testimony of George McNeill" before the *United States Industrial Commission*, Vol. 7, 56th Cong., 2d Sess., House Doc. No. 495 (Washington, D.C.: 1900), p. 117.

28. Statement of William Mullen, secretary of the Amalgamated Card Room Operatives of Lancashire, quoted in *Fall River Daily Globe*, April 18, 1904.

29. Immigration Commission, *Immigrants in Industry*, Vol. 72, 61st Cong., 2d Sess., S. Doc. No. 633 (Washington, D.C.: 1909-1910), pp. 123-125. For a description of how the French Canadians arrived as strikebreakers but soon became strong unionists, see "Testimony of Rufus Wade," *Industrial Commission*, p. 70.

30. Immigration Commission, *Immigrants in Industry*, Vol. 72, pp. 123-124.

31. Taped interview with Manuel Mellow, a retired textile worker and organizer in Fall River.

32. *Fall River Daily Herald*, February 13, 20, 1884.

33. Ibid., February 18, 1884.

34. Ibid., February 20, 1884.

35. Immigration Commission, *Immigrants in Industry*, Vol. 72, pp. 125, 273.

36. *Fall River Daily Herald*, March 14, 1889.

37. Ibid., January 30, 1884.

38. Ibid., August 10, 1894.

39. Ibid., February 4, 1884.

40. Ibid.

41. Ibid., February 8, 1884.

42. Ibid.

43. Ibid., February 11, 1884.

44. Ibid., February 9, 1884.

45. Ibid., February 11, 1884.

46. Ibid., February 12, 1884.

47. Ibid.

48. Ibid., March 1, 1884.

49. Ibid., March 15, 1884. The loomfixers, with the highest percentage of English and Irish workers, were considered the aristocracy of the textile operatives and the least likely to unionize. Under the influence of community support for united class action, even this aristocracy joined the union enthusiasm.

50. Ibid., February 11, 1884.
51. Ibid.
52. Ibid., February 6, 18, 1884.
53. Ibid., February 28, 1884.
54. Ibid., March 31, 1884.
55. Ibid., February 28, 1884.
56. Ibid., April 26, 1884.
57. Ibid., April 28, 1884.
58. Ibid., May 2, 1884.
59. Ibid.
60. Ibid., February 20, 1884.
61. Ibid., February 28, 1884.
62. Ibid., February 15, 19, 1884.
63. Ibid., March 10, 15, 1884.
64. Ibid., March 18, 22, 1884.
65. Ibid., March 25, 1884.
66. Ibid., April 25, 1884.
67. Ibid., May 24, 26, 1884.
68. Ibid., June 7, 1884.
69. Ibid., February 18, 1884.
70. Ibid., March 19, 1884.

71. Karl Marx, "Value, Price, and Profit," in *The Essential Left* (New York: Barnes Barnes and Noble, 1961), p. 94.

72. *Fall River Daily Herald,* March 11, 1884.

73. For a discussion of the weavers prior to 1880 and how they were too diffuse and semiskilled to organize, see Lintner, "Social History."

74. *Fall River Daily Herald,* March 14, 1889.

75. Gertrude Barnum, "The Story of a Fall River Mill Girl," *The Independent* 15 (February 21, 1905): 243; tape sessions with retired garment worker Mary Felix, located at the Fall River local, International Ladies Garment Workers Union.

76. *Fall River Daily Herald,* March 21, 1884.

77. Massachusetts Bureau of Statistics of Labor, *Massachusetts Labor Bulletin,* No. 36 (June 1905): 63.

78. *Fall River Daily Herald,* March 8, 9, 1889.

79. Ibid., March 11, 1889.

80. Ibid.

81. Ibid., March 12, 1889.

82. Ibid.

83. Ibid., March 13, 15, 1889.

84. Ibid., March 14, 1889.

85. Ibid., March 15, 1889.

86. John Higham, *Strangers in the Land* (New York: Atheneum, 1963), describes the general hostility of the country towards any violence by labor and radicals after the Haymarket riot, the incident to which the weaver was referring.

87. *Fall River Daily Herald,* March 15, 1889.

88. Ibid., March 16, 1889.

89. Ibid., March 19, 1889.

90. Ibid., March 20, 1889.

91. Ibid., March 21, 1889.

92. Ibid., March 22, 1889.

93. Ibid.

94. Ibid., March 25, 1889.

95. Ibid., March 27, 1889.

96. This unity was marred by the fact that the spinners union, under the conservative leadership of Howard who would not let the issue come before the membership, did not support the strike.

97. Lahne, *Cotton Mill Worker*, p. 179; *Fall River Daily Herald*, August 7, 1894; "Testimony of James Tansey, secretary of the Carders Union" before the *United States Industrial Commission*, Vol. 17, 56th Cong., 2d Sess., House Doc. No. 185 (Washington, D.C.: 1901), p. 579; Fenner, *History*, p. 140.

98. Arthur Phillips, *The Phillips History of Fall River* (Fall River: Dover Press, 1945), p. 145; *Fall River Daily Herald*, August 7, 1894.

99. *Fall River Daily Herald*, August 10, 1894.

100. Ibid., August 13, 14, 1894.

101. Ibid., August 17, 20, 1894.

102. Ibid., August 21, 1894.

103. Phillips, *Phillips History*, p. 145; *Fall River Daily Herald*, September 4, 1894.

104. *Fall River Daily Herald*, September 12, 13, 1894.

105. Ibid., September 15, 1894.

106. Ibid., September 26, 27, 1894.

107. Ibid., October 11, 1894.

108. Ibid., October 12, 1894.

109. Ibid., October 13, 1894.

110. Ibid., October 15, 1894.

111. Ibid., October 17, 1894.

112. Ibid., October 22, 1894.

113. Ibid.

114. Ibid., October 24, 26, 1894.

115. Ibid., October 25, 1894.

116. Ibid., October 29, 1894.

CHAPTER 10

1. In 1901, the Fall River operatives organized the United Textile Union which was chartered by the American Federation of Labor and located in Fall River.

2. Herbert Lahne, *The Cotton Mill Worker* (New York: Farrar and Rinehart, 1944), pp. 78, 179, 195; Arthur Phillips, *The Phillips History of Fall River* (Fall River: Dover Press, 1945), p. 145; Massachusetts Bureau of Statistics of Labor, *Massachusetts Labor Bulletin*, No. 59, May 1908 (Boston: 1908): 225.

3. *National Labor Relations Board, Decisions*, Vol. 36 (December 1941), decision Nos. R.2979, R.2980, R.2981, p. 683.

4. Ibid., p. 678.

5. Ibid., p. 683; Lahne, *Cotton Mill Worker*, p. 7.

6. Stanley Howard, *The Movement of Wages in the Cotton Manufacturing Industry of New England* (Boston: National Council of American Cotton Manufacturers, 1920).

7. Taped interview with Manuel Mellow, April 1973.

8. Tape sessions with retired garment workers of Fall River, whose parents were textile workers and many of whom began working as textile workers. The tapes are available at the Fall River local, International Ladies Garment Workers Union, and University of Louisville, Oral History Archives.

9. Lahne, *Cotton Mill Worker*, pp. 8, 189; *Phillips History*, p. 145.

10. Ibid.

11. Gertrude Barnum, "The Story of a Fall River Mill Girl," *The Independent* 58 (February 21, 1905): 243; *Charities* 14 (February 4, 1905): 415.

12. *Fall River Globe*, April 7, 1904.

13. See Eliot Dunlop Smith, *Technology and Labor* (New Haven, Conn.: Yale University Press, 1939), which contains a more detailed discussion of the stretchouts in textiles.

14. *Massachusetts Labor Bulletin*, No. 37 (September 1905): 186.

15. Barnum, "Fall River Mill Girl," p. 243.

16. Donald Taft, *Two Portuguese Communities in New England* (New York: Longmans, Green, and Co., 1923), p. 208.

17. Quoted as the opinion of an operative in Fall River in *Charities* 14, p. 415.

18. *Fall River Daily Herald*, July 25, 1904, emphasis mine.

19. *Massachusetts Labor Bulletin*, No. 34 (December 1904): 330.

20. Martin Segal, "The Case of the Fall River Textile Worker," *Quarterly Journal of Economics* (August 1956): 468.

21. Hayes Rubbins, *Springfield Weekly Republican*, December 25, 1904, quoted in *Current Literature* 38 (March 1905): 200; Edward Porritt, "A Labor Conflict Without Violence," *Outlook* (December 17, 1904): 972-977; "Relief Work in the Fall River Strike," *Charities* 13 (January 21, 1905): 392; *The Boston Globe*, August 8, 1904.

22. *Massachusetts Labor Bulletin*, No. 36 (June 1905): 63; Fall River manufacturers became intimately tied to the interests of the Kilburn-Lincoln Textile Machinery Company early in its own development. This tie with the local company discouraged the adoption of more modern machinery from other manufacturers. See Jonathan Thayer Lincoln, "Material for a History of American Textile Machinery," *Journal of Economic and Business History* 3 (February 1932): 259-280.

23. Barnum, "Fall River Mill Girl," p. 243.

24. *Massachusetts Labor Bulletin*, No. 36 (June 1905): 63.

25. Ibid.

26. Ibid.

27. Porritt, "Labor Conflict Without Violence," p. 973; *Fall River Globe*, April 2, 5, 6, 1904.

28. *Fall River Globe*, April 21, 1904.

29. Ibid., May 4, 13, 1904.

30. Ibid., May 23, 1904.

31. Ibid., June 8, 1904.

32. Ibid., June 14, 1904.

33. Ibid., June 14, 25, 1904.

34. Ibid., May 4, 1904.

35. Ibid., July 16, 24, 1904.

36. Ibid., July 14, 1904.

37. Ibid.

38. Ibid., July 15, 1904.

39. Ibid.

40. *Fall River Daily Herald*, July 21, 1904; *Fall River Globe*, July 18, 1904.

41. *Fall River Globe*, July 21, 1904.

42. *Fall River Daily Herald*, July 26, 1904; *Fall River Globe*, July 25, 1904.

43. Ibid.

44. *Fall River Globe*, July 25, 1904.

45. Ibid., July 27, 1904.

46. *Charities* 14, p. 415; Barnum, "Fall River Mill Girl," p. 243; *Fall River Globe*, July 25, 1904.

47. *Fall River Globe*, August 4, 1904.

48. *Fall River Daily Herald*, August 4, 1904.

49. *Fall River Globe*, September 21, 1904.

50. Ibid.

51. Ibid., July 30, 1904.

52. *Massachusetts Labor Bulletin*, No. 34 (December 1904): 311.

53. It is from this perspective that one can understand Golden's behavior during the Lawrence strike of 1912, when he tried to break the strike of unskilled immigrants by offering union men as scabs.

54. *Fall River Daily Herald*, August 16, 1904.

55. *Fall River Globe*, August 1, 3, 1904.

56. Ibid., August 3, 1904.

57. Ibid., August 17, 1904.

58. Ibid., August 16, 18, 1904.

59. Ibid., September 1, 1904.

60. *Fall River Daily Herald*, August 10, 1904; *Fall River Globe*, September 6, 1904.

61. *Fall River Globe*, September 9, 1904.

62. Ibid., October 3, 1904.

63. Ibid., October 4, 1904.

64. Ibid., November 10, 11, 14, 1904.

65. Ibid., November 22, 23, 30, December 1, 2, 1904.

66. Ibid., December 1, 1904.

67. Ibid., November 9, 1904, January 14, 1905.

68. *Current Literature* 38 (January 28, 1905): 214.

69. Ibid.

70. *Fall River Globe*, November 25, 26, 1904.

71. Porritt, "Labor Conflict Without Violence," p. 975; *Fall River Globe*, September 6, 24, November 19, 1904.

72. *Massachusetts Labor Bulletin*, No. 34 (December 1904): 330; *Fall River Globe*, July 1, 29, August 1, 2, 4, 6, 22, 1904.

73. *Fall River Globe*, September 28, 1904.

74. Ibid.

75. *Fall River Daily Herald*, July 26, September 6, 17, 1904.

76. *Fall River Globe*, August 1, December 12, 1904.

77. Ibid., December 10, 1904.

78. Inaugural address of John T. Coughlin, Fall River, Massachusetts, January 2, 1905. Papers of the city of Fall River.

79. *Massachusetts Labor Bulletin*, No. 34 (December 1904); *Fall River Globe*, January 19, 1905; *Current Literature* 38 (March 1905): 200.

80. *Massachusetts Labor Bulletin*, No. 59 (May 1908): 225.

81. Ibid.

82. Lahne, *Cotton Mill Worker*, p. 189.

83. Segal, "Case," p. 446; Lahne, *Cotton Mill Worker*, p. 7.

84. Taped interview with Manuel Mellow, a retired doffer, and his wife in April 1973. Both were organizers for the Textile Workers Organizing Committee.

85. Taped interviews with retired garment workers; taped interview with Manuel Mellow and his wife, April 1973.

86. Taped interview with Manuel Mellow and his wife, April 1973.

87. Taped interview with retired garment workers.

88. Report No. Two, National Industrial Conference Board, "The Cost of Living Among Wage Earners in Fall River, Massachusetts, October, 1919" (Boston: November 1919), p. 3; Richard Kelly, *Nine Lives of Labor* (New York: Frederick A. Praeger, 1956), pp. 42-43, 46.

89. Taped interview with Manuel Mellow; Taft, *Two Portuguese Communities*, p. 337; *Monthly Labor Review* 63 (July 1946): 13-14.

90. *Fall River Herald News*, August 30, 1934.

91. Ibid., September 1, 4, 1934. Ironically, at this time Tansey's son was an agent for one of the city's mills, a factor which demonstrated the pull of the skilled workers away from the working-class community and toward the manufacturer.

92. Ibid., September 4, 1934.

93. Ibid., August 30, 1934.

94. Ibid., September 5, 1934.

95. Ibid., September 7, 1934; Kelly, *Nine Lives*, pp. 51-52.

96. *Fall River Herald News*, September 7, 1934.

97. Ibid.

98. Ibid., September 10, 1934.

99. Ibid., September 8, 1934.

100. Ibid., September 17, 1934.

101. Kelly, *Nine Lives*, pp. 54-55.

102. Ibid., pp. 55-56.

103. Ibid., pp. 51-53, 56-57.
104. Ibid., pp. 40-55.
105. *National Labor Relations Board, Decisions,* Vol. 36, pp. 678, 682-683.

CHAPTER 11

1. The argument that the American experience was unique because the American working class was ethnically heterogeneous fails to hold up when a comparison is made to the European working class. Indeed, our immigrant work force was not so unique. See Godula Kosack and Stephen Castles, *Immigrant Workers and Class Structure in Western Europe* (London: Oxford University Press, 1972), which discusses the role of recent immigrants in all developing capitalist economies.

2. Tape sessions with retired shoe workers.

3. John Cumbler, "Labor, Capital, and Community," *Labor History* 15, No. 3 (Summer 1974): 397. As late as 1905, based on a sample of 104 shoe workers, 51 or just under 50 percent were living within a half mile of Central Square, the major location of both the shoe shops and the social gathering spots. Eighty-four or just under 81 percent lived within a mile of Central Square (sample from *Lynn City Directory,* 1905).

4. Robert Blauner *Alienation and Freedom* (Chicago: University of Chicago Press, 1968), pp. 15-17. See map.

5. See George Friedmann, *The Anatomy of Work* (New York: Free Press, 1964) and Blauner, *Alienation and Freedom,* which discuss the importance of the worker's role in the total production process in minimizing alienation.

6. The shoe workers were on piece time but had effective control over the machine speed and the number of batches they could handle. Through this control, piece time, rather than alienating the worker or stretching out his work, allowed him greater control over the pace and structure of his job. Like metal polishers, shoe workers manipulated piece time so that when a set of batches was completed they could help others and all could leave the shop together with common pay. Tape sessions with retired shoe workers.

7. "Minutes Book, Lynn Lasters Benefit Association," Vol. 27, September 10, 1894, Lynn Lasters Union Papers; *Lynn Daily Bee,* September 27, October 6, 9, 1890, January 1, 1891; "Lynn Lasters Union, Treasurers Cash Book," Vols. 3, 4, September 5, 29, October 13, 28, November 25, December 23, 1890; January 20, February 21, June 1, 1891, Lasters Union Papers.

8. Blauner, *Alienation and Freedom,* pp. 58-86. Although Fall River textile workers fit Blauner's model of on-the-job alienation, there are significant off-the-job differences which can be related to the differences in the size of the work force and the urban environment. Blauner's study, which reveals strong off-the-job community support for textile workers, deals with small milling (relative to Fall River), located in small mill towns and villages. Blauner examines mills with 130 workers, while Fall River's mills employed 200 to 2,000 workers. Blauner's villages had one or two mills, while Fall River had over a hundred mills.

9. William Hale, "The Importance of Churches in a Manufacturing Town," *Forum* 18 (September 1894-February 1895): 295. Jonathan Harrison, *Certain Dangerous Tendencies in Amiercan Life* (Boston: Houghton, Osgood, and Co., 1880), pp. 163-164.

10. "Testimony of Thomas O'Donnell" before the Senate Committee, Relations Between Labor and Capital, 1883, quoted in John Garraty, ed., *Labor and Capital in the Gilded Age* (Boston: Little, Brown, 1968), p. 36; Gertrude Barnum, "The Story of a Fall River Mill Girl," *The Independent* 58 (February 1905): 243.

11. Despite the antagonism between the English and Irish and French Canadians, the community had earlier managed to transcend ethnic divisions and to unite as members of a common working class through its community institutions. With the increased dispersion of the workers and the speedups, these institutions became less active as integrating and unifying class elements. The Portuguese put the final strain on the community. Racist and ethnic divisions emerged, and the darker Portuguese were seen as outside the community. See David Montgomery, "The Shuttle and the Cross: Weavers and Artisans in the Kensington Riots of 1844," *Journal of Social History* 5 (1972), which examines how class institutions united the working class and how the absence of these institutions set the stage for ethnic clashes.

12. Although these institutions were not purely functional and had cultural as well as job-specific roles, when the process of urban dispersion and suburbanization of the work force removed the Lynn worker from the downtown institutions, it became more difficult for these institutions to continue as informal socializing centers. See Daniel Luria, "Suburbanization, Ethnicity, and the Party Base: Spatial Aspects of the Decline of American Socialism," Working Paper No. 26, Elliott Sclar's Brandeis University Project, "Boston Studies in Urban Political Economy," which investigates the effect of urban dispersion on working-class political activity. See also Charles Levenstein, "Notes for a Theory of Social-Spatial Stratification," Working Paper No. 24, Sclar project.

Bibliographical Essay

Since the notes to this work should provide the scholar with an ample guide to the literature on the subject, this bibliography confines itself to a short essay on available and significant primary and secondary sources.

The Lynn Library's Scrapbooks Collection and their indexed local newspapers supply even scholars with a limited interest in the city with a great deal of easily accessible information. These sources are complemented by the rich collection of the Lynn Historical Society, David Johnson's *Sketches of Lynn* (Lynn: Thomas Nichols, 1880), and Alonzo Lewis and James Newhall's *History of Lynn* (Lynn, 1897). The newspapers of the Lynn workers—the *Knights of Labor, The Union Leader, The Union Worker,* and *The Electrical Union News,* all of which are available at the Lynn Historical Society and the local union hall (IUE 201)—provide the labor historian with a perspective on labor, although not necessarily on the laborer. The papers of the Lynn Lasters Union, available at the Baker Library, Harvard University, contain information on the union's response to mechanization and on the functioning of the union, both informally and formally. The dues records are also invaluable for anyone interested in the ethnic makeup of the union movement. The *City Directories* and the membership rolls of the various fraternal organizations, available in the Lynn Library, are also important in evaluating the role of ethnicity and class and social institutions in the city's working-class community. These sources, combined with the U.S. manuscript census and the published Massachusetts state census, provide a picture of the ethnic and social characteristics of the work force in Lynn.

The annual reports of the Massachusetts Bureau of Statistics of Labor and of the U.S. Commissioner General of Immigration, as well as the

U.S. Senate's *Immigration Commission Report, 1901-1910*, the *Report of the Committee of the Senate Upon Relations Between Labor and Capital, 1885*, and the *Report on Condition of Women and Child Wage-earners in the United States, 1910-1913*, and the House's nineteen-volume *Report of the Industrial Commission, 1901, 1902*, provide information not only on the working conditions in several industrial cities besides Lynn and Fall River, but also on the immigrant workers.

New England Magazine, Forum, Charities, The Atlantic Monthly, Everybody, Independent, Outlook, and other popular magazines of the late nineteenth and early twentieth centuries commonly ran articles on working conditions and life in industrial cities, including several on Lynn and Fall River. These articles contain data that are rarely available in newspapers or official documents and papers, but they should be used with caution considering their middle-class bias.

The papers of the Lynn settlement house, the Gregg House, available at the Swedenberg School of Religion; the Associated Charities of Lynn; Joseph Cook's *Outlines of Music Hall Lectures, Embracing Five Addresses on Factory Reform* (Boston: W. H. Halliday, 1871); and Bessie Van Vorst and Marie Van Vorst's *The Woman Who Toils* (New York: Doubleday, Page and Co., 1903), although often giving information about the city's poor, also suffer from that same middle-class bias. *Calander* offers the official perspective of the Catholic church on local issues of the day, many of which involved the working class.

Important secondary works on Lynn are Paul Faler, "Workingmen, Mechanics and Social Change: Lynn, Massachusetts," Ph.D. dissertation, University of Wisconsin, 1970, and Alan Dawley, *Class and Community: The Industrial Revolution in Lynn* (Cambridge, Mass.: Harvard University Press, 1976). Henry Bedford, *Socialism and the Workers in Massachusetts* (Amherst, Mass: University of Massachusetts Press, 1967), John R. Commons, "American Shoemakers, 1648-1895," *Quarterly Journal of Economics* 24 (November 1909), Blanch Hazard, *The Organization of the Boot and Shoe Industry in Massachusetts Before 1875* (Cambridge, Mass.: Harvard University Press, 1921), and John Laslett, *Labor and the Left* (New York: Basic Books, 1970) are important secondary works on the shoe industry in Lynn. Robert Billups and Phillip Jones, *Labor and Conditions in the Shoe Industry in Massachusetts, 1920-1924* (Washington, D.C.: U.S. Government Printing Office, 1925), describes the decline of Lynn's shoe industry, and A. E. Galster, *The Labor Movement in the Shoe*

Industry, With Special References to Philadelphia (New York: Ronald Press Co., 1924), deals with the various conflicts within the shoe workers' union.

For Fall River several important secondary as well as primary materials are available for the researcher. The records of the Fall River Iron Works, housed at the Baker Library, include those of several of the more important mills in Fall River. These immense, important records provide a picture of the work process, wages, family employment patterns, housing costs, and ethnic makeup of the mill work force. The newspapers of Fall River, as well as the *Cotton Factory Times* (the paper of the English textile workers before migrating), although incomplete in depicting working-class life, do relate (with all the biases of these sources) the major strikes and events within the working-class community. *Fall River City Directories* furnish the occupations of those residents listed, as well as a limited amount of information on fraternal and ethnic organizations. Hugo Dubuque's directory of the city's French Canadian population and ethnic organizations adds important information on the role and membership of French Canadian fraternal organizations within the city.

Fall River generated several local histories which are of use to historians of the city, particularly Henry Fenner, *History of Fall River* (New York: F. T. Smiley Publishing Co., 1906), Henry Earl, *Fall River and Its Manufacturies, 1803-1910* (Fall River: George Bamford, 1910), Jonathan Lincoln, *The City of the Dinner Pail* (Boston: Houghton-Mifflin Co., 1909), Thomas Smith, *The Cotton Textile Industry of Fall River* (New York: King's Crown, 1944), and Donald Taft, *Two Portuguese Communities in New England* (New York: Longmans, Green, and Co., 1923). Three doctoral dissertations have been completed on Fall River, namely, Robert Lamb, "Development of Entrepreneurship in Fall River, 1813-1850," Harvard University, 1935; Sylvia Lintner, "A Social History of Fall River, 1859-1879," Radcliffe College, 1945; and Philip Silvia, "The Spindle City: Labor, Politics, and Religion in Fall River, Massachusetts, 1870-1905," Fordham University, 1973.

In addition to the documents mentioned earlier, there are several important public documents of particular interest to Fall River: the Massachusetts Department of Labor and Industry, "Hearings on the Conditions Affecting the Textile Industry in this Commonwealth, 1930"; Bureau of Statistics of Labor's 1882 study of three textile centers; and the U.S. Congress, Cabinet Commission, *Report on Cotton Textile Industry,*

1935. Carol Aronovici's commissioned study of housing in Fall River, *Housing Conditions in Fall River* (Fall River: Associated Charities, Housing Committee, 1912), elucidates the various reports on the city's high mortality which found their way into magazine articles and into official health congresses and meetings. Jonathan Harrison, *Certain Dangerous Tendencies in American Life* (Boston: Houghton, Osgood, and Co., 1880), and William Hale, "The Importance of Churches in a Manufacturing Town," *Forum* 18 (September 1894-February 1895): 288-300, contain full discussions of Fall River's working-class community, although, like many of the articles which appeared on Fall River in the magazines mentioned above, they involve a certain amount of sensationalizing.

Important secondary works on Fall River include Rowland Berthoff's excellent *British Immigrants in Industrial America* (Cambridge, Mass.: Harvard University Press, 1953), Herbert Lahne, *The Cotton Mill Worker* (New York: Farrar and Rinehart, 1944), Thomas Young, *The American Cotton Industry* (New York: Charles Scribner's and Son, 1903), Stanley Howard, *The Movement of Wages in the Cotton Manufacturing Industry of New England Since 1860* (Boston: National Council of American Cotton Manufacturers, 1920), J. Herbert Burgy, *The New England Cotton Textile Industry* (Baltimore: Waverly Press, 1932, Melvin Copelan, *The Cotton Manufacturing Industry in the United States* (Cambridge, Mass.: Harvard Economics Studies No. 8, 1912), and Caroline Ware, *Early New England Cotton Manufacturing, A Study in Industrial Beginnings* (Boston: Houghton-Mifflin Co., 1931).

Index

About the Author
John T. Cumbler is Assistant Professor of History and American
Studies at the University of Louisville, Kentucky. His articles have ap-
peared in the *Journal of Urban History* and *Labor History*.